Celebrate Joyous Occasions In Simple, Scrumptious Style!

Warmly welcoming family and friends to your home...offering a special spread of festive fare...creating merry moments to remember for years. All too often, however, there's a lot of pressure on the hostess to make things "just right"—especially on holidays and special occasions.

With *Taste of Home Holiday & Celebrations 2010*, party planners don't need to panic! Inside the colorful pages are 259 simply delicious recipes—as well as mouthwatering menu ideas and handy meal planning guides—to make gatherings throughout the year memorable for the guests...and hassle-free for the hostess.

'TIS THE SEASON. Take the worry out of what to present guests at each Christmas event with this chapter's 112 dazzling dishes, including Mini Gorgonzola Stuffed Potatoes, Roasted Garlic & Herb Prime Rib, Gingerbread Muffin Tops, Special Mushroom Lasagna, White Chocolate Candy Cane Parfaits and Sugar Plums. We even offer complete menu ideas for an English-inspired Christmas dinner, a casual supper for Christmas Eve and a family-friendly North Pole party. Or bring a fresh twist to the table by preparing Orange Cream Meringue Cups, Kumquat Margaritas and Mexican Grilled Salmon, all starring winter citrus fruits.

GIVING THANKS. Take your taste buds on a trip to Dixie with a Southern-style Thanksgiving dinner featuring Smoky Shrimp with Creamy Grits, Bacon Mac & Cheese and Hazelnut Pumpkin Pie. For smaller dinner parties, you'll find a lovely dinner showcasing Chili-Roasted Turkey Breast, Winter Squash Puff and Topsy-Turvy Cranberry Cakes. Cooks can also complete any fall dinner with succulent sides centering on seasonal produce and desserts highlighting sweet and juicy pears.

EASTER GATHERINGS. Early-day dining is wonderful and worry-free when you offer Almond-Crusted French Toast, Cilantro-Lime Fruit Salad and So-Easy Cheese Danish. Or invite guests for Easter dinner complete with Plum & Chutney Glazed Ham, Fennel au Gratin and Mini Carrot Cake Tortes.

SPECIAL CELEBRATIONS. You'll also find 82 family-favorite recipes for occasions throughout the year, such as a bridal party barbecue, New England clam bake, Cuban-themed dinner party, fortune-telling Halloween and more!

CAN-DO DECORATING IDEAS. There are dozens of ideas for stunning centerpieces (turn to page 171 for Fresh-as-a-Daisy Table Toppers), dazzling decorating ideas (check out page 15 for a Christmas Kissing Ball) and fun party favors (see Silver Screen Swag Bags on page 185).

With flavorful foods, easy decorating tips and perfect party ideas, *Taste of Home Holiday & Celebrations 2010* helps make magical memories for family and friends all year long!

Would you like to see one of your family-favorite recipes featured in a future edition of this timeless treasury? See page 256 for details!

taste of home
HOLIDAY &
Celebrations
2010

SENIOR VICE PRESIDENT, EDITOR IN CHIEF:
Catherine Cassidy

VICE PRESIDENT, EXECUTIVE EDITOR/BOOKS:
Heidi Reuter Lloyd

FOOD DIRECTOR: Diane Werner RD

SENIOR EDITOR/BOOKS: Mark Hagen

PROJECT EDITOR: Julie Schnittka

ASSOCIATE EDITOR: Sara Lancaster

CRAFT EDITOR: Jane Craig

ASSOCIATE FOOD EDITOR: Annie Rundle

ART DIRECTOR: Gretchen Trautman

CONTENT PRODUCTION SUPERVISOR: Julie Wagner

PROOFREADER: Linne Bruskewitz

RECIPE ASSET MANAGEMENT SYSTEM: Coleen Martin

PREMEDIA SUPERVISOR: Scott Berger

RECIPE TESTING & EDITING: Taste of Home Test Kitchen

FOOD PHOTOGRAPHY: Taste of Home Photo Studio

ADMINISTRATIVE ASSISTANT: Barb Czysz

GRAPHIC DESIGN ASSOCIATE: Juli Schnuck

NORTH AMERICAN CHIEF MARKETING OFFICER: Lisa Karpinski

VICE PRESIDENT/BOOK MARKETING: Dan Fink

CREATIVE DIRECTOR/CREATIVE MARKETING: James Palmen

The Reader's Digest Association, Inc.

PRESIDENT AND CHIEF EXECUTIVE OFFICER:
Mary G. Berner

PRESIDENT, NORTH AMERICAN AFFINITIES:
Suzanne M. Grimes

Taste of Home Books
©2010 Reiman Media Group, Inc.
5400 S. 60th Street, Greendale WI 53129

International Standard Book Number (10):
0-89821-758-X
International Standard Book Number (13):
978-0-89821-758-2
International Standard Serial Number:
1535-2781

Cover photo of Baked Alaskas
with Tipsy Cherry Centers
(p. 67) by Dan Roberts.
Food styled by Diane Armstrong.
Set styled by Stephanie Marchese.

Back cover photos: Roasted
Cornish Hens with Vegetables
(p. 61), Pineapple Cider Wassail
(p. 9), Fresh-as-a-Daisy Table
Toppers (p. 171) and Roasted
Garlic & Herb Prime Rib (p. 12).

For other Taste of Home books and products, visit:
ShopTasteofHome.com.

table of CONTENTS

'TIS THE
season

A formal Yuletide dinner...comforting potpies for a cozy Christmas Eve supper...a family-friendly North Pole celebration...appealing appetizers at a fun ornament-making party. This chapter makes it easy to entertain during the bustling holiday season. We also present a merry selection of breads, entrees, desserts, cookies, candies...and dazzling dishes starring winter's citrus fruits.

*S*inging some carols...decorating evergreens...kissing under the mistletoe...hanging stockings. Many Christmas customs celebrated throughout the world have their origins in England.

Why not bring a bit of old-time tradition to your holiday table by serving a customary English Christmas dinner?

With a dollop of zesty horseradish sauce, slices of Roasted Garlic & Herb Prime Rib will impress dinner guests.

Take a break from ordinary dinner rolls and prepare savory Yorkshire Pudding with Bacon and Sage. Simply seasoned Brussels Sprouts with Pancetta are an easy yet satisfying side dish.

CULINARY CUSTOMS
(PICTURED AT RIGHT)

Roasted Garlic & Herb Prime Rib (p. 12)
Yorkshire Pudding with Bacon and Sage (p. 10)
Brussels Sprouts with Pancetta (p. 12)

elegant english
CHRISTMAS DINNER

Christmas Day
Dinner Plan

A Few Weeks Before:
- Prepare two grocery lists—one for nonperishable items to purchase now and another one for perishable items to purchase a few days before Christmas Day.
- Order a 6- to 8-pound bone-in beef rib roast.

Two Days Before:
- Buy all the remaining grocery items, including the rib roast.
- Roast the chestnuts for New England Green Beans; peel and chop. Refrigerate in a covered container.
- Make the fruit mixture for Christmas Pudding; cover and chill.

Christmas Eve:
- Set the table.
- For Roasted Garlic & Herb Prime Rib, roast the garlic and make the horseradish sauce. Refrigerate in separate covered containers.
- For Brussels Sprouts with Pancetta, wash and halve the brussels sprouts; chop the pancetta. Place in different containers; cover and chill.
- Prepare and puree the Creamy Rutabaga Soup. Cover and store in the refrigerator.
- Wash and trim the green beans for New England Green Beans; chill in a resealable plastic bag.

- Cook the bacon for Yorkshire Pudding with Bacon and Sage. Cover and chill. Add the melted butter to the bacon drippings and pour into muffin cups; refrigerate.
- Assemble the Old English Trifle; cover and chill.
- Prepare the Christmas Pudding; let cool and refrigerate.

Christmas Day:
- In the morning, wash and peel the potatoes, rutabaga, turnip and parsnip for Root Vegetable au Gratin. Cover with cold water and chill.
- An hour before guests arrive, make the Pineapple Cider Wassail; keep warm on low setting in a slow cooker.
- Make the Roasted Garlic & Herb Prime Rib.
- Prepare Root Vegetable au Gratin.
- When you remove the rib roast from the oven, bake Yorkshire Pudding with Bacon and Sage. Reheat the bacon before sprinkling over the top.
- Prepare the New England Green Beans.
- Reheat the Creamy Rutabaga Soup in a saucepan over low heat; stir in the milk, salt, pepper and remaining broth. Garnish and serve.
- Carve the rib roast and serve with the horseradish sauce.
- Reheat the Christmas Pudding; serve for dessert along with Old English Trifle.

pineapple cider wassail

(PICTURED AT RIGHT)

Pineapple juice prevents this hot drink from becoming overly sweet. Skip the rum—without sacrificing flavor—for a beverage that's ideal for guests of all ages.

Lori Schmeling | *HARTLAND, WI*

1 cinnamon stick (3 inches)

1 teaspoon whole cloves

1/4 teaspoon cardamom seeds, crushed

4 cups apple cider or juice

4 cups unsweetened pineapple juice

1-1/2 cups apricot nectar

1 cup orange juice

1/2 cup rum, optional

Place the cinnamon stick, cloves and cardamom on a double thickness of cheesecloth; bring up corners of cloth and tie with string to form a bag.

In a large saucepan, combine the apple cider, pineapple juice, apricot nectar and orange juice. Add spice bag. Bring to a boil. Reduce the heat; simmer, uncovered, for 15-20 minutes or until the flavors are blended. Discard spice bag. Stir in rum if desired. Serve warm. **YIELD:** 14 servings (about 2-1/2 quarts).

yorkshire pudding with bacon and sage

(PICTURED ON PAGE 6)

*Individual souffles are a nice change from traditional dinner rolls.
The savory treats are tastefully topped with crumbled bacon and fresh sage.*

Melissa Jelinek | MENOMONEE FALLS, WI

5 bacon strips, chopped

2 tablespoons butter, melted

1-1/2 cups all-purpose flour

3 tablespoons minced fresh sage, divided

1/2 teaspoon salt

1-1/2 cups whole milk

3 eggs

In a large skillet, cook bacon over medium heat until crisp. Remove to paper towels with a slotted spoon; drain, reserving drippings.

Transfer drippings to a measuring cup; add enough melted butter to measure 1/4 cup. Pour into 12 ungreased muffin cups. Place in a 450° oven until hot.

Meanwhile, in a small bowl, combine the flour, 2 tablespoons sage and salt; beat in milk and eggs until smooth. Fold in two-thirds of the bacon. Divide batter among prepared muffin cups.

Bake at 450° for 10 minutes. Reduce heat to 350° (do not open oven door). Bake 10-12 minutes longer or until puffed and golden brown. Sprinkle with remaining bacon and sage. **YIELD:** 1 dozen.

YORKSHIRE PUDDING

Similar to a popover or souffle, Yorkshire pudding was originally used as first-course filler for folks who couldn't afford much meat. Over the years, Yorkshire pudding has become a common accompaniment to roast beef dinners.

root vegetable au gratin

*I make root vegetables even more enticing by combining them
with a creamy cheese sauce. This casserole is a favorite at our holiday buffets.*

Lizela Sabiranju | LYNNWOOD, WA

3 medium Yukon Gold potatoes, peeled and thinly sliced

1 medium rutabaga, peeled, halved and thinly sliced

1 medium turnip, peeled and thinly sliced

1 medium parsnip, peeled and thinly sliced

2 cups heavy whipping cream

2 tablespoons minced fresh rosemary or 2 teaspoons dried rosemary, crushed

1 tablespoon all-purpose flour

1 teaspoon seasoned salt

1/2 cup shredded Gruyere or Swiss cheese

Arrange the potatoes, rutabaga, turnip and parsnip in a greased 13-in. x 9-in. baking dish.

In a small saucepan, combine the cream, rosemary, flour and seasoned salt. Bring to a gentle boil. Remove from the heat; pour over vegetables. Sprinkle with cheese.

Cover and bake at 375° for 30 minutes. Uncover; bake for 20-25 minutes longer or until bubbly and vegetables are tender. **YIELD:** 10 servings.

christmas pudding

(PICTURED AT RIGHT)

Packed with fruits, nuts and spices, our Test Kitchen's pudding is rich and delicious.

2-1/2 cups soft bread crumbs

1-1/2 cups raisins

2/3 cup chopped dates

1 medium apple, shredded

1 large carrot, shredded

1/2 cup brandy

1/3 cup dried currants

1/3 cup maraschino cherries

1/4 cup chopped almonds

1/4 cup red candied cherries

1/4 cup green candied cherries

2 tablespoons chopped candied citron

1/3 cup butter, softened

2/3 cup packed brown sugar

2 eggs

1/2 cup all-purpose flour

1 teaspoon baking soda

1/2 teaspoon ground cinnamon

1/4 teaspoon salt

1/8 teaspoon ground cloves

1/8 teaspoon ground nutmeg

1/4 cup orange juice

1/4 cup maraschino cherry juice

SAUCE:

1/2 cup packed brown sugar

1/4 cup butter, cubed

1 egg yolk

1/4 cup half-and-half cream

1/8 teaspoon salt

1/4 cup heavy whipping cream

1 tablespoon brandy

In a large bowl, combine the first 12 ingredients. Cover and refrigerate for 8 hours or overnight.

In a large bowl, cream butter and brown sugar until light and fluffy. Beat in eggs. Combine the flour, baking soda, cinnamon, salt, cloves and nutmeg; add to creamed mixture alternately with orange and cherry juices, beating well after each addition. Stir in fruit mixture.

Pour into two well-greased 8-in. x 4-in. loaf pans. Cover with foil. Place on a rack in each of two stockpots. Add 2 in. of boiling water to each stockpot; cover and boil gently for 2-1/4 to 2-3/4 hours or until a toothpick inserted near the center comes out clean, adding water as needed. Let stand for 5 minutes before unmolding.

Meanwhile for the sauce, in a small saucepan, combine the brown sugar, butter, egg yolk, half-and-half and salt. Bring to a boil. Cook and stir for 1-2 minutes or until thickened. Cool the sauce to room temperature.

In a large bowl, beat whipping cream until stiff peaks form. Fold whipped cream and brandy into brown sugar mixture. Serve with pudding. **YIELD:** 10 servings (1-1/4 cups sauce).

EDITOR'S NOTE: This pudding can be baked in a water bath at 325° for the same amount of time.

roasted garlic & herb prime rib

(PICTURED ON PAGE 7)

An easy herb rub creates a delicious crust over an impressive rib roast.
The creamy horseradish sauce adds a bit of zest to each delectable bite.

Michele Solomon | CRESTVIEW, FL

1 whole garlic bulb

1/4 teaspoon plus 2 tablespoons olive oil, divided

3 green onions, finely chopped

1 tablespoon dried rosemary, crushed

1 teaspoon dried thyme

1 teaspoon dill weed

1 teaspoon onion powder

1/2 teaspoon salt

1/4 teaspoon pepper

1/2 cup dry red wine or beef broth

1 bone-in beef rib roast (6 to 8 pounds)

2 cups beef broth

SAUCE:

1 cup (8 ounces) sour cream

1 tablespoon prepared horseradish

1-1/2 teaspoons dill weed

Remove papery outer skin from garlic (do not peel or separate cloves). Cut top off of garlic bulb. Brush with 1/4 teaspoon oil. Wrap garlic bulb in heavy-duty foil. Bake at 425° for 30-35 minutes or until softened. Cool for 10-15 minutes.

Squeeze softened garlic into a small bowl; stir in the onions, herbs, onion powder, salt and pepper. Add wine and remaining oil. Place roast fat side up in a shallow roasting pan. Cut slits into roast; spoon garlic mixture into slits. Rub remaining garlic mixture over roast. Pour beef broth into bottom of pan.

Bake, uncovered, at 450° for 15 minutes. Reduce heat to 325°; bake 2-1/4 to 2-3/4 hours longer or until the meat reaches desired doneness (for medium-rare, a meat thermometer should read 145°; medium, 160°; well-done, 170°).

Meanwhile, in a small bowl, combine sauce ingredients. Cover and chill until serving. Remove roast to a serving platter and keep warm; let stand for 15 minutes. Serve with sauce. **YIELD:** 12 servings.

brussels sprouts with pancetta

(PICTURED ON PAGE 7)

The addition of pancetta lends a wonderful smoky flavor to crisp-tender brussels sprouts, giving them mass appeal.

Mandy Rivers | LEXINGTON, SC

6 ounces sliced pancetta, chopped

2 pounds fresh brussels sprouts, halved

3 garlic cloves, minced

1 cup chicken broth

1/4 teaspoon salt

1/4 teaspoon pepper

In a large skillet, cook pancetta over medium heat until slightly crisp. Add brussels sprouts and garlic; cook and stir for 5 minutes.

Add the broth, salt and pepper, stirring to loosen browned bits from pan. Bring to a boil. Reduce heat; simmer, uncovered, for 8-10 minutes or until brussels sprouts are tender. **YIELD:** 8 servings.

old english trifle

(PICTURED AT RIGHT)

Loaded with cake cubes and fruit, a lovely layered trifle is always welcome at a holiday dinner. The smooth, homemade custard is well worth the effort.

Nancy O'Connor | *GLEN RIDGE, NJ*

2 cups cubed sponge cake

5 macaroon cookies, crumbled

2 tablespoons sherry or orange juice

2 tablespoons brandy or orange juice

3 cups heavy whipping cream, divided

4 egg yolks

2 tablespoons sugar

1/4 teaspoon vanilla extract

1 cup fresh raspberries

1 cup sliced fresh strawberries

1 cup sliced peeled fresh or frozen peaches, thawed

1/2 cup sliced almonds, toasted

Place cake cubes and crumbled cookies in a 3-qt. glass bowl. Drizzle with the sherry and brandy.

In a small saucepan, heat 1-3/4 cups cream until bubbles form around sides of pan. In a small bowl, whisk the egg yolks and sugar. Remove cream from heat; stir a small amount of hot cream into egg mixture. Return all to the pan, stirring constantly. Cook and stir until mixture is thickened and coats the back of a spoon; stir in vanilla.

Layer the raspberries, strawberries and peaches over the cake cubes and crumbled cookies; spoon custard over the fruit. Cover and refrigerate for at least 1 hour.

In a large bowl, beat remaining cream until stiff peaks form. Pipe over custard; sprinkle with almonds. **YIELD:** 12 servings (1 cup each).

creamy rutabaga soup

I attended a dinner party where this smooth, nutty soup was served as an appetizer in demitasse cups. No one guessed that rutabagas were the main ingredient.

Cappy Hall Rearick | ST. SIMONS ISLAND, GA

1 medium onion, chopped

1 celery rib, chopped

1 tablespoon butter

4 cups cubed peeled rutabagas (about 2 medium)

1-1/2 cups uncooked long grain rice

1-1/2 cups water

5-1/2 cups chicken broth, divided

1-1/4 cups whole milk

1/2 teaspoon salt

1/4 teaspoon pepper

Sour cream and minced fresh chives

In a Dutch oven, saute onion and celery in butter until tender. Add the rutabagas, rice, water and 2-1/2 cups broth. Bring to a boil. Reduce heat; simmer, uncovered, for 25-35 minutes or until rutabagas are tender.

In a blender, cover and process soup in batches until smooth. Return all to the pan. Stir in the milk, salt, pepper and remaining broth; heat through (do not boil). Garnish servings with sour cream and chives. YIELD: 10 servings (2-1/2 quarts).

new england green beans

Smokey and sweet green beans are flavored with bacon, cranberries and maple syrup. The addition of roasted chestnuts brings a bit of crunch.

Brandi Fisher | FORT WORTH, TX

1/2 cup chestnuts

1-1/2 pounds fresh green beans, trimmed

3/4 cup dried cranberries

4 thick-sliced bacon strips, chopped

1 small onion, finely chopped

2 tablespoons butter

2 tablespoons maple syrup

1/4 teaspoon salt

1/4 teaspoon pepper

With a small sharp knife, score an "X" on the rounded side of each chestnut, being careful not to cut through the nutmeat. Place the chestnuts on an ungreased baking sheet. Bake at 425° for 15-20 minutes or until tender. When cool enough to handle, peel and chop.

Place beans in a large saucepan and cover with water. Bring to a boil. Cover and cook for 6-7 minutes or until crisp-tender. Add cranberries during the last minute of cooking time.

Meanwhile, in a large skillet, cook bacon and onion over medium heat until bacon is crisp; drain. Drain bean mixture; add to the skillet. Stir in the chestnuts, butter, maple syrup, salt and pepper; heat through. YIELD: 8 servings.

christmas kissing ball

(PICTURED AT RIGHT)

Instead of a simple sprig of mistletoe, hang an herb- and holly-adorned kissing ball in your entryway and greet guests with a hug...and peck on the cheek!

4-inch moss-covered or green Styrofoam ball

Three 16-inch lengths of 20-gauge craft wire

Fresh or artificial holly

Fresh or artificial boxwood

Fresh or artificial rosemary

Greening pins

Red artificial berries

1 yard of gold ribbon

Insert three lengths of craft wire into the top center of the moss or Styrofoam ball, extending it out of the bottom by about 1 inch.

At the bottom, individually bend each wire end to make a "U" shape. Push the bent wire ends into the bottom of the ball to secure. At the top, twist the wire ends together to form a small loop for hanging. Cut away any excess wire.

Cut or break the holly into pieces about 3 inches long and secure them to the ball with greening pins. Add boxwood and rosemary in the same way until entire ball is covered. Add red berries where desired.

Thread a length of ribbon through the wire hanging loop and knot the ends together. Tie another piece into a bow at the base of the hanging loop and a piece to the bottom of the kissing ball.

EDITOR'S NOTE: Greening pins are available in the floral section of craft stores. Fresh holly will last for about a week at room temperature. Refrigerate kissing ball or mist it with water periodically to keep it longer.

THE SYMBOLISM OF KISSING BALLS

At Christmastime, the Victorians hung "kissing balls" in their doorways as a symbol of love for their visitors. The attractive orbs were made from greenery (like holly, ivy and mistletoe) as well as from herbs, all which held special meaning.

In our Christmas Kissing Ball above, we used holly (symbolizing good will and everlasting life), boxwood (constancy in love) and rosemary (loyalty and fidelity). You can also tuck in other herbs such as sage (long life and good health), lavender (devotion, loyalty and luck) and oregano (happiness).

Before you and the kids get all nestled snug in your beds for a long winter's nap on Christmas Eve, treat everyone to a hot and hearty holiday dinner.

There's no need to fuss...feed your family a casual yet delicious meal that will make tummies happy as they anticipate the arrival of Santa.

Bubbling with an Italian-style veggie filling and topped with a from-scratch bread crust, Ratatouille Pizza Potpies will be a delight to everyone's wondering eyes.

Round out the Yuletide dinner with Pepperoni-Stuffed Mushrooms, Fried Mozzarella Cheese Appetizers, Puttanesca Salad, Easy Italian Bread-sticks and a selection of sweets.

...AND TO ALL A GOOD NIGHT!
(PICTURED AT RIGHT)

Ratatouille Pizza Potpies (p. 20)

'twas the night
BEFORE CHRISTMAS

Countdown to
Christmas Eve Dinner

A Few Weeks Before:
- Prepare two grocery lists—one for nonperishable items to purchase now and another one for the perishable items to purchase a few days before Christmas Eve.

One Week Before:
- Prepare Raspberry Hard Candy; store in an airtight container.

Three Days Before:
- Buy remaining grocery items.
- Prepare the Mocha-Almond Snack Mix and Sugar Plums; store in separate airtight containers.

The Day Before:
- Make the sauce for Fried Mozzarella Cheese Appetizers; refrigerate in a covered container.
- Bake Easy Italian Breadsticks. Let cool, then store in an airtight container.
- For the Puttanesca Salad, prepare the dressing; cover and chill.

Christmas Eve:
- In the morning, assemble the filling for Ratatouille Pizza Potpies; place in ramekins. Cover and refrigerate.

- An hour and a half before serving, coat the Fried Mozzarella Cheese Appetizers with bread crumbs; chill.
- Prepare the Pepperoni-Stuffed Mushrooms; cover with a damp paper towel and refrigerate. Bake them when guests arrive.
- Make the Butterscotch Hot Cocoa. Keep warm on the low setting in a slow cooker.
- Fry the mozzarella cheese squares as directed. Reheat the tomato sauce before serving.
- An hour before baking, make the dough for Ratatouille Pizza Potpies. Let rise, then assemble the potpies and bake as directed.
- Remove the dressing from the refrigerator 30 minutes before using; whisk, then assemble the Puttanesca Salad, tossing to coat.
- Wrap the Easy Italian Breadsticks in foil; reheat in the oven with the Ratatouille Pizza Potpies for 10 minutes.
- Serve the breadsticks, salad and potpies. For dessert, pass around Sugar Plums, Raspberry Hard Candy and Mocha-Almond Snack Mix.

fried mozzarella cheese appetizers

(PICTURED AT RIGHT)

Holidays are times to wow guests with awesome recipes like this. A crisp coating holds marvelous melted cheese, which tastes terrific when dipped into a homemade tomato sauce.

Jay Davis | *KNOXVILLE, TN*

1 pound part-skim mozzarella cheese

2 eggs, beaten

2/3 cup all-purpose flour

3/4 cup seasoned bread crumbs

1 garlic clove, minced

1 tablespoon plus 1/4 cup olive oil, divided

1 can (28 ounces) Italian crushed tomatoes

1 teaspoon dried oregano

2 teaspoons sugar

1/4 teaspoon dried basil

1/8 teaspoon pepper

Cut cheese into twenty-four 1/4-in. slices. Place the eggs, flour and bread crumbs in separate shallow bowls. Dip cheese slices in eggs, then coat with flour. Dip cheese again in eggs and coat with crumbs. Place on waxed paper-lined baking sheets; refrigerate for at least 1 hour.

Meanwhile, in a small saucepan, saute garlic in 1 tablespoon oil for 1 minute; add the tomatoes, oregano, sugar, basil and pepper. Bring to a boil. Reduce heat; simmer, uncovered, for 40-45 minutes or until slightly thickened.

In a large skillet, cook cheese slices in remaining oil over medium heat for 30-60 seconds on each side or until golden brown. Drain on paper towels. Serve with sauce. YIELD: 2 dozen appetizers (2-1/2 cups sauce).

ratatouille pizza potpies

(PICTURED ON PAGE 17)

A homemade bread crust covers a bubbly, Italian-style stew featuring pizza sauce, vegetables and cheese. The individual pies are so hearty, you'll want to eat them with a knife and fork.

Bev Batty | FOREST LAKE, MN

1-1/2 teaspoons active dry yeast

1 cup warm water (110° to 115°)

1 tablespoon olive oil

1 tablespoon honey

1-1/2 teaspoons salt

2-1/2 to 3 cups bread flour

FILLING:

1 jar (14 ounces) pizza sauce

1 small eggplant, peeled and cut into 1/2-inch cubes

1 small zucchini, cut into 1/2-inch cubes

1 medium sweet red pepper, chopped

1 medium sweet yellow pepper, chopped

1 small onion, chopped

4 ounces sliced pepperoni

1 cup (4 ounces) shredded part-skim mozzarella cheese

3/4 cup shredded provolone cheese

3/4 cup shredded Asiago cheese

3/4 cup grated Parmesan cheese

2 teaspoons honey

1 garlic clove, minced

1 teaspoon garlic salt

1 teaspoon pizza or Italian seasoning

1 teaspoon dried oregano

1 tablespoon olive oil

In a large bowl, dissolve yeast in warm water. Add the oil, honey, salt and 1-1/2 cups flour. Beat until smooth. Stir in enough remaining flour to form a soft dough (dough will be sticky).

Turn onto a floured surface; knead until smooth and elastic, about 6-8 minutes. Place in a greased bowl, turning once to grease the top. Cover and let rise in a warm place until doubled, about 1 hour.

In a large bowl, combine the pizza sauce, vegetables, pepperoni, cheeses, honey, garlic and seasonings; divide among eight 10-oz. ramekins or custard cups.

Punch dough down. Divide dough into eight portions. On a lightly floured surface, roll out dough to fit ramekins. Cut out a decorative center with a small holiday-shaped cookie cutter. Place dough over filling; trim and seal edges. Brush with oil.

Place ramekins on a baking sheet. Bake at 375° for 20-25 minutes or until filling is bubbly and crust is golden brown. **YIELD:** 8 servings.

POTPIE IN ONE PAN

To make Ratatouille Pizza Potpies in one dish, transfer filling to a greased 11-in. x 7-in. baking dish. Roll out the dough to fit the dish. If desired, cut out a decorative center or cut slits in the top to vent. Place dough over filling; brush with oil. Bake at 375° for 30-35 minutes or until filling is bubbly and crust is golden brown.

sugar plums

(PICTURED AT RIGHT)

While working as a secretary in a library, I got a request from someone looking for a sugar plum recipe. I searched high and low but eventually stumbled upon this cookie in a local publication.

Virginia Barber | WAYNESVILLE, GA

2 eggs

1-1/4 cups sugar, divided

1 cup chopped almonds

1 cup flaked coconut

1 cup chopped dates

1 teaspoon vanilla extract

1/4 teaspoon almond extract

In a large bowl, beat eggs for 1 minute. Gradually add 1 cup sugar; beat 1 minute longer or until thickened. Stir in almonds, coconut, dates and extracts. Transfer to an ungreased 11-in x 7-in. baking dish.

Bake at 350° for 20-25 minutes or until browned and a thermometer reads 160°. Remove from the oven; stir. Let stand for 6-8 minutes or until cool enough to handle. Roll into 1-in. balls; roll in remaining sugar. Cool completely on waxed paper. Store in an airtight container. **YIELD:** 3 dozen.

butterscotch hot cocoa

(PICTURED ABOVE)

Most people are used to adding mint flavoring to their hot cocoa. But your family just may favor our recipe specialists' version, which calls for brown sugar and butterscotch ice cream topping.

4 cups 2% milk

3/4 cup half-and-half cream

1/2 cup packed brown sugar

1/2 cup baking cocoa

1/2 cup butterscotch ice cream topping

1 teaspoon vanilla extract

Miniature marshmallows

In a large saucepan, heat milk and cream over medium heat until bubbles form around sides of pan (do not boil). Remove from heat; whisk in brown sugar, cocoa, butterscotch topping and vanilla until smooth. Return to heat; cook and stir until heated through. Pour into mugs; sprinkle with marshmallows. **YIELD:** 5 servings.

easy italian breadsticks

(PICTURED AT FAR RIGHT)

Need two great reasons to make these crisp and chewy breadsticks for your family?
They're simple and delicious! The recipe has been in my family for more than 40 years.

Pamela Hawkins | GASTON, OR

2-1/4 cups all-purpose flour

3-1/2 teaspoons baking powder

1 tablespoon sugar

1/2 teaspoon seasoned salt

1/2 teaspoon dried basil

1 cup 2% milk

1/3 cup butter, melted

1/4 cup grated Parmesan cheese

1/2 teaspoon garlic salt

In a small bowl, combine the first five ingredients. Gradually add milk, tossing with a fork until dough forms a ball. Turn onto a lightly floured surface; knead 8-10 times.

Roll dough into a 14-in. x 10-in. rectangle. Cut in half lengthwise; cut each half widthwise into 1-in. strips. Place butter in a shallow bowl. Dip each strip into butter; twist two to three times.

Place 1 in. apart on greased baking sheets. Sprinkle with cheese and garlic salt. Bake at 450° for 8-10 minutes or until golden brown. Serve warm. YIELD: about 2 dozen.

pepperoni-stuffed mushrooms

No one can resist stuffed mushrooms with the fantastic taste of pizza.
The Italian-style appetizers disappear as fast as I can put them on a plate.

Trisha Kruse | EAGLE, ID

24 large fresh mushrooms

1 medium onion, chopped

2/3 cup chopped pepperoni

2 tablespoons butter

1 garlic clove, minced

1/4 cup seasoned bread crumbs

2 tablespoons grated Parmesan cheese

1 teaspoon Italian seasoning

1/8 teaspoon salt

1/4 cup shredded part-skim mozzarella cheese

Remove the stems from the mushrooms. Finely chop the stems and set caps aside.

In a large skillet, saute the onion, pepperoni and mushroom stems in butter until tender. Add garlic; cook 1 minute longer. Stir in the bread crumbs, Parmesan cheese, Italian seasoning and salt; remove from the heat and cool slightly. Spoon into mushroom caps.

Place on an ungreased baking sheet. Bake at 325° for 15 minutes. Sprinkle with mozzarella cheese; bake 5-10 minutes longer or until mushrooms are tender. YIELD: 2 dozen.

puttanesca salad

(PICTURED AT RIGHT)

Instead of offering dinner guests an ordinary lettuce salad, serve this zesty vegetable dish. With pepperoncinis, anchovy fillets, olives and artichoke hearts, each colorful bite is brimming with flavor.

Gretchen Barnes | *FAIRFAX, VA*

6 medium tomatoes, quartered

1 medium sweet red pepper, chopped

1 jar (7-1/2 ounces) marinated quartered artichoke hearts, drained

1 cup chopped cucumber

2/3 cup chopped red onion

1/2 cup pitted Greek olives, chopped

1/2 cup pepperoncinis

1/3 cup minced fresh parsley

1/3 cup minced fresh basil

5 anchovy fillets, chopped

DRESSING:

2 tablespoons olive oil

2 tablespoons red wine vinegar

2 garlic cloves, minced

1/2 teaspoon salt

1/2 teaspoon fennel seed, crushed

1/4 teaspoon dried oregano

1/4 teaspoon crushed red pepper flakes

1/4 teaspoon pepper

In a large bowl, combine the first ten ingredients. In a small bowl, whisk the remaining ingredients. Pour over tomato mixture; toss to coat. Serve with a slotted spoon. **YIELD:** 10 servings.

mocha-almond snack mix

(PICTURED AT FAR RIGHT)

Coated with coffee-flavored chocolate, cereal, almonds and popcorn turn into sweet clusters.
It's a hard-to-resist snack during the holidays. Enlist the kids to help pour and stir!

Niki Plourde | GARDNER, MA

4 cups Corn Chex

4 cups popped popcorn

2 cups sliced almonds

1-1/2 pounds white candy coating, chopped

2 tablespoons instant espresso powder

1 teaspoon almond extract

1/4 teaspoon salt

In a large bowl, combine the cereal, popcorn and almonds. In a microwave, melt candy coating; stir until smooth. Add the espresso powder, extract and salt. Pour over cereal mixture and toss to coat.

Immediately spread onto waxed paper; let stand until set. Break into pieces. Store in an airtight container. YIELD: 3-1/2 quarts.

raspberry hard candy

Old-fashioned hard candy appeals to old and young alike. Everyone is thrilled with the awesome raspberry flavor of this confection. Feel free to try other kinds of food coloring.

Joe Caden | SUTTON, WV

1 teaspoon butter

3-3/4 cups sugar

1-1/2 cups light corn syrup

1 cup water

2 teaspoons raspberry extract

8 to 10 drops neon purple food coloring

Line a 15-in. x 10-in. x 1-in. pan with foil. Grease the foil with butter; set aside.

In a large heavy saucepan, combine the sugar, corn syrup and water. Cook and stir over high heat until sugar is dissolved. Bring to a boil. Cook, without stirring, until a candy thermometer reads 300° (hard-crack stage). Remove from the heat. Stir in extract and food coloring. Immediately pour into prepared pan without scraping the saucepan (do not spread mixture).

Cool for 1-2 minutes or until candy is almost set. Using a sharp knife, score into 1/2-in. squares; cool completely. Break squares apart. Store in an airtight container. YIELD: about 2 pounds.

EDITOR'S NOTE: We recommend that you test your candy thermometer before each use by bringing water to a boil; the thermometer should read 212°. Adjust your recipe temperature up or down based on your test.

candy christmas tree

(PICTURED AT RIGHT)

The young and young at heart will surely have visions of sugar plums dancing in their heads when they catch sight of an evergreen adorned with candies and other treats.

During the Yuletide season, you can find small, foil-wrapped chocolates in festive shapes, such as snowmen, Santas, ornaments and bells. Glue or tape a string or ribbon to the back for hanging.

You can also fill small cellophane or fabric bags with assorted candies. Secure with a ribbon, then hang from the tree.

Individually wrapped candy canes are easy decorations to drape over branches.

If you're serving a sweet snack mix, present it in Candy-Coated Waffle Cones dangling from the evergreen. (Directions for making the cute cones are below.)

Because unwrapped food may come in contact with the branches, use a sap- and chemical-free artificial tree. It should be sturdy and stable...and be able to withstand being touched by tiny hands!

CANDY-COATED WAFFLE CONES

Decorated waffle cones are a colorful and clever way to offer party guests individual servings of sweet treats, such as Mocha-Almond Snack Mix (recipe on opposite page).

Pipe canned white frosting around the top edge of the cone; sprinkle with colored sugar, chocolate sprinkles, colored jimmies or nonpareils. Place the cones on a wire rack until frosting is set. Store in an airtight container.

To hang the cones from a tree, tie a length of gold metallic cord around the widest part of the top of the cone. Turn the knot to the back of the cone; trim cord ends. Cut a length of cord for the hanging loop. On opposite sides of the cone, tie each end of the hanging loop cord to the cord that is tied around the cone; trim ends.

With so much to accomplish during the Christmas season, multitaskers are sure to love the idea of gathering their girlfriends for a party that combines both food and fun(ction)!

As you and your guests catch up with each other and craft some easy handmade ornaments, nibble on a merry array of elegant hors d'oeuvres, including Bistro Appetizer Bundles.

To take the chill out of the wintry evening, also offer hot-from-the-oven options like Chorizo Poppers, Inside-Out French Onion Soup, Ham & Cheese Bites, Mini Gorgonzola Stuffed Potatoes and Crab Rangoon Cheese Spread.

FESTIVE FINGER FOODS

(PICTURED AT RIGHT)

Bistro Appetizer Bundles (p. 31)
Crab Rangoon Cheese Spread (p. 32)
Mini Gorgonzola Stuffed Potatoes (p. 30)
Ham & Cheese Bites (p. 34)
Inside-Out French Onion Soup (p. 28)
Chorizo Poppers (p. 28)

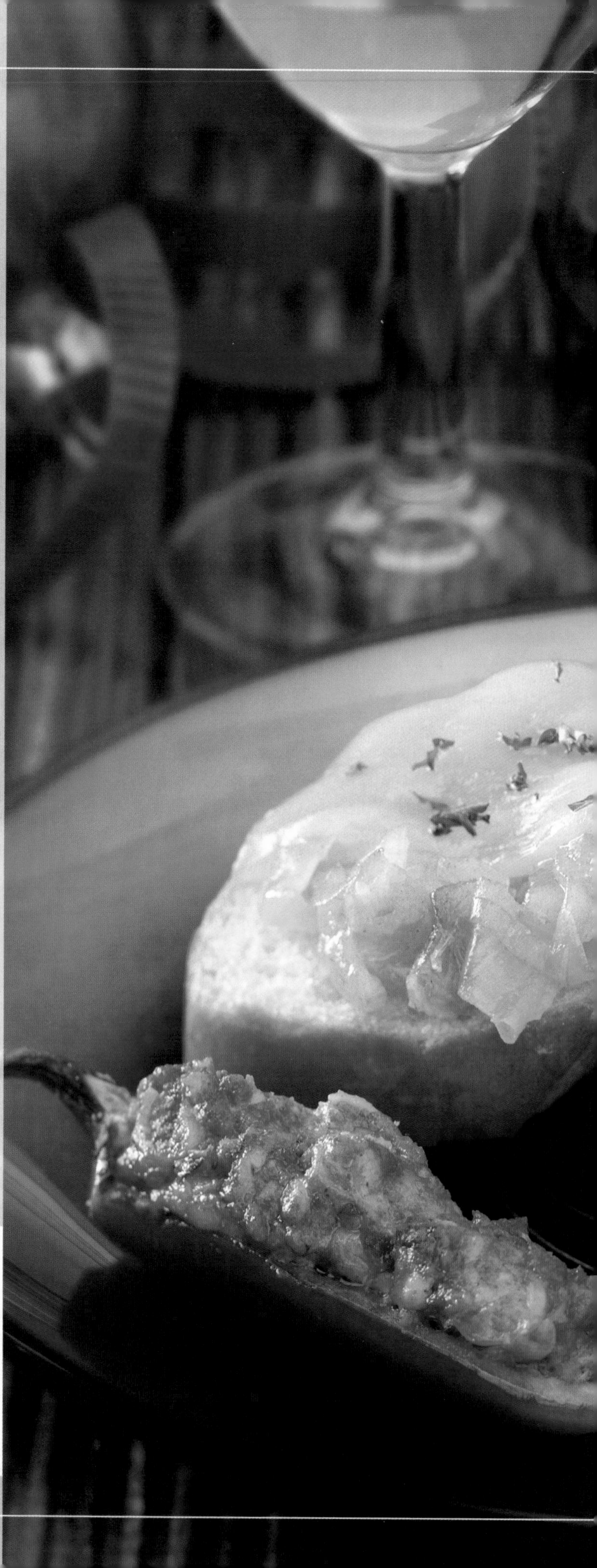

ornament making
APPETIZER PARTY

chorizo poppers

(PICTURED ON PAGE 27)

Chorizo sausage adds even more zip to jalapeno popper snacks bursting with cheese.
Guests are glad to see them at my get-togethers throughout the year.

Daniel Brock | SARASOTA, FL

24 jalapeno peppers

3/4 pound uncooked chorizo or bulk spicy pork sausage

1 small onion, chopped

1 package (8 ounces) cream cheese, softened

1/2 cup shredded Italian cheese blend

1/2 cup shredded Mexican cheese blend

2 tablespoons minced fresh cilantro

2 tablespoons lime juice

2 garlic cloves, minced

Cut jalapenos in half lengthwise; remove seeds and membranes.

In a small skillet, cook chorizo and onion over medium heat until meat is fully cooked and onion is tender; drain. Place in a small bowl; add the remaining ingredients.

Stuff mixture into pepper halves, a scant tablespoonful in each. Place on a greased baking sheet. Bake at 350° for 18-20 minutes or until heated through. **YIELD:** 4 dozen.

EDITOR'S NOTE: When cutting hot peppers, disposable gloves are recommended. Avoid touching your face.

inside-out french onion soup

(PICTURED ON PAGE 27)

I came up with this innovative recipe in an attempt to capture the rich flavor of
French onion soup in an impressive party starter. It's comfort food with a festive twist!

Alana Puentes | HOWARD BEACH, NY

3 large onions, thinly sliced

2 tablespoons butter

2 teaspoons plus 3 tablespoons olive oil, divided

1 garlic clove, minced

1/4 cup sherry or beef broth

2 cups beef broth

1 bay leaf

30 slices French bread baguette (1/2 inch thick)

1/4 teaspoon pepper

2 garlic cloves, peeled and halved

1/2 pound provolone cheese, thinly sliced

2 tablespoons minced fresh parsley

In a Dutch oven, cook onions in butter and 2 teaspoons oil over low heat for 20-25 minutes or until onions are golden brown, stirring occasionally. Add minced garlic and sherry, stirring to loosen browned bits from pan. Add broth and bay leaf. Bring to a boil over medium heat; cook until liquid is evaporated. Discard bay leaf.

Place bread on ungreased baking sheets; brush with remaining oil. Sprinkle with pepper.

Bake at 400° for 4-6 minutes or until lightly browned. Rub cut sides of halved garlic over toast; top slices with onion mixture and cheese. Bake for 1-2 minutes or until cheese is melted. Sprinkle with parsley. **YIELD:** 2-1/2 dozen.

chicken focaccia pizzas

(PICTURED AT RIGHT)

Our home economists top homemade focaccia with chicken, olives and cheese for an incredible appetizer pizza. The recipe feeds a crowd, so it's great for parties.

1 package (1/4 ounce) active dry yeast

1 cup warm water (110° to 115°)

4 tablespoons olive oil, divided

1 teaspoon sugar

1 teaspoon Italian seasoning

1/2 teaspoon salt

3 to 3-1/2 cups all-purpose flour

4 teaspoons cornmeal

2 garlic cloves, minced

2 teaspoons dried basil

2 cups cubed cooked chicken breast

2 plum tomatoes, thinly sliced

1 can (2-1/4 ounces) sliced ripe olives, drained

1 cup (4 ounces) shredded part-skim mozzarella cheese

2 tablespoons grated Parmesan cheese

Ranch salad dressing, optional

In a large bowl, dissolve yeast in warm water. Add 2 tablespoons oil, sugar, Italian seasoning, salt and 2-1/2 cups flour. Beat on medium speed for 3 minutes or until smooth. Stir in enough remaining flour to form a soft dough (dough will be sticky).

Turn onto a floured surface; knead until smooth and elastic, about 6-8 minutes. Place in a greased bowl, turning once to grease the top. Cover and let rise in a warm place until doubled, about 40 minutes.

Sprinkle cornmeal over two greased 12-in. pizza pans. Punch dough down; turn onto a lightly floured surface. Divide in half; roll each portion into a 13-in. circle. Transfer to the prepared pans; build up the edges slightly. Cover and let rise until doubled, about 40 minutes.

Brush crusts with remaining oil; sprinkle with garlic and basil. Top with the chicken, tomatoes, olives and cheeses. Bake at 400° for 22-26 minutes or until crusts are golden brown. Serve with ranch dressing if desired. **YIELD:** 2 pizzas (8 slices each).

mini gorgonzola stuffed potatoes

(PICTURED ON PAGE 27)

*Give twice-baked potatoes a tasty twist by using red potatoes,
filling them with a rich filling and then serving them as an elegant appetizer.*

Janis Scharnott | FONTANA, WI

48 small red potatoes

4 ounces cream cheese, softened

1/3 cup sour cream

1/4 cup butter, softened

2 garlic cloves, minced

1/4 teaspoon salt

1/4 teaspoon pepper

1-1/2 cups (6 ounces) crumbled Gorgonzola cheese

4 thick-sliced bacon strips, cooked and crumbled

1/4 cup grated Parmesan cheese

2 tablespoons minced chives

Scrub potatoes; place in a Dutch oven and cover with water. Bring to a boil. Reduce heat; cover and simmer for 10-12 minutes or until tender. Drain.

When cool enough to handle, cut a thin slice off the top of each potato and discard. Scoop out the pulp, leaving thin shells. Cut thin slices from potato bottoms to level if necessary.

In a large bowl, mash the pulp with cream cheese, sour cream, butter, garlic, salt and pepper. Stir in Gorgonzola cheese and bacon. Spoon mixture into potato shells; sprinkle with Parmesan cheese.

Place in two ungreased 15-in. x 10-in. x 1-in. baking pans. Bake at 350° for 10-15 minutes or until heated through. Sprinkle with chives. **YIELD:** 4 dozen.

warm blue cheese, bacon & garlic dip

*This is a favorite snack of mine that I serve when hosting my husband's office parties.
Crunchy smoked almonds complement the creamy cheese dip.*

Barb Whatley | FREMONT, NE

7 bacon strips, chopped

2 garlic cloves, minced

1 package (8 ounces) cream cheese, softened

1/4 cup half-and-half cream

1 cup (4 ounces) crumbled blue cheese

2 tablespoons minced chives

3 tablespoons coarsely chopped smoked almonds

Bagel chips

In a large skillet, cook bacon over medium heat until crisp. Using a slotted spoon, remove the bacon to paper towels; drain, reserving 1/2 teaspoon drippings.

Saute garlic in reserved drippings for 1 minute; transfer to a small bowl. Add cream cheese and cream; beat until smooth. Stir in the blue cheese, chives and bacon.

Transfer to a 1-qt. baking dish; cover and bake at 350° for 25 minutes. Uncover and bake 5-10 minutes longer or until lightly browned. Sprinkle with almonds; serve with chips. **YIELD:** 2 cups.

bistro appetizer bundles

(PICTURED AT RIGHT AND ON PAGE 27)

Packed with enoki mushrooms, asparagus, peppers and carrots, these prosciutto-wrapped bundles are sure to satisfy. They add a fancy touch to holiday parties.

Roxanne Chan | ALBANY, CA

10 fresh asparagus spears

10 thin slices prosciutto or deli ham

1 package (3-1/2 ounces) fresh enoki mushrooms

1 medium sweet red pepper, cut into strips

10 carrot sticks

10 green onion tops

DIPPING SAUCE:

1/4 cup sour cream

1/4 cup Mascarpone cheese

1 tablespoon minced fresh thyme

2 teaspoons honey mustard

1 garlic clove, minced

1/4 teaspoon grated lemon peel

1/4 teaspoon freshly ground pepper

In a large saucepan, bring 3 cups water to a boil. Add asparagus; cover and cook for 3 minutes. Drain and immediately place asparagus in ice water. Drain and pat dry.

Place prosciutto slices on a work surface; divide the asparagus, mushrooms, pepper strips and carrot sticks among slices. Roll up tightly; tie bundles with green onion tops.

Combine the sauce ingredients; serve sauce with bundles. **YIELD:** 10 appetizers (1/2 cup sauce).

ABOUT ENOKI MUSHROOMS

Sometimes called velvet shanks, enoki mushrooms have long, slender stems with little caps and a mild, delicate flavor. You can purchase them at specialty grocery stores or Asian food markets. Avoid mushrooms that are slimy or brown...they should be firm and white. Refrigerate enoki mushrooms in a paper bag for up to 2 weeks. Before using, rinse in cold water and trim the stems at the base.

crab rangoon cheese spread

(PICTURED ON PAGE 27)

*Crisp, deep-fried wonton strips are a perfect accompaniment
to a classic, cheesy crab spread. Sweet-and-sour sauce adds fantastic flavor.*

Gina Muller | MONROE, IA

1 package (12 ounces) wonton wrappers

Oil for deep-fat frying

1 teaspoon salt

2 packages (8 ounces each) cream cheese, softened

1 tablespoon sugar

3 pouches (3.53 ounces each) premium crabmeat, drained

6 green onions, finely chopped

1 jar (10 ounces) sweet-and-sour sauce

Cut wonton wrappers into thirds. In an electric skillet or deep-fat fryer, heat oil to 375°. Fry the wonton strips, a few at a time, for 10-20 seconds on each side or until golden brown. Drain on paper towels; sprinkle with salt.

In a large bowl, beat cream cheese and sugar until smooth. Stir in crab and onions. Transfer to a serving plate; shape into a 6-in. disk. Top with sweet-and-sour sauce. Serve with wonton chips. **YIELD:** 3 cups spread (180 chips).

goat cheese & onion pastries

*A flaky puff pastry crust holds caramelized onions and creamy goat cheese
for an easy—yet upscale—recipe that's a "must" on all of our entertaining menus.*

Heidi Ellis | MONUMENT, CO

6 bacon strips, chopped

2 large onions, finely chopped

3 shallots, thinly sliced

1/2 teaspoon sugar

1/2 cup white wine

2 teaspoons minced fresh thyme or 1/2 teaspoon dried thyme

2 garlic cloves, minced

1/4 teaspoon pepper

1 sheet frozen puff pastry, thawed

1 egg white, beaten

1 log (4 ounces) fresh goat cheese, cut into 12 slices

In a large skillet, cook bacon over medium heat until crisp. Remove to paper towels with a slotted spoon; drain, reserving 2 teaspoons drippings. Add the onions, shallots and sugar to the pan; cook and stir over medium heat for 15-20 minutes or until golden brown.

Add wine, stirring to loosen browned bits from pan. Stir in the thyme, garlic and pepper. Cook, uncovered, for 2-3 minutes or until liquid is evaporated. Stir in bacon; set aside.

On a lightly floured surface, unfold puff pastry. Cut into three 9-in. x 3-in. rectangles. Transfer to a parchment paper-lined baking pan. Brush dough with egg white; top with onion mixture and goat cheese.

Bake at 400° for 16-20 minutes or until golden brown. Cut each rectangle into four appetizers. **YIELD:** 1 dozen.

broiled tomato-mozzarella dip

(PICTURED AT RIGHT)

This eye-catching and palate-pleasing dip features zippy tomatoes topped with plenty of mozzarella cheese.

Connie Barszcz | ELMVALE, ON

1 medium onion, finely chopped

2 tablespoons olive oil

1 can (28 ounces) diced tomatoes, drained

1/2 cup dry red wine or chicken broth

1 tablespoon dried basil

1 tablespoon fennel seed, crushed

1 tablespoon dried oregano

3 garlic cloves, minced

2 teaspoons sugar

1/2 teaspoon crushed red pepper flakes

1/2 teaspoon salt

2 cartons (8 ounces each) fresh mozzarella cheese pearls, drained

Toasted sliced Italian bread

In a large saucepan, saute onion in oil until tender. Stir in the tomatoes, wine, basil, fennel, oregano, garlic, sugar, pepper flakes and salt. Bring to a boil. Reduce heat; cover and simmer for 10 minutes.

Uncover and cook 10-15 minutes longer or until thickened. Transfer mixture to a 10-in. baking dish; sprinkle with cheese.

Broil 6 in. from the heat for 3-5 minutes or until cheese is golden brown. Serve with toasted bread. YIELD: 5 cups.

ham & cheese bites

(PICTURED ON PAGE 27)

I can double the recipe for these easy-to-prepare appetizers and still come home with empty platters. Apple butter and Dijon mustard lend a sweet and savory taste to every bite.

Carre Czemierys | *BROOKFIELD, WI*

1 loaf (14 ounces) ciabatta bread

2 tablespoons olive oil

6 tablespoons apple butter

1 tablespoon Dijon mustard

1/2 pound white cheddar cheese, thinly sliced

1/2 pound yellow cheddar cheese, thinly sliced

9 slices deli ham, cut into 1-inch strips

2 tablespoons minced chives

Cut bread into 1-in. cubes; place cut side up on a baking sheet. Brush the tops with oil. Broil 4 in. from the heat for 1-2 minutes or until toasted.

Combine apple butter and mustard; spread over toast. Layer with cheeses and ham. Broil for 1-2 minutes or until cheese is melted. Sprinkle with chives. **YIELD:** 3 dozen.

sweet and spicy stuffed portobellos

You'll need a knife and fork to dig into these hearty portobellos topped with sauteed sliced mushrooms, goat cheese, pesto and sun-dried tomatoes.

Gilda Lester | *MILLSBORO, DE*

1 pound sliced baby portobello mushrooms

4 shallots, peeled and sliced

1 jalapeno pepper, seeded and chopped

1/4 teaspoon crushed red pepper flakes

5 tablespoons olive oil, divided

1/4 cup white wine or chicken broth

2 tablespoons Dijon mustard

1 tablespoon Worcestershire sauce

1 tablespoon soy sauce

1 tablespoon honey

8 large portobello mushrooms, stems removed

8 ounces fresh goat cheese

1/2 cup chopped oil-packed sun-dried tomatoes

1/4 cup prepared pesto

Fresh basil leaves, optional

In a large skillet, saute the sliced mushrooms, shallots, jalapeno and pepper flakes in 2 tablespoons oil until mushrooms are tender. Add the wine, mustard, Worcestershire sauce, soy sauce and honey; cook 3-4 minutes longer or until slightly thickened.

Brush the whole mushrooms with 2 tablespoons oil. Place in a 15-in. x 10-in. x 1-in. baking pan. Bake at 350° for 8-10 minutes or until tender.

Fill mushroom caps with shallot mixture. Combine the goat cheese, tomatoes and pesto; spoon over the tops. Bake for 5-7 minutes or until heated through. Drizzle with remaining oil; garnish with basil if desired. **YIELD:** 8 servings.

EDITOR'S NOTE: When cutting hot peppers, disposable gloves are recommended. Avoid touching your face.

wasabi bacon-wrapped shrimp

(PICTURED AT RIGHT)

If you have a shrimp-loving crowd, you must serve this appetizer! When weather permits, I cook the shrimp out on the grill.

Angela Buchanan | *LONGMONT, CO*

6 bacon strips

12 uncooked large shrimp

1/4 cup reduced-fat mayonnaise

1 tablespoon wasabi mustard

1/4 cup thawed orange juice concentrate

1/4 cup reduced-sodium soy sauce

1 green onion, chopped

In a large skillet, cook bacon over medium heat until partially cooked but not crisp. Remove to paper towels to drain.

Peel and devein shrimp, leaving tails on. Combine mayonnaise and mustard; brush over shrimp on both sides. Cut each bacon strip in half widthwise. Wrap a piece of bacon around each shrimp. Secure with toothpicks. Place in a foil-lined 15-in. x 10-in. x 1-in. baking pan.

Bake at 375° for 12-15 minutes or until the bacon is crisp and the shrimp is no longer pink.

In a small bowl, combine the orange juice concentrate, soy sauce and onion; serve with shrimp. **YIELD:** 1 dozen (1/2 cup sauce).

WHAT IS WASABI?

Wasabi is a Japanese root vegetable that is similar to horseradish except that it is green in color and is more expensive. Use wasabi sparingly until you determine how much heat you can handle.

roast beef potato planks

For an appetizer that's more like a meal, I deep-fry potato slices and then top them with roast beef and cheese before baking. Sun-dried tomatoes add appealing color.

Michaela Rosenthal | WOODLAND HILLS, CA

4 medium potatoes, peeled

Oil for deep-fat frying

1-1/2 pounds shaved deli roast beef

1 pound white cheddar cheese, thinly sliced

1/4 cup chopped oil-packed sun-dried tomatoes

2 tablespoons minced fresh parsley

2 teaspoons prepared horseradish

1/2 teaspoon grated lemon peel

1/8 teaspoon pepper

Cut potatoes lengthwise into 1/4-in. slices; cover with cold water and let stand for 30 minutes.

Drain potatoes and pat dry with paper towels. In an electric skillet or deep-fat fryer, heat oil to 375°. Fry potatoes, a few at a time, for 3-4 minutes on each side or until lightly browned. Remove with a slotted spoon; drain on paper towels.

Top potato slices with roast beef and cheese; place on a baking sheet. Broil 3-4 in. from the heat for 1-2 minutes or until cheese is melted. In a small bowl, combine the remaining ingredients. Spoon over the tops. YIELD: about 2-1/2 dozen.

gorgonzola & artichoke spread

Friends and family favor this cool and creamy spin on hot artichoke dip. Spoon it onto celery sticks or sturdy crackers for a satisfying snack.

Susi Mitchell | LEAKEY, TX

1 cup (4 ounces) crumbled Gorgonzola cheese

1/2 cup mayonnaise

1 can (14 ounces) water-packed artichoke hearts, rinsed, drained and quartered

1 medium sweet red pepper, chopped

6 green onions, thinly sliced

1/2 cup chopped walnuts

2 garlic cloves, minced

Celery ribs and assorted crackers

In a small bowl, combine cheese and mayonnaise. Stir in the artichokes, pepper, onions, walnuts and garlic. Serve with celery and crackers. YIELD: 3 cups.

gorgeous glass ornaments

(PICTURED AT RIGHT)

Everyday items transform ordinary clear glass ornaments into beautiful baubles for your evergreen.

FESTIVE FILLERS. Remove the cap of the ornament; set aside. Roll ribbon pieces, a stamped plastic circle or foam stickers around a pencil; slip inside the ornament. Add artificial snow if desired; replace cap. You can also fill ornaments with artificial greens, pieces of glitter garland or any other Christmas decorations.

MAKE IT PRETTY WITH GLITTER 'N' PAINT. Remove the cap of the ornament; set aside. Pour craft varnish inside the ornament, rotating it until the entire inside is coated. Pour the excess varnish back into the container; stand the ornament upside down in a small disposable cup until no more varnish comes out.

Pour one or more colors of fine glitter or acrylic paint inside the ornament. Cover the opening with your finger; shake (for glitter) or rotate (for paint) until the inside is completely covered. Shake out excess glitter. Stand ornament upside down until dry. Replace cap. If desired, decorate outside of ornaments with sequins or stickers.

TISSUE PAPER WRAP-UP. Tear tissue paper into small pieces. With a sponge brush, apply glue to a small area on the ornament; place a piece of the tissue paper over it. Continue adding the glue and tissue paper, overlapping pieces slightly, until the entire ornament is covered. Let dry.

You don't need to spend a lot of dough during the Christmas season to show your sweet sentiments to family, teachers, friends and neighbors.

Skip the trip to the mall. Head to the kitchen and bake a bounty of from-the-heart breads instead!

From lovely loaves (like Raspberry Butter Braids, shown at right) and coffee cakes to cinnamon rolls and muffins, the home-baked goodies in this chapter will warm the hearts and souls of the recipients.

(And they won't break the bank of the baker!)

OVEN-FRESH FAVORITE
(PICTURED AT RIGHT)

Raspberry Butter Braids (p. 40)

yuletide
SWEET BREADS

raspberry butter braids

(PICTURED ON PAGE 39)

Looking for an eye-catching sweet bread to give as a gift?
With tender, raspberry-filled layers, this lovely, two-loaf recipe is sure to impress.

Robin Stout | AMHERSTVIEW, ON

1 package (1/4 ounce) active dry yeast

1/4 cup warm water (110° to 115°)

1 cup warm 2% milk (110° to 115°)

1/2 cup butter, cubed

1/2 cup sugar

1 egg

1/2 teaspoon salt

4 to 4-1/2 cups all-purpose flour

3/4 cup seedless raspberry jam

EGG WASH:

1 egg

2 tablespoons water

GLAZE:

1-1/4 cups confectioners' sugar

1/4 cup butter, melted

1/2 teaspoon vanilla extract

2 to 3 teaspoons water

In a large bowl, dissolve yeast in warm water. Add the milk, butter, sugar, egg, salt and 2 cups flour; beat until smooth. Add enough remaining flour to form a soft dough.

Turn onto a floured surface; knead until smooth and elastic, about 6-8 minutes. Place in a greased bowl, turning once to grease the top. Cover and let rise in a warm place until doubled, about 1 hour.

Punch dough down. Turn onto a lightly floured surface; divide dough in half. On greased baking sheets, roll each portion into a 14-in. x 12-in. rectangle. Cut each rectangle into three 14-in. x 4-in. strips. Spoon 2 tablespoons jam down the center of each strip. Bring long edges together over filling; pinch to seal. Braid three strips together; pinch ends to seal and tuck under. Repeat with the remaining strips. Cover and let rise until doubled, about 45 minutes.

Beat the egg and water; brush over the loaves. Bake at 350° for 20-25 minutes or until golden brown. Transfer to wire racks.

For glaze, combine the confectioners' sugar, butter, vanilla and enough water to achieve desired consistency. Brush over warm loaves. **YIELD:** 2 loaves (15 slices each).

coconut cranberry muffins

To me, a perfect day includes time in the kitchen baking a batch of goodies...and my husband would agree!

Janice Christofferson | EAGLE RIVER, WI

2 cups all-purpose flour

2/3 cup plus 2 teaspoons sugar, divided

2 teaspoons baking powder

1/4 teaspoon salt

1 egg, lightly beaten

2/3 cup light coconut milk

1/4 cup butter, melted

1/2 teaspoon vanilla extract

1 cup dried cranberries

1 teaspoon grated lemon peel

In a large bowl, combine the flour, 2/3 cup sugar, baking powder and salt. In a small bowl, combine egg, milk, butter and vanilla. Stir into dry ingredients just until moistened. Fold in cranberries and peel.

Fill paper-lined muffin cups half full; sprinkle with remaining sugar. Bake at 400° for 16-20 minutes or until a toothpick comes out clean. Cool for 5 minutes before removing to a wire rack. **YIELD:** 1 dozen.

buttermilk berry fritters

(PICTURED AT RIGHT)

Your family's mouths will start watering when they dream about the crispy outside and soft inside of these fantastic fritters. They're definitely worth waking up for.

Janice Moore | EAST PALATKA, FL

2 cups all-purpose flour

1/2 cup sugar

3 teaspoons baking powder

1/2 teaspoon salt

2 eggs, beaten

1 cup buttermilk

1/4 cup butter, melted

1 teaspoon vanilla extract

1 cup dried cranberries

Oil for deep-fat frying

Confectioners' sugar

In a small bowl, combine the flour, sugar, baking powder and salt. Combine the eggs, buttermilk, butter and vanilla; add to dry ingredients just until moistened. Fold in the cranberries.

In an electric skillet or deep-fat fryer, heat oil to 375°. Drop batter by tablespoonfuls, a few at a time, into hot oil. Fry until golden brown, about 1-2 minutes on each side. Drain on paper towels. Dust fritters with confectioners' sugar. YIELD: 3-1/2 dozen.

DEEP-FRYING FACTS

- If you don't have a deep-fat fryer or electric fry pan with a thermostat, you can use a kettle or Dutch oven together with a thermometer so you can accurately regulate the temperature of the oil.
- Always follow the oil temperature recommended in recipes. If the oil is too hot, the foods will brown too fast and not be done in the center. If the oil is below the recommended temperature, the foods will absorb oil and taste greasy.
- To avoid splattering, carefully place foods into the hot oil and never add any liquids to hot oil.
- Don't overload your fryer. You'll have better results if you fry in small batches.
- To keep fried foods warm until the entire recipe is cooked, drain fried foods on paper towels, then place on an ovenproof platter. Cover loosely with foil and place in a 200° oven.

coconut-apricot sweet rolls

You'll appreciate the fact that this recipe makes a big batch of yummy yeast rolls. I often put half of the baked rolls in the freezer. When thawed and reheated, they taste just as good as the day they were made!

Candice Scholl | WEST SUNBURY, PA

2 packages (1/4 ounce each) active dry yeast

1 teaspoon sugar

2-1/2 cups warm water (110° to 115°), divided

1 package (18-1/4 ounces) yellow cake mix

1-1/2 cups whole wheat flour

1/2 cup canola oil

2 eggs

1 teaspoon vanilla extract

3/4 teaspoon salt

4-1/2 to 5 cups all-purpose flour

FILLING:

2 cups dried apricots, chopped

1 cup water

2 cups packed brown sugar

1 cup finely chopped walnuts

1 cup flaked coconut

2 tablespoons all-purpose flour

2 tablespoons ground cinnamon

1/2 cup butter, melted

4 tablespoons honey, divided

GLAZE:

2-1/2 cups confectioners' sugar

3 tablespoons milk

3 tablespoons butter, melted

1-1/4 teaspoons vanilla extract

Flaked coconut, toasted

In a large bowl, dissolve yeast and sugar in 1 cup warm water; let stand for 5 minutes. Add the dry cake mix, whole wheat flour, oil, eggs, vanilla, salt and remaining water. Beat until smooth. Stir in enough all-purpose flour to form a soft dough.

Turn onto a floured surface; knead until smooth and elastic, about 6-8 minutes. Place in a greased bowl, turning once to grease the top. Cover and let rise in a warm place until doubled, about 1 hour.

In a large saucepan, bring apricots and water to a boil. Reduce heat; simmer, uncovered, for 10 minutes or until apricots are tender. Drain. In a bowl, combine the apricots, brown sugar, walnuts, coconut, flour and cinnamon; set aside.

Punch dough down. Turn onto a lightly floured surface; divide in half. Roll each half into an 18-in. x 12-in. rectangle. Brush melted butter to within 1/2 in. of edges; sprinkle with apricot mixture. Drizzle each with 1 tablespoon honey. Roll up jelly-roll style, starting with a long side; pinch seams to seal.

Cut each into 15 rolls. Place cut side up in two greased 13-in. x 9-in. baking pans and one 9-in. square baking pan. Drizzle with remaining honey. Cover and let rise in a warm place until doubled, about 30 minutes.

Bake at 350° for 20-25 minutes or until golden brown. Combine the confectioners' sugar, milk, butter and vanilla; drizzle over rolls. Sprinkle with coconut. Serve warm. **YIELD:** 2-1/2 dozen.

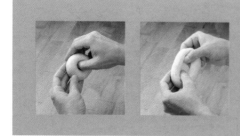

SHAPING BAGELS

1. Shape dough into balls. Push your thumb through the center of each to form a 1-1/2-in. hole.

2. Stretch and shape the dough to form a ring.

eggnog bagels

(PICTURED AT RIGHT)

Crispy and chewy bagels from our recipe specialists rival any gourmet bakery brand. The fantastic spiced spread complements the cinnamon-sugar goodies.

2 packages (1/4 ounce each) active dry yeast

1/2 cup warm water (110° to 115°)

1 cup eggnog

2 tablespoons sugar, divided

5 teaspoons salt, divided

3/4 teaspoon ground nutmeg

3 to 3-1/2 cups bread flour

8 cups water

TOPPING:

1 egg white

1 tablespoon water

2 tablespoons sugar

1/4 teaspoon ground cinnamon

1/8 teaspoon ground nutmeg

SPICED CREAM CHEESE:

1 package (8 ounces) cream cheese, softened

1 tablespoon sugar

3/4 teaspoon rum extract

1/8 teaspoon ground cinnamon

1/8 teaspoon ground nutmeg

In a large bowl, dissolve yeast in warm water. Add the eggnog, 1 tablespoon sugar, 3 teaspoons salt, nutmeg and 1-1/2 cups of flour; mix well. Stir in enough of the remaining flour to form a stiff dough; beat 1 minute longer.

Turn onto a floured surface; knead until smooth and elastic, about 6-8 minutes. Place in a greased bowl, turning once to grease the top. Cover and let rise in a warm place until doubled, about 1 hour.

Punch dough down. Shape into 12 balls. Push thumb through centers to form a 1-1/2-in. hole. Stretch and shape dough to form an even ring. Place on parchment paper-lined baking sheets. Cover and let rest for 30 minutes, then refrigerate overnight.

Let stand at room temperature for 30 minutes; flatten bagels slightly. In a non-aluminum Dutch oven, bring water to a boil with the remaining sugar and salt. Drop bagels, one at a time, into water. Cook for 30 seconds; turn and cook 30 seconds longer. Remove with a slotted spoon; drain well on paper towels.

Place bagels 2 in. apart on greased baking sheets. In a small bowl, combine egg white and water; brush over bagels. Combine the sugar, cinnamon and nutmeg; sprinkle over the tops.

Bake at 425° for 10-14 minutes or until golden brown. Remove from pans to wire racks to cool completely.

In a small bowl, combine the cream cheese, sugar, extract, cinnamon and nutmeg; serve with bagels. **YIELD:** 1 dozen bagels (3/4 cup cream cheese).

EDITOR'S NOTE: This recipe was tested with commercially prepared eggnog.

butterscotch-pecan cinnamon rolls

Our children and grandchildren gobble up my cinnamon rolls as fast as the
bread machine can make the dough! Butterscotch pudding mix gives them a distinctive taste.

Jane Quinnell | WISCONSIN RAPIDS, WI

1 cup warm 2% milk (70° to 80°)

1/4 cup warm water (70° to 80°)

1 egg

1/4 cup butter, softened

1/4 cup instant butterscotch pudding mix

1 tablespoon sugar

1 teaspoon salt

4-1/4 cups bread flour

1 tablespoon active dry yeast

1/4 cup finely chopped pecans

1/4 cup milk chocolate chips

FILLING:

1/4 cup butter, softened

1 cup packed brown sugar

1/4 cup finely chopped pecans

1/4 cup milk chocolate chips

2 teaspoons ground cinnamon

ICING:

3/4 cup confectioners' sugar

2 tablespoons butter, softened

1-1/2 teaspoons 2% milk

1/4 teaspoon vanilla extract

In bread machine pan, place the first nine ingredients in order suggested by manufacturer. Select dough setting (check dough after 5 minutes of mixing; add 1 to 2 tablespoons of water or flour if needed). Just before the final kneading (your machine may audibly signal this), add pecans and chips. When cycle is completed, turn dough onto a well-floured surface.

Roll into an 18-in. x 12-in. rectangle; spread with butter. Combine the brown sugar, pecans, chips and cinnamon; sprinkle over dough to within 1/2 in. of edges. Roll up jelly-roll style, starting with a long side; pinch seam to seal. Cut into 12 slices.

Place cut side down in a greased 13-in. x 9-in. baking pan. Cover and let rise until doubled, about 30 minutes. Bake at 350° for 25-30 minutes or until golden brown. Cool in pan for 5 minutes before inverting onto a serving plate.

In a small bowl, combine the icing ingredients. Drizzle over warm rolls. YIELD: 1 dozen.

KEEPING CINNAMON ROLLS TOGETHER

To keep homemade cinnamon rolls from separating or unrolling, dust off any excess flour from your dough after rolling it out. Then be careful not to spread or sprinkle too much filling over the dough—abundant filling does not allow the roll to seal as it rises. Tightly roll up the dough and allow the rolls to rise until doubled before baking.

gingerbread muffin tops

(PICTURED AT RIGHT)

Our Test Kitchen came up with this unique recipe for muffin tops that doesn't require a special baking pan. The flavor is similar to mouthwatering molasses cookies.

1/3 cup butter, softened

1/3 cup packed brown sugar

1 egg

3/4 cup molasses

2 cups all-purpose flour

1-1/2 teaspoons ground ginger

1 teaspoon baking soda

1 teaspoon ground cinnamon

1/2 teaspoon salt

1 tablespoon coarse sugar

In a large bowl, cream butter and brown sugar until light and fluffy. Beat in egg and molasses. Combine the flour, ginger, baking soda, cinnamon and salt; gradually add to creamed mixture and mix well.

Drop by 1/4 cupfuls 2 in. apart onto a parchment paper-lined baking sheet. Sprinkle with coarse sugar. Bake at 350° for 15-20 minutes or until set. Cool for 5 minutes before removing from pan to a wire rack. Serve warm. **YIELD:** 7 muffin tops.

christmas morning coffee cake

Bananas and cranberry sauce make every slice of this pretty coffee cake moist and marvelous.

Rosemary Snyder | KENOSHA, WI

2 cups biscuit/baking mix

2 tablespoons sugar

1/2 teaspoon ground cinnamon

1/4 teaspoon ground allspice

2 eggs, beaten

2/3 cup mashed ripe bananas (about 2 medium)

1/4 cup milk

1 teaspoon vanilla extract

1 can (14 ounces) whole-berry cranberry sauce

TOPPING:

1/2 cup packed brown sugar

1/2 cup coarsely chopped pecans

2 tablespoons all-purpose flour

2 tablespoons butter, melted

In a large bowl, combine the baking mix, sugar, cinnamon and allspice. Combine eggs, bananas, milk and vanilla; stir into dry ingredients just until moistened. Pour into a greased 9-in. square baking pan.

Place the cranberry sauce in a bowl; stir. Spread over batter. Combine topping ingredients; sprinkle over cranberry sauce. Bake at 400° for 25-30 minutes or until a toothpick inserted near the center comes out clean. Remove to a wire rack. **YIELD:** 9 servings.

glazed lemon-anise bread

When I was growing up, anise was one of my favorite Christmas flavors, so my mother always made this bread for the holidays. Now my own family enjoys the tasty tradition.

Eileen Falk | CUTLER, IN

3 to 3-1/2 cups all-purpose flour

1/3 cup sugar

1 package (1/4 ounce) quick-rise yeast

1/2 teaspoon salt

1/3 cup 2% milk

1/3 cup butter, cubed

1/4 cup water

1 egg

2 tablespoons lemon juice

2 to 3 teaspoons aniseed

1 teaspoon grated lemon peel

GLAZE:

1 cup confectioners' sugar

1/4 teaspoon vanilla extract

2 to 3 tablespoons 2% milk

In a large bowl, combine 1-1/2 cups flour, sugar, yeast and salt. In a small saucepan, heat the milk, butter and water to 120°-130°; add to dry ingredients. Beat on medium speed for 2 minutes. Add egg, lemon juice, aniseed, lemon peel and 1/2 cup flour; beat 2 minutes longer. Stir in enough remaining flour to form a soft dough.

Turn onto a floured surface; knead until smooth and elastic, about 6-8 minutes. Place in a greased bowl, turning once to grease the top. Cover and let rise in a warm place until doubled, about 1 hour.

Punch dough down. Place in a greased 8-in. x 4-in. loaf pan. Cover and let rise until doubled, about 40 minutes.

Bake at 375° for 25-30 minutes or until golden brown. Cool for 10 minutes before removing from pan to a wire rack.

For glaze, combine the confectioners' sugar, vanilla and enough milk to achieve desired consistency. Spread over top of warm loaf, allowing glaze to drape down the sides. Cool. **YIELD:** 1 loaf (12 slices).

almond-studded chocolate loaf

(PICTURED AT RIGHT)

With rich chocolate flavor and a nutty topping, this luscious loaf could be served as a dessert or a sweet snack. I've also been known to give it as a gift.

Lisa Varner | CHARLESTON, SC

2 cups all-purpose flour

1/4 cup baking cocoa

2 teaspoons baking powder

1/2 teaspoon salt

1/4 teaspoon baking soda

1 egg

1 cup 2% milk

3/4 cup packed dark brown sugar

1/3 cup canola oil

1/2 teaspoon almond extract

1 cup plus 2 tablespoons chopped almonds, divided

3/4 cup plus 2 tablespoons miniature semisweet chocolate chips, divided

In a large bowl, combine the flour, cocoa, baking powder, salt and baking soda. In a small bowl, whisk the egg, milk, brown sugar, oil and extract. Stir mixture into dry ingredients just until moistened. Fold in 1 cup almonds and 3/4 cup chocolate chips.

Spoon into a greased 9-in. x 5-in. loaf pan. Sprinkle with remaining almonds and chips. Bake at 350° for 55-60 minutes or until a toothpick inserted near the center comes out clean. Cool for 10 minutes before removing from pan to a wire rack. **YIELD:** 1 loaf (16 slices).

gumdrop loaves

I dress up traditional fruitcake by stirring in colorful, chewy gumdrops. No one can resist this moist bread!

JoAnn Renze | OMAHA, NE

1 cup butter, softened

1 cup sugar

1 cup packed brown sugar

4 eggs

2 cups unsweetened applesauce

1 teaspoon vanilla extract

3 cups small gumdrops

1-1/2 cups chopped pecans

1-1/2 cups chopped dates

1 cup raisins

1/3 cup red candied cherries, cut in half

4 cups all-purpose flour, divided

2 teaspoons baking soda

2 teaspoons ground cinnamon

1 teaspoon pumpkin pie spice

In a large bowl, cream butter and sugars until light and fluffy. Beat in the eggs, applesauce and vanilla (batter will appear curdled). Remove black gumdrops and save for another use. In a large bowl, combine the gumdrops, pecans, dates, raisins, cherries and 1 cup flour; toss to coat. Combine the baking soda, cinnamon, pie spice and remaining flour; gradually add to the creamed mixture. Fold in gumdrop mixture.

Pour into two greased 9-in. x 5-in. loaf pans. Bake at 300° for 45 minutes; cover loosely with foil. Bake 45 minutes longer or until a toothpick inserted near the center comes out clean. Cool for 10 minutes before removing from pans to wire racks to cool completely. **YIELD:** 2 loaves.

bing cherry & orange coffee cake

Dotted with flecks of juicy cherries, every slice of this coffee cake is infused with refreshing citrus flavor.

Leah MacDonald | CALGARY, AB

2 cans (15 ounces each) pitted dark sweet cherries, drained and chopped

2 tablespoons plus 3 cups all-purpose flour, divided

2 tablespoons plus 1-3/4 cups sugar, divided

1 cup butter, softened

3 eggs

1 tablespoon grated orange peel

1-1/2 teaspoons baking powder

1/2 teaspoon ground cinnamon

1/4 teaspoon ground ginger

1/8 teaspoon salt

1/2 cup orange juice

ICING:

3/4 cup confectioners' sugar

2 tablespoons butter, softened

1/4 teaspoon vanilla extract

1-1/2 to 2 teaspoons 2% milk

In a small bowl, combine the cherries, 2 tablespoons of flour and 2 tablespoons of sugar; set aside.

In a large bowl, cream butter and remaining sugar until light and fluffy. Add eggs, one at a time, beating well after each addition. Beat in orange peel. Combine the baking powder, cinnamon, ginger, salt and remaining flour; add to the creamed mixture alternately with orange juice, beating well after each addition. Fold in cherry mixture.

Transfer to a greased and floured 10-in. fluted tube pan. Bake at 350° for 50-60 minutes or until a toothpick inserted near the center comes out clean. Cool for 10 minutes before removing from pan to a wire rack to cool completely.

For icing, in a small bowl, beat the confectioners' sugar, butter, vanilla and enough milk to achieve desired consistency. Drizzle over bread. **YIELD:** 12 servings.

cranberry cobblescones

(PICTURED AT RIGHT)

My clever, scone-like treats signal the start of the Christmas season at our house. The whole family loves the sweet-tart taste of cranberries sandwiched between tender dough.

Lori Steward | DULUTH, MN

2 cups all-purpose flour

1 tablespoon sugar

2 teaspoons baking powder

1/2 teaspoon salt

1/4 cup cold butter

2 eggs

About 1/3 cup heavy whipping cream

FILLING:

1/4 cup sugar

1 tablespoon brown sugar

2 teaspoons cornstarch

1/4 teaspoon ground cinnamon

3/4 cup whole-berry cranberry sauce

TOPPING:

1 tablespoon milk

2 tablespoons sugar

1/2 teaspoon ground cinnamon

Grease a 16-in. sheet of heavy-duty aluminum foil; set aside. In a large bowl, combine the flour, sugar, baking powder and salt. Cut in butter until mixture resembles fine crumbs. Place eggs in a measuring cup. Add enough cream to measure 3/4 cup; stir into crumb mixture. Knead just until dough forms a ball, about 1 minute. Turn onto prepared foil; roll out into a 16-in. x 8-in. rectangle.

For filling, combine the sugars, cornstarch and cinnamon in a small saucepan. Stir in cranberry sauce. Bring to a boil over medium heat, stirring constantly. Boil for 1 minute or until thickened; remove from the heat and cool slightly.

Spread filling widthwise over half of the rectangle. Fold dough over filling, forming an 8-in. square; seal edges. Transfer foil with dough to a greased baking sheet.

Brush with milk. Combine the sugar and cinnamon; sprinkle over top. Cut into 2-in. squares (do not separate). Bake at 425° for 16-18 minutes or until golden brown. **YIELD:** 16 scones.

When planning menus for occasions throughout the year, cooks first focus on the main course, then round out the meal with a selection of sides.

During the Christmas season, choosing just the right entree is especially important.

There's no need to worry about making the wrong main course choice when you turn to this lovely recipe-packed chapter.

For a showstopping success, Crown Roast with Broccoli Mushroom Stuffing is guaranteed to elicit oohs, aahs...and recipe requests.

From elegant oven dinners to special skillet suppers, you're certain to find an inviting entree to serve as the star attraction on your table.

STAR OF WONDER
(PICTURED AT RIGHT)

Crown Roast with
Broccoli Mushroom Stuffing (p. 52)

dazzling
MAIN COURSES

crown roast with broccoli mushroom stuffing

(PICTURED ON PAGE 51)

When I need an eye-catching entree to impress guests on special occasions, I reach for a pork crown roast.
It may take some time to put together, but it easily bakes in the oven and feeds a crowd.

Carol Sue Bullick | ROYERSFORD, PA

1 pork crown roast (14 ribs and about 9 pounds)

3 tablespoons all-purpose flour

1 teaspoon salt

1 teaspoon dried thyme

1 teaspoon dried parsley flakes

1/4 teaspoon pepper

STUFFING:

1 chicken bouillon cube

1/2 cup boiling water

1 bunch broccoli, cut into 1/2-inch pieces

1 pound sliced fresh mushrooms

1 large onion, chopped

3 tablespoons canola oil

3/4 teaspoon salt

1/4 teaspoon dried thyme

1/4 teaspoon pepper

10 slices white bread, cubed

GRAVY:

2-1/2 cups water

3 tablespoons all-purpose flour

1/2 teaspoon salt

1/8 teaspoon pepper

Place roast on a rack in a large shallow roasting pan. In a small bowl, combine the flour, salt, thyme, parsley and pepper; rub over roast. Cover rib ends with foil. Bake, uncovered, at 350° for 1-1/2 hours.

Meanwhile, dissolve bouillon cube in water. In a large skillet, saute broccoli, mushrooms and onion in oil until tender; stir in salt, thyme, pepper and dissolved bouillon. Add bread cubes; toss to coat.

Carefully spoon the stuffing into the center of the roast. Bake 30-60 minutes longer or until a meat thermometer reads 160°. Place remaining stuffing in a greased 2-1/2-qt. baking dish; refrigerate until ready to bake.

Bake additional stuffing, covered, for 30-40 minutes. Uncover; bake 10 minutes longer or until lightly browned.

Transfer roast to a serving platter. Remove foil. Let stand for 10-15 minutes.

Meanwhile, pour drippings and loosened brown bits into a measuring cup. Skim fat, reserving 3 tablespoons. Add enough water to measure 3 cups. In a large saucepan, combine flour and reserved fat until smooth. Gradually stir in the salt, pepper and drippings. Bring to a boil; cook and stir for 2 minutes or until thickened. Remove stuffing to a bowl and cut between ribs. Serve with gravy. **YIELD:** 14 servings (14 cups stuffing).

hearty tomato-olive penne

(PICTURED AT RIGHT)

*Who needs meat when you have a pasta
dish loaded with fresh tomatoes,
Greek olives and Havarti cheese?
I often assemble this casserole in advance
and bake the next day, adding
a few minutes to the cooking time.*

Jacqueline Frank | GREEN BAY, WI

2 large onions, chopped

6 tablespoons olive oil

3 garlic cloves, minced

3 pounds plum tomatoes, seeded and chopped (about 10 tomatoes)

1 cup vegetable or chicken broth

1 tablespoon dried basil

1 teaspoon crushed red pepper flakes

1/2 teaspoon salt

1/4 teaspoon pepper

1 package (16 ounces) uncooked penne pasta

1 block (24 ounces) Havarti cheese, cut into 1/2-in. cubes

1 cup pitted Greek olives

1/3 cup grated Parmesan cheese

In a Dutch oven, saute onions in oil until tender. Add garlic; cook 1 minute longer. Stir in the tomatoes, broth, basil, pepper flakes, salt and pepper. Bring to a boil. Reduce heat; cover and simmer for 25-30 minutes or until sauce is slightly thickened.

Meanwhile, cook penne according to package directions; drain.

Stir the Havarti cheese, olives and cooked penne into the sauce. Transfer to a greased 13-in. x 9-in. baking dish; sprinkle with the Parmesan cheese.

Cover and bake at 375° for 20 minutes. Uncover; bake 5 minutes longer or until cheese is melted. YIELD: 8 servings.

HEARD ABOUT HAVARTI?

Havarti is semi-soft cow's milk cheese. The Danish delicacy has a buttery, creamy texture and mildly tangy taste. Refrigerate Havarti in your refrigerator's crisper drawer for about 2 weeks.

favorite chicken marsala

The slightly sweet flavor of marsala wine pairs well with the earthy taste of mushrooms.
My version of a classic main course also features heavy whipping cream.

Cyndy Gerken | NAPLES, FL

1/2 cup plus 1 tablespoon all-purpose flour, divided

1/4 teaspoon salt

1/4 teaspoon pepper

1-1/2 pounds boneless skinless chicken breasts, cut into 1/2-inch strips

1/4 cup olive oil

1/4 cup butter, divided

1 cup sliced fresh shiitake mushrooms

1 cup sliced baby portobello mushrooms

2 large shallots, chopped

1 cup marsala wine

1 cup chicken broth

1 cup heavy whipping cream

2 tablespoons minced fresh parsley

PASTA:

1 package (16 ounces) angel hair pasta

1 whole garlic bulb, minced

1/4 cup olive oil

3 tablespoons butter

1/2 cup grated Parmesan cheese

1/2 teaspoon salt

1/4 teaspoon pepper

Dash crushed red pepper flakes

Place 1/2 cup flour, salt and pepper in a large resealable plastic bag. Add chicken, a few pieces at a time, and shake to coat. In a large skillet, cook chicken in oil and 2 tablespoons butter in batches until no longer pink. Remove and keep warm.

Saute mushrooms and shallots in remaining butter until tender. Add wine, stirring to loosen browned bits from pan. Sprinkle with remaining flour; stir until blended. Gradually stir in broth and cream. Bring to a boil. Reduce heat; cook and stir for 5-10 minutes or until slightly thickened.

Meanwhile, in a Dutch oven, cook pasta according to package directions. Drain, reserving 1/2 cup cooking liquid. In the same Dutch oven, saute garlic in oil and butter for 2 minutes. Return pasta to the pan; stir in the cheese, salt, pepper, pepper flakes and reserved cooking liquid.

Place the pasta on a serving platter; top with chicken and sauce. Sprinkle with parsley. **YIELD:** 6 servings.

peach glaze for ham

Five ingredients easily become a fruity, spiced glaze for ham.
My family enjoys the entree so much that I serve it at both Christmas and Easter.

Christine Eiberts | TULSA, OK

1 can (8-1/2 ounces) sliced peaches in heavy syrup

1 fully cooked bone-in ham (6 pounds)

1 tablespoon whole cloves

1-1/2 cups packed brown sugar

3 tablespoons cider vinegar

1/4 to 1/2 teaspoon ground cloves

Drain peaches, reserving syrup (save peaches for another use). Place ham on a rack in a shallow roasting pan. Score the surface of the ham, making diamond shapes 1/2 in. deep; insert a clove in each diamond. Cover and bake at 325° for 2 hours.

Meanwhile, in a small bowl, combine the brown sugar, vinegar, cloves and reserved syrup.

Brush ham with 1/2 cup brown sugar mixture. Bake, uncovered, 25-35 minutes longer or until a meat thermometer reads 140°. Let stand for 15 minutes before slicing. Serve with remaining brown sugar mixture. **YIELD:** 10 servings.

lobster-stuffed beef wellington

(PICTURED AT RIGHT)

Instead of stuffing beef tenderloin with mushrooms, I use lobster for a more elegant feel. A side of potatoes and salad completes the festive meal.

Terry Smigielski | BOOTHBAY HARBOR, ME

3 lobster tails (8 to 10 ounces each)

1/2 cup heavy whipping cream

2 fresh thyme sprigs

1-1/4 teaspoons salt, divided

1-1/8 teaspoons pepper, divided

2/3 cup dry bread crumbs

1 beef tenderloin roast (4 to 5 pounds)

1 package (17.3 ounces) frozen puff pastry, thawed

1 egg white

3 tablespoons butter, melted

Using kitchen scissors, cut through lobster shells; carefully remove lobster and chop. In a small skillet, combine the lobster, cream, thyme, 1/4 teaspoon salt and 1/8 teaspoon pepper. Bring to a boil over medium heat, cook 3-5 minutes or until lobster is firm and opaque. Discard thyme sprigs. Stir in bread crumbs; set aside to cool.

Make a lengthwise slit down the center of tenderloin to within 1/2 in. of bottom. Open meat so it lies flat. Place lobster mixture down the center. Close tenderloin; tie several times with kitchen string. Sprinkle with remaining salt and pepper.

Place the tenderloin in a greased 15-in. x 10-in. x 1-in. baking pan; fold ends under tenderloin. Bake, uncovered, at 475° for 20-25 minutes or until browned.

Cool to room temperature; refrigerate until chilled.

On a lightly floured surface, unfold one puff pastry sheet; cut lengthwise along one fold line, forming two rectangles. Cut smaller rectangle into a 6-in. x 3-in. rectangle; use remaining piece for decorations if desired. Moisten a 6-in. edge of large rectangle with water. Attach smaller rectangle along that edge, pressing lightly to seal. Roll out 2 in. longer than the tenderloin on each side. Transfer to an ungreased baking sheet. Brush with egg white.

Remove and discard kitchen string from tenderloin; place onto the pastry. Roll out remaining puff pastry into a rectangle 8 in. wide and 5 in. longer than the tenderloin; place over the meat. Brush pastry edges with water; fold edges under meat. With a sharp knife, make four slashes across top of pastry. Brush with butter.

Bake, uncovered, at 425° for 40 minutes (meat will be cooked to medium doneness); cover loosely with foil to prevent over-browning if necessary. Transfer to a serving platter. Let stand for 15 minutes before slicing. YIELD: 14 servings.

pancetta sage turkey with cream sauce

I turn ordinary boneless turkey breasts into something special by filling them with pancetta and fresh sage. Draping pretty slices with creamy sauce is the crowning touch.

Erin Duff | OSLER, SK

2 boneless skinless turkey breast halves (2 pounds each)

12 pancetta slices or bacon strips

10 fresh sage leaves

1/2 cup all-purpose flour

1 teaspoon salt

1 teaspoon pepper

3 tablespoons butter

SAUCE:

2 shallots, finely chopped

2 garlic cloves, minced

1 cup white wine or chicken broth

1 cup heavy whipping cream

2 fresh rosemary sprigs

6 fresh sage leaves

Dash each salt and pepper

Cover one turkey half with plastic wrap; flatten to 1/2-in. thickness. Remove plastic; place half of pancetta and sage over turkey. Roll up jelly-roll style, starting with a short side; tie with kitchen string. Repeat with the remaining turkey, pancetta and sage. Combine the flour, salt and pepper; sprinkle over each turkey.

In a large skillet, brown turkey in butter on all sides. Place on a rack in a shallow roasting pan. Bake, uncovered, at 325° for 1-1/4 to 1-1/2 hours or until a meat thermometer reads 170°. Let stand for 15 minutes before slicing.

Meanwhile, in the same skillet, saute shallots and garlic, stirring to loosen browned bits from pan. Add wine; bring to a boil. Cook until liquid is reduced by half. Stir in the cream, rosemary, sage, salt and pepper; cook for 3-4 minutes or until thickened. Serve with turkey. **YIELD:** 12 servings.

SUBSTITUTING BACON FOR PANCETTA

Unlike American bacon, pancetta is unsmoked pork belly that has been salt cured, spiced and dried. If you can't find pancetta at your local grocery store, you can use bacon. But to reduce the bacon's smoky flavor, blanch it before using.

Put the bacon in a saucepan. Cover with 3 inches of cold water. Bring to a boil; reduce heat and simmer for 5 minutes. Drain the bacon and rinse in cold running water. Pat dry with paper towels.

baked salmon steaks

(PICTURED AT RIGHT)

This delightful recipe finally convinced my husband that fish is fantastic! The entree is quick enough for weekday dinners yet impressive enough for holiday guests.

Jill Anderson | *SLEEPY EYE, MN*

2 tablespoons water

2 tablespoons olive oil

1 tablespoon minced fresh oregano or 1 teaspoon dried oregano

2 teaspoons sugar

2 teaspoons lime juice

2 teaspoons minced chipotle pepper in adobo sauce

2 garlic cloves, minced

1 teaspoon salt

4 salmon steaks (8 ounces each)

Lime wedges

In a small bowl, combine the first eight ingredients. Place salmon in a greased 15-in. x 10-in. x 1-in. baking pan. Spoon chipotle mixture over fish. Bake, uncovered, at 350° for 20-25 minutes or until fish flakes easily with a fork. Serve with lime wedges. YIELD: 4 servings.

festive rack of lamb

Rack of lamb isn't an entree you prepare every day. So when you do, it needs to be outstanding. Our Test Kitchen staff guarantees the citrus-garlic sauce served alongside roasted lamb is sure to please. This recipe can easily be doubled or tripled.

2 tablespoons all-purpose flour

1 teaspoon salt

1/2 teaspoon pepper

1 rack of lamb (1-1/2 pounds and 8 ribs), trimmed

2 tablespoons butter

1 cup white wine or chicken broth

1 teaspoon grated lemon peel

1 garlic clove, minced

1/2 teaspoon dried rosemary, crushed

1 bay leaf

Place the flour, salt and pepper in a shallow bowl. Coat lamb in flour mixture. In a large skillet over medium-high heat, cook lamb in butter for 2 minutes on each side. Place on a greased baking sheet.

Bake, uncovered, at 375° for 15-20 minutes or until meat reaches desired doneness (for medium-rare, a meat thermometer should read 145°; medium, 160°; well-done, 170°).

Meanwhile, add the wine, lemon peel, garlic, rosemary and bay leaf to skillet. Bring to a boil; cook until liquid is reduced by half, about 8 minutes.

Remove lamb from oven and loosely cover with foil. Let stand for 5 minutes before slicing. Serve sauce with lamb. YIELD: 2 servings.

bbq beef brisket with horseradish cream

Chipotle peppers give a nice hint of heat to tender slices of oven-braised brisket.
The cool, creamy horseradish sauce also adds a bit of zip.

Janine Talley | ORLANDO, FL

1 fresh beef brisket (4 pounds)

1/2 teaspoon pepper

1/4 teaspoon salt

3 tablespoons olive oil

2 large onions, chopped

4 garlic cloves, sliced

3 cups beef broth

1 bottle (18 ounces) barbecue sauce

6 fresh thyme sprigs

1/4 cup chopped chipotle peppers in adobo sauce

HORSERADISH CREAM:

1/2 cup heavy whipping cream

1/2 cup sour cream

1/4 cup cider vinegar

1/4 cup prepared horseradish

1/2 teaspoon salt

Sprinkle brisket with pepper and salt. In an ovenproof Dutch oven, brown meat in oil on all sides. Remove and keep warm.

In the same pan, saute onions until crisp-tender. Add garlic; cook 1 minute longer. Return brisket to the pan. Add the broth, barbecue sauce, thyme and chipotle peppers. Bring to a boil. Cover and bake at 350° for 3 to 3-1/2 hours or until meat is tender.

In a small bowl, beat the cream, sour cream, vinegar, horseradish and salt until thickened. Cover and refrigerate until serving.

Remove brisket to a serving platter. Skim the fat from cooking juices; discard thyme sprigs. Thinly slice meat across the grain. Serve with cooking juices and horseradish cream. **YIELD:** 10 servings (1-1/4 cups horseradish cream).

EDITOR'S NOTE: This is a fresh beef brisket, not corned beef.

prosciutto-wrapped haddock

A friend made this main dish for me when I was in college. It redefined my idea of Italian cooking.
Prosciutto and pesto complement the mild-flavored fish.

Kendra Doss | KANSAS CITY, MO

1/3 cup fresh basil leaves

2 tablespoons grated Parmesan cheese

2 garlic cloves, halved

1 tablespoon pine nuts, toasted

1/8 teaspoon salt

Dash crushed red pepper flakes

Dash pepper

1/4 cup plus 3 tablespoons olive oil, divided

1/4 cup chopped tomatoes

4 haddock fillets (6 ounces each)

4 thin slices prosciutto or deli ham

Place the basil, cheese and garlic in a food processor; cover and pulse until chopped. Add the pine nuts, salt, pepper flakes and pepper; cover and process until blended. While processing, gradually add 1/4 cup oil in a steady stream. Stir in tomatoes.

Spread 1 tablespoon pesto over each fillet; wrap with a prosciutto slice. Place on a greased 15-in. x 10-in. x 1-in. baking pan and brush with remaining olive oil. Bake at 400° for 10-15 minutes or until fish flakes easily with a fork. **YIELD:** 4 servings.

bold citrus shrimp

(PICTURED AT RIGHT)

This is the only way my finicky teenagers will eat seafood. They love the robust citrus taste of the skillet-prepared shrimp.

Suzanne Kesel | COHOCTON, NY

2 pounds uncooked jumbo shrimp

2/3 cup lemon juice

1/3 cup lime juice

3 tablespoons brown sugar

3/4 teaspoon ground ginger

1 jalapeno pepper, seeded and diced

2 tablespoons grated lemon peel

4-1/2 teaspoons grated lime peel

1 tablespoon whole white peppercorns, crushed

3/4 teaspoon salt

4 tablespoons olive oil, divided

Peel and devein shrimp, leaving the tails on. Butterfly shrimp along outside curve.

In a small saucepan, combine the lemon juice, lime juice, brown sugar and ginger. Bring to a boil; cook until liquid is reduced by half, about 10 minutes. Stir in the jalapeno, lemon peel, lime peel, peppercorns and salt; cook 1 minute longer. Remove from heat. Stir in 1 tablespoon olive oil. When cool, coat shrimp with sauce mixture.

In a large skillet, cook shrimp in remaining oil in batches over medium-high heat for 1-2 minutes on each side or until shrimp turn pink. **YIELD:** 5 servings.

EDITOR'S NOTE: When cutting hot peppers, disposable gloves are recommended. Avoid touching your face.

pork loin roast with sour cream sauce

*I use roasted parsnips, celery and onions to create a mouthwatering,
rustic sauce for pork. This is home cooking at its very best!*

Donna Noel | GRAY, ME

1 large parsnip, peeled and grated

2 medium onions, chopped

1 celery rib, chopped

1 cup water

1 cup white wine or chicken broth

1 boneless rolled pork loin roast (4 pounds)

2 tablespoons butter

1 tablespoon all-purpose flour

1 cup (8 ounces) sour cream

1/2 teaspoon salt

1/8 teaspoon white pepper

Place the parsnip, onions and celery in a greased shallow roasting pan. Pour water and wine over vegetables. Place roast fat side up over top. Bake, uncovered, at 350° for 1-3/4 hours to 2-1/4 hours or until a meat thermometer reads 160°. Transfer to a warm serving platter. Let stand for 10-15 minutes before slicing.

Place pan drippings and vegetables in a blender. Cover and process until blended. Meanwhile, in a large saucepan, melt butter. Stir in flour until smooth; gradually add vegetable mixture. Bring to a boil; cook and stir for 1-2 minutes or until thickened. Remove from the heat. Stir in the sour cream, salt and pepper. Serve with pork. **YIELD:** 10 servings (2-1/2 cups sauce).

pei pah duck

*Fans of duck will fall for this Asian-inspired recipe.
Basting the bird with a honey and soy sauce mixture creates moist, tender slices.*

Jennifer Yanfen Sadjadi | HIGH POINT, NC

1 domestic duck (5 to 6 pounds)

1 tablespoon Chinese five-spice powder

2 garlic cloves, minced

2 teaspoons salt

2 teaspoons sugar

2 teaspoons ground ginger

2 teaspoons pepper

2 teaspoons ground cloves

4 green onions, cut into 2-inch pieces

2 tablespoons minced fresh gingerroot

4 garlic cloves, peeled

1 tablespoon hoisin sauce

1/4 cup honey

1/4 cup soy sauce

2 tablespoons cider vinegar

Prick skin of duck well with a fork. Combine the five-spice powder, garlic, salt, sugar, ginger, pepper and cloves; rub over the outside and inside of duck. Combine the green onions, gingerroot, garlic cloves and hoisin; place inside the cavity.

Combine the honey, soy sauce and vinegar. Bake at 350° for 2-1/2 to 3 hours or until a meat thermometer reads 180°, basting occasionally with honey mixture. Cover loosely with foil if duck browns too quickly. Cover and let stand for 15 minutes before carving. **YIELD:** 6 servings.

roasted cornish hens with vegetables

(PICTURED AT RIGHT)

Roasting simply seasoned Cornish game hens and vegetables in one pan results in a full-flavored meal in one.

Lillian Julow | GAINESVILLE, FL

6 medium potatoes, quartered

6 medium carrots, cut in half lengthwise and cut into chunks

1 large sweet onion, cut into wedges

1/2 cup butter, melted

2 teaspoons dried oregano

2 teaspoons dried rosemary, crushed

1-1/2 teaspoons garlic salt

6 Cornish game hens (20 ounces each)

1 tablespoon olive oil

1/4 teaspoon salt

1/4 teaspoon pepper

6 bacon strips

In a large bowl, combine the first seven ingredients. Transfer to a shallow roasting pan.

Brush hens with oil; sprinkle with salt and pepper. Wrap a bacon strip around each hen; secure with a wooden toothpick. Tie legs together. Place, breast side up, over the vegetables.

Bake, uncovered, at 350° for 1-1/2 to 2 hours or until a meat thermometer reads 180° and vegetables are tender. Remove hens to serving platter; serve with the vegetables. **YIELD:** 6 servings.

GET TO KNOW GAME HENS

Contrary to the name, Cornish hens are not game birds but are young chickens that typically weigh 1-1/2 pounds or less. They were originally bred to offer consumers small, individual-serving chickens with mostly white meat.

Cornish game hens look elegant, have tender meat and take less time to cook than whole chickens. But they are more expensive, making them appropriate for special occasions.

Good things come in small packages. Never has that phrase been truer than when it's referring to diminutive desserts.

Bite-sized beauties allow folks to indulge in something sweet with moderate restraint. They may be mini, but they offer major satisfaction!

Individual Toffee Dream Cheesecakes and Croissant Pudding with Chocolate Kahlua Sauce are updated versions of two all-time classic, comforting favorites.

For refreshing flavor, White Chocolate-Candy Cane Parfaits and Berry Napoleons will put smiles on both big and small guests gathered around your table.

SMALL AND SWEET

(PICTURED AT RIGHT)

Individual Toffee Dream Cheesecakes (p. 66)
White Chocolate-Candy Cane Parfaits (p. 68)
Croissant Pudding with Chocolate Kahlua Sauce (p. 70)
Berry Napoleons (p. 64)

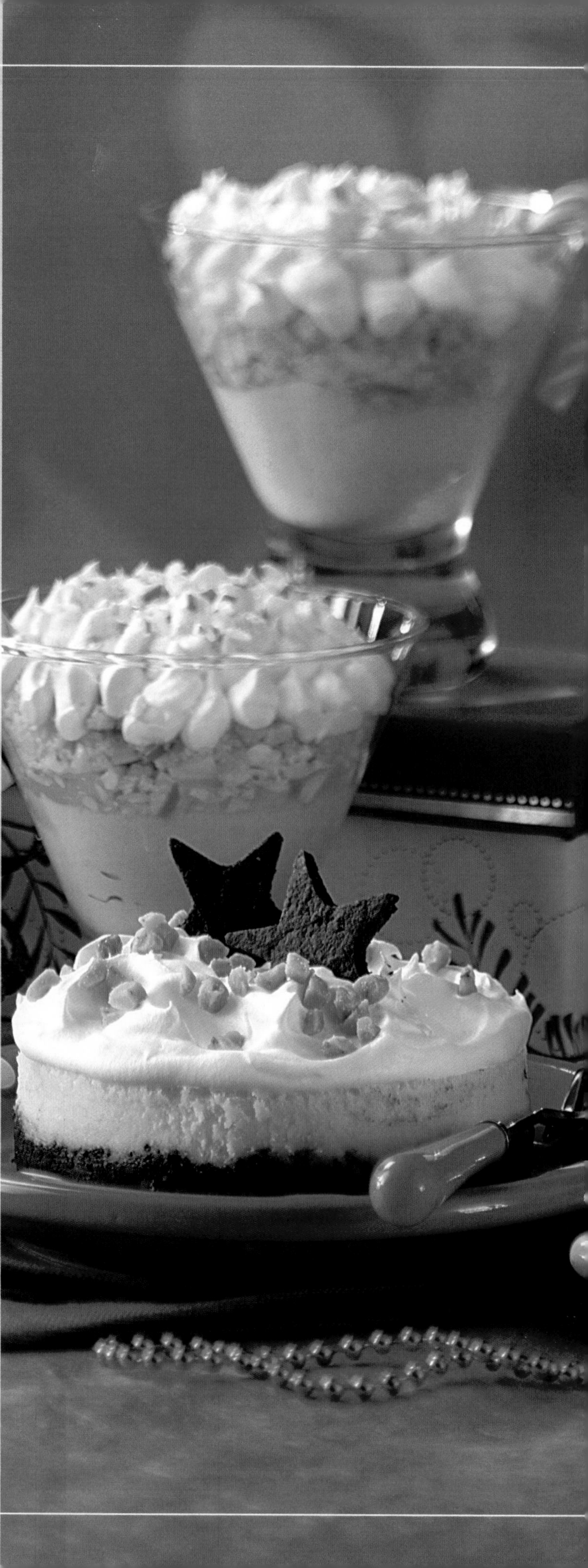

merry
MINI DESSERTS

berry napoleons

(PICTURED ON PAGE 63)

Top flaky phyllo dough with a beautiful blend of berries and sweetened whipped cream for a lovely, fresh-tasting finale. Each element of the recipe can be prepared in advance.

Wolfgang Hanau | WEST PALM BEACH, FL

1 package (10 ounces) frozen sweetened raspberries

1 tablespoon port wine

1 tablespoon raspberry liqueur

1 package (16 ounces) frozen phyllo dough, thawed

1 cup butter, melted

FRESH BERRIES:

2 cups fresh raspberries

2 cups fresh blueberries

2 cups sliced fresh strawberries

3 to 4 tablespoons orange liqueur

WHIPPED CREAM:

1-1/2 cups heavy whipping cream

3 tablespoons confectioners' sugar

1/4 teaspoon vanilla extract

Place the raspberries, wine and raspberry liqueur in a blender; cover and process until pureed. Strain the raspberry mixture, reserving juice; discard seeds. Set aside.

Layer two sheets of phyllo dough on a baking sheet; brush with butter. Keep remaining phyllo covered with plastic wrap and a damp towel to prevent it from drying out. Repeat layers four times. Cut stack in half lengthwise, then cut widthwise, forming 12 rectangles. Repeat with remaining dough on three additional baking sheets. Bake at 375° for 6-8 minutes or until golden brown. Cool on pans on wire racks.

In a large bowl, combine berries, orange liqueur and 2 tablespoons reserved raspberry juice; toss to coat. Cover and refrigerate for 30 minutes.

Meanwhile, in a large bowl, beat cream until it begins to thicken. Add confectioners' sugar and vanilla; beat until stiff peaks form.

Drizzle 1 tablespoon remaining raspberry sauce over each serving plate. Place one phyllo rectangle over sauce; layer each with 1/4 cup berries and 2 tablespoons whipped cream. Top with remaining phyllo. **YIELD:** 24 servings.

LIQUEUR SUBSTITUTE

The recipe for Berry Napoleons calls for orange and raspberry liqueurs, both of which are made from Cognac. Grand Marnier (orange) and Chambord (raspberry) are the two most popular brands. Orange juice concentrate and syrup from frozen raspberries can be substituted for the liqueurs, but the flavor may be affected.

molten peppermint-chocolate cakes

(PICTURED AT RIGHT)

With a warm chocolate sauce inside, these moist little cakes are perfect for cold winter nights. The addition of peppermint extract provides a special touch.

Genise Krause | *STURGEON BAY, WI*

1/2 cup butter, cubed

4 ounces bittersweet chocolate, chopped

2 eggs

2 egg yolks

1/3 cup sugar

1/2 teaspoon peppermint extract

1/4 cup all-purpose flour

1/8 teaspoon salt

Confectioners' sugar

In a small saucepan, melt the butter and chocolate; transfer to a large bowl. Add the eggs, egg yolks and sugar; mix well. Stir in extract. Add flour and salt; stir until blended. Pour into four greased 6-oz. custard cups or ramekins.

Place the custard cups on a baking sheet. Bake at 425° for 10-12 minutes or until a thermometer inserted near the center reads 160° and cake sides are set. Remove from the oven and let stand for 1 minute. Run a knife around edge of custard cups; invert onto individual dessert plates. Garnish with confectioners' sugar. Serve immediately. **YIELD:** 4 servings.

baked cinnamon apples

After a heavy meal, I like to serve a little lighter dessert. Cinnamon liqueur, butter and brown sugar infuse naturally sweet apples with wonderful flavor.

Kenna Jo Lambertsen | *NEVADA, IA*

4 large apples

1/4 cup butter

1/2 cup packed brown sugar

1 cup cinnamon schnapps liqueur

Core the apples and peel top two-thirds of each. Place in an ungreased 8-in. baking dish. Fill each apple with 1 tablespoon butter and 2 tablespoons brown sugar. Pour liqueur over apples.

Bake, uncovered, at 350° for 55-60 minutes or until the apples are tender, basting occasionally. **YIELD:** 4 servings.

individual toffee dream cheesecakes

(PICTURED ON PAGE 62)

Tasty toffee bits are a sweet surprise inside individual, creamy cheesecakes.
I often drizzle chocolate syrup over the whipped cream garnish.

Marla Hyatt | ST. PAUL, MN

1 cup chocolate wafer crumbs

3 tablespoons butter, melted

1/2 cup toffee bits

FILLING:

1 cup sweetened condensed milk

6 ounces cream cheese, softened

1 teaspoon vanilla extract

2 eggs, lightly beaten

Optional toppings: chocolate wafers, whipped cream and additional toffee bits

Place each of four greased 4-in. springform pans on a double thickness of heavy-duty foil (about 12 in. square). Securely wrap foil around pans.

In a small bowl, combine cracker crumbs and butter. Press onto bottoms of prepared pans; sprinkle with toffee bits.

In a large bowl, beat the condensed milk, cream cheese and vanilla until smooth. Add the eggs; beat on low speed just until combined. Pour filling over crusts. Place springform pans in a large baking pan; add 1 in. of hot water to larger pan.

Bake at 350° for 24-28 minutes or until centers are just set and tops appear dull. Remove springform pans from water bath. Cool on a wire rack for 10 minutes. Carefully run a knife around edges of pans to loosen; cool 1 hour longer. Refrigerate overnight.

To make decorative stars, place a chocolate wafer on a small piece of waxed paper; microwave on high for 30-60 seconds or until softened. Immediately cut with a 1-1/2-in. star-shaped cookie cutter. Garnish the cheesecakes with whipped cream, additional toffee bits and stars as desired. **YIELD:** 4 servings.

key lime puddings

While in the oven, this refreshing, lime-infused confection creates a custard with a cake-like topping.
I sometimes prepare the treat in an 8-inch square baking dish...just bake a little longer.

Peggy Lee | CHESAPEAKE, VA

3 tablespoons butter, softened

1 cup sugar, divided

5 tablespoons all-purpose flour

2 eggs, separated

1 cup 2% milk

1/4 cup key lime juice

In a small bowl, beat butter and 3/4 cup sugar until crumbly. Beat in flour and egg yolks until smooth. Gradually beat in milk and lime juice.

In another small bowl, beat egg whites on medium speed until soft peaks form. Gradually add remaining sugar, 1 tablespoon at a time, beating on high until stiff peaks form. Gently fold into key lime mixture.

Pour into five ungreased 6-oz. ramekins or custard cups. Place in a shallow baking dish; add 1 in. of hot water to dish. Bake, uncovered, at 350° for 30-35 minutes or until a thermometer reaches 170°. Serve warm. **YIELD:** 5 servings.

baked alaskas with tipsy cherry centers

(PICTURED AT RIGHT)

When I need an outstanding dessert for a celebration, I turn purchased pound cake into individual Baked Alaskas. Guests beam when this eye-catching treat is set in front of them.

Diane Halferty | *CORPUS CHRISTI, TX*

1/2 cup cherry preserves

3 teaspoons cherry brandy, divided

2 cups cherry ice cream, softened

1 loaf (10-3/4 ounces) frozen pound cake, thawed

3 egg whites

1/2 cup sugar

In a small bowl, combine preserves and 1 teaspoon brandy. Line four 6-oz. ramekins with plastic wrap; spoon ice cream into ramekins. Make an indentation in the center of each; fill with cherry mixture. Freeze until firm.

Split pound cake horizontally into thirds. Using a 6-oz. ramekin, cut the pound cake into four circles (save the remaining cake for another use). Brush circles with the remaining brandy.

In a large heavy saucepan, combine egg whites and sugar. With a hand mixer, beat on low speed for 1 minute. Continue beating over low heat until egg mixture reaches 160°, about 8 minutes. Transfer to a bowl; beat until stiff glossy peaks form and sugar is dissolved.

Place cake circles on an ungreased foil-lined baking sheet; top each with an inverted ice cream mold. Remove plastic. Immediately spread meringue over ice cream, sealing to edges of cakes.

Heat with a creme brulee torch or broil 8 in. from the heat for 3-4 minutes or until the meringue is lightly browned. Serve immediately. **YIELD:** 4 servings.

white chocolate-candy cane parfaits

(PICTURED ON PAGE 62)

Candy canes add some crunch and a burst of mint flavor in these lovely parfaits
from our home economists. The delightful desserts are fun for the holidays.

1/4 cup sugar

3 tablespoons cornstarch

1/8 teaspoon salt

1-1/2 cups heavy whipping cream, divided

1 cup 2% milk

3 egg yolks, beaten

3 ounces white baking chocolate, chopped

1/2 teaspoon vanilla extract

2 tablespoons confectioners' sugar

1/4 teaspoon peppermint extract

2 tablespoons plus 1/3 cup finely crushed
candy canes, divided

1/3 cup crushed shortbread cookies

Additional crushed candy canes

In a large heavy saucepan, combine the sugar, cornstarch and salt. Gradually add 1 cup heavy whipping cream and milk. Bring to a boil over medium-high heat, stirring constantly. Reduce heat; cook and stir with a wire whisk 2-3 minutes longer or until thickened.

Remove from the heat. Whisk a small amount of hot mixture into egg yolks; return all to the pan, stirring constantly. Bring to a gentle boil; cook and stir for 2 minutes. Remove from the heat; stir in white chocolate until melted. Stir in vanilla. Transfer to a large bowl. Cool to room temperature without stirring. Press waxed paper onto surface of pudding; refrigerate until chilled.

In a small bowl, beat remaining cream until it begins to thicken. Add confectioners' sugar and peppermint extract; beat until soft peaks form. Fold in 2 tablespoons crushed candies.

In each of the eight dessert dishes, layer 1/4 cup pudding and 2 teaspoons crushed candies and cookie crumbs. Top with whipped cream. Garnish with additional crushed candies. **YIELD:** 8 servings.

custard puddings

Traditional custard pudding is old-fashioned comfort food at its finest.
The appealing taste of almond comes through in every spoonful.

Bonnie Simpson | *BATON ROUGE, LA*

2-1/2 cups whole milk

4 eggs

1/2 cup sugar

1/4 teaspoon salt

Dash ground nutmeg

1/2 teaspoon vanilla extract

1/8 teaspoon almond extract

In a small saucepan, heat milk until bubbles form around sides of pan. In a small bowl, whisk the eggs, sugar, salt and nutmeg. Remove milk from the heat; stir a small amount of hot milk into egg mixture.

Return all to the pan, stirring constantly. Stir in the extracts.

Transfer to nine 4-oz. ramekins or custard cups. Place cups in a baking pan; add 1 in. of boiling water to pan. Bake, uncovered, at 325° for 25-30 minutes or until center is just set (mixture will jiggle). Remove ramekins from water bath; cool for 10 minutes. Refrigerate until chilled. **YIELD:** 9 servings.

chocolate cheesecake triangles

(PICTURED AT RIGHT)

I love this tasty twist on cheesecake. The creamy, chocolaty triangles are served with a luscious raspberry sauce for an easy, impressive finale.

Pat Habiger | SPEARVILLE, KS

1-1/4 cups chocolate wafer crumbs

1/3 cup butter, melted

3 tablespoons plus 1/2 cup sugar, divided

2 packages (8 ounces each) cream cheese, softened

2 tablespoons all-purpose flour

1 can (5 ounces) evaporated milk

1 egg

2 teaspoons vanilla extract

1 cup (6 ounces) semisweet chocolate chips, melted

RASPBERRY SAUCE:

1 package (10 ounces) frozen sweetened raspberries, thawed and undrained

1 teaspoon cornstarch

2 tablespoons cold water

Line the bottom and sides of a 9-in. square baking pan with heavy-duty foil. In a small bowl, combine the wafer crumbs, butter and 3 tablespoons sugar; press onto the bottom of prepared pan.

In a large bowl, beat the cream cheese, flour and remaining sugar until smooth. Beat in milk. Add egg; beat on low speed just until combined. Stir in vanilla.

In another bowl, combine 3/4 cup cream cheese mixture and melted chocolate; set aside. Pour remaining cream cheese mixture over crust. Top with spoonfuls of chocolate mixture; cut through batter with a knife to swirl. Bake at 325° for 35-40 minutes or until center is almost set. Cool on a wire rack. Refrigerate until chilled.

Meanwhile, for sauce, place raspberries in a blender; cover and process until well blended. Press through a sieve over a small saucepan. Discard seeds. Combine cornstarch and water; stir into raspberry juice. Bring to a boil. Cook and stir for 2 minutes or until thickened. Refrigerate until serving.

Using foil, lift cheesecake out of pan; discard foil. Cut into four squares; cut each square diagonally into four triangles. Serve with sauce. **YIELD:** 16 servings.

croissant pudding with chocolate kahlua sauce

(PICTURED ON PAGE 63)

These custards puff up slightly while baking, creating beautiful, golden crowns.
Kahlua brings a mild coffee taste to the heavenly chocolate sauce.

Cheryl Tucker | HOUSTON, TX

6 croissants, torn into pieces

4 egg yolks

2 eggs

3 cups heavy whipping cream

2-1/4 cups sugar

1-1/2 cups half-and-half cream

4-1/2 teaspoons vanilla extract

1-1/2 teaspoons salt

SAUCE:

2 ounces unsweetened chocolate, coarsely chopped

2 tablespoons butter

1 cup sugar

1/2 cup evaporated milk

Dash salt

3 tablespoons Kahlua

Divide the croissant pieces among nine greased 10-oz. ramekins or custard cups. Place on baking sheets.

In a large bowl, combine the egg yolks, eggs, cream, sugar, half-and-half, vanilla and salt. Pour over croissant pieces; let stand for 15 minutes or until croissants are softened. Bake at 325° for 40-45 minutes or until a knife inserted near the center comes out clean.

For sauce, in a small saucepan, melt chocolate and butter over medium-low heat. Add the sugar, milk and salt; cook and stir for 3-4 minutes or until thickened. Remove from the heat; stir in Kahlua. Serve with warm pudding. YIELD: 9 servings.

caribbean wontons

I first served these fresh and fruity treats as an appetizer at a summer luau.
But family and friends also enjoy them as a dessert for occasions throughout the year.

Melissa Birdsong | GILBERT, SC

4 ounces cream cheese, softened

1/4 cup flaked coconut

1/4 cup mashed ripe banana

2 tablespoons chopped walnuts

2 tablespoons canned crushed pineapple

1 cup marshmallow creme

24 wonton wrappers

Oil for deep-fat frying

SAUCE:

1 pound fresh strawberries, hulled

1/4 cup sugar

1 teaspoon cornstarch

Confectioners' sugar and ground cinnamon

In a small bowl, beat cream cheese until smooth. Stir in the coconut, banana, walnuts and pineapple. Fold in marshmallow creme.

Position a wonton wrapper with one point toward you. Keep remaining wrappers covered with a damp paper towel until ready to use. Place 2 teaspoons of filling in the center of wrapper. Moisten edges with water; fold opposite corners together over filling and press to seal. Repeat with remaining wrappers and filling.

In an electric skillet or deep-fat fryer, heat oil to 375°. Fry the wontons, a few at a time, for 15-20 seconds on each side or until golden brown. Drain on paper towels.

Place strawberries in a food processor; cover and process until pureed. In a small saucepan, combine sugar and cornstarch. Stir in pureed strawberries. Bring to a boil; cook and stir for 2 minutes or until thickened. Strain mixture, reserving sauce; discard seeds. Sprinkle wontons with confectioners' sugar and cinnamon. Serve with sauce. YIELD: 2 dozen (1-1/4 cups sauce).

tiffany cups

(PICTURED AT RIGHT)

This mouthful is delightful and so cute in mini-ramekins. Vanilla is comforting with a strong Irish cream accent.

Tiffany Rampey | *CHICAGO, IL*

2/3 cup heavy whipping cream

2 egg yolks

5-1/2 teaspoons sugar

4 teaspoons Irish cream liqueur or refrigerated nondairy creamer

1 teaspoon vanilla extract

Coarse sugar and orange curls, optional

In a small saucepan, heat the cream over medium heat until bubbles form around sides of pan. In a small bowl, whisk egg yolks and sugar. Remove from the heat; stir a small amount of hot cream into egg yolk mixture. Return all to the pan, stirring constantly. Stir in liqueur and vanilla.

Transfer to four stoneware demitasse cups or 2-oz. ramekins. Place cups in a baking pan; add 1 in. of boiling water to pan. Bake, uncovered, at 325° for 20-25 minutes or until centers are just set (mixture will jiggle). Remove the cups from water bath; cool for 10 minutes. Cover and refrigerate for at least 4 hours. Garnish with coarse sugar and orange curls if desired. YIELD: 4 servings.

chocolate raspberry mousse

The addition of whipping cream lends to the spectacular, smooth texture of this rich and creamy mousse. You just can't beat the chocolate-and-raspberry flavor combination.

Steffany Lohn | *BRENTWOOD, CA*

2-1/2 cups heavy whipping cream, divided

1/2 cup sugar

4 egg yolks

12 ounces bittersweet chocolate, chopped

1/4 cup raspberry liqueur

2 teaspoons vanilla extract

Fresh raspberries

In a large saucepan, heat 1-1/2 cups cream and sugar over medium heat until bubbles form around sides of pan. Whisk a small amount of the hot mixture into the egg yolks. Return all to the pan, whisking constantly. Cook and stir over low heat until mixture reaches at least 160° and coats the back of a metal spoon. Remove from the heat. Stir in the chocolate, liqueur and vanilla.

In a large bowl, beat remaining cream until stiff peaks form; fold into chocolate mixture. Spoon into dessert glasses. Cover and refrigerate for 2 hours before serving. Garnish with raspberries. YIELD: 10 servings.

apricot-almond tartlets

These delicate, buttery tarts melt in your mouth. With their jeweled apricot tops,
they make a pretty presentation on your holiday cookie tray.

Julie Dunsworth | OVIEDO, FL

1 cup all-purpose flour

3 tablespoons confectioners' sugar

1/3 cup cold butter

1 egg yolk

1 to 2 tablespoons water

FILLING:

1/2 cup almond paste

1/4 cup butter, softened

1 egg white

1/4 teaspoon almond extract

1/2 cup apricot preserves

In a large bowl, combine flour and confectioners' sugar; cut in butter until mixture resembles coarse crumbs. Add the egg yolk and water; stir until dough forms a ball. Roll into 1-in. balls. Press onto the bottoms and up the sides of greased miniature muffin cups.

In a small bowl, beat almond paste and butter until blended; beat in egg white and almond extract. Spoon into tart shells, about 2 teaspoons in each.

Bake at 350° for 20-25 minutes or until golden brown. Cool for 5 minutes before removing from pans to wire racks. Top with apricot preserves. **YIELD:** 2 dozen.

spiced pumpkin ice cream puffs

(PICTURED AT RIGHT)

This extraordinary dessert showcases four homemade components: pumpkin ice cream,
candy, cream puffs and a wine sauce. The effort is worthwhile...and each part has a make-ahead aspect.

Richard Lasher | STUARTS DRAFT, VA

ICE CREAM:

1-1/2 cups heavy whipping cream

1 cup whole milk, divided

1/2 cup sugar

6 egg yolks

1 can (15 ounces) solid-pack pumpkin

2 teaspoons vanilla extract

1 teaspoon ground cinnamon

1/4 teaspoon ground nutmeg

CANDY PIECES:

1/2 cup sugar

CREAM PUFFS:

1 cup all-purpose flour

1/4 teaspoon ground cinnamon

1/8 teaspoon ground ginger

1/8 teaspoon ground nutmeg

1 cup water

6 tablespoons butter, cubed

1/4 teaspoon salt

4 eggs

SAUCE:

3 cups dry red wine

1/2 cup butter, cubed

1/4 cup packed brown sugar

1/4 cup honey

1/4 cup orange juice

5 fresh mint leaves

4 whole cloves

4-1/2 teaspoons lemon juice

1 teaspoon ground cinnamon

1 teaspoon minced fresh gingerroot

1 cinnamon stick (3 inches)

5 teaspoons cornstarch

2 tablespoons water

In a large saucepan, heat the cream and 1/2 cup milk to 175°; stir in the sugar until dissolved. Whisk a small amount of the hot mixture into the egg yolks. Return all to the pan, whisking constantly. Cook and stir over low heat until mixture reaches at least 160° and coats the back of a metal spoon. Remove from the heat. Cool quickly by placing pan in a bowl of ice water; stir for 2 minutes. Stir in the pumpkin, vanilla, cinnamon, nutmeg and remaining milk. Press waxed paper onto surface of custard. Refrigerate for several hours or overnight.

Fill the cylinder of ice cream freezer two-thirds full; freeze according to the manufacturer's directions. When ice cream is frozen, transfer to a freezer container; freeze for at least 2 hours before serving.

Meanwhile, in a heavy saucepan over medium-low heat, cook sugar until melted, about 20 minutes. Do not stir. Reduce heat to low; cook for 5 minutes or until syrup is golden brown, stirring occasionally. Quickly pour onto an ungreased baking sheet; cool and coarsely crush.

For cream puffs, in a small bowl, combine flour, cinnamon, ginger and nutmeg; set aside. In a large saucepan, bring water, butter and salt to a boil. Add flour mixture all at once and stir until a smooth ball forms. Remove from the heat; let stand for 5 minutes. Add eggs, one at a time, beating well after each addition. Continue beating until mixture is smooth and shiny.

Drop by rounded tablespoonfuls 3 in. apart onto greased baking sheets. Bake at 400° for 20-25 minutes or until the puffs are golden brown.

Remove to wire racks. Immediately split puffs open; remove tops and set aside. Discard soft dough from inside. Cool puffs.

For sauce, in a large saucepan, combine the wine, butter, brown sugar, honey, orange juice, mint, cloves, lemon juice, cinnamon, gingerroot and cinnamon stick. Bring to a boil; cook until liquid is reduced by half. Strain wine mixture, discarding cloves and cinnamon stick. Return wine mixture to pan. Combine cornstarch and water until smooth. Gradually stir into wine mixture. Bring to a boil; cook and stir for 2 minutes or until thickened.

To serve, scoop ice cream into cream puffs; replace tops. Drizzle with sauce and sprinkle with candy pieces. YIELD: 32 cream puffs.

The Christmas season is about sharing...especially when it comes to all the yummy home-baked goodies. Spread the good cheer even further by sharing your delicious creations with those who might not otherwise get to enjoy homemade treats during the holidays.

Invite your friends and family over for a fun and casual charitable Christmas bake. Whip up batches of Chocolate-Dipped Orange Spritz, Honey-Nut Swirls, Cranberry Pistachio Biscotti, Cashew Crunch or any other confections in this chapter.

Then package your sweets and deliver them to the elderly or to a local homeless shelter. It's sure to be an experience that helps everyone get a taste of the season's true meaning.

FROM THE HEART
(PICTURED AT RIGHT)

Honey-Nut Swirls (p. 80)
Cranberry Pistachio Biscotti (p. 76)
Chocolate-Dipped Orange Spritz (p. 78)
Cashew Crunch (p. 76)

charitable
COOKIES & CANDIES

cranberry pistachio biscotti

(PICTURED ON PAGE 74)

*Wonderful for dunking but just as delicious alone, these slightly crunchy biscotti
feature the irresistible flavorful combo of cranberries and pistachios.*

Ruth Knol | ANNVILLE, PA

1/2 cup dried cranberries

1/2 cup boiling water

1/2 cup butter, softened

1 cup sugar

4 eggs

2 teaspoons vanilla extract

3 cups all-purpose flour

2 teaspoons baking powder

1/2 teaspoon salt

1/2 cup chopped pistachios

3 tablespoons coarse sugar

Place cranberries in a small bowl. Cover with boiling water; let stand for 5 minutes. Drain and set aside. In a large bowl, cream butter and sugar until light and fluffy. Add 3 eggs, one at a time, beating well after each addition. Stir in vanilla. Combine the flour, baking powder and salt; gradually add to creamed mixture and mix well. Stir in pistachios and cranberries with liquid.

Divide dough into three portions. On a parchment paper-lined baking sheet, shape each portion into a 12-in. x 1-1/2-in. rectangle. Beat remaining egg; brush over rectangles and sprinkle with coarse sugar. Bake at 375° for 18-22 minutes or until set and lightly browned. Carefully remove to wire racks; cool for 15 minutes.

Transfer to a cutting board; cut diagonally with a serrated knife into 3/4-in. slices. Place cut side down on ungreased baking sheets. Bake for 6-8 minutes on each side or until edges are browned. Remove to wire racks to cool completely. Store in an airtight container. YIELD: 3-1/2 dozen.

cashew crunch

(PICTURED ON PAGE 75)

*Folks can't stop eating this buttery, brittle-like candy. Try using almonds or
your favorite nut in place of the cashews as an equally tasty alternative.*

Kim Croft | SAN DIEGO, CA

2 teaspoons plus 10 tablespoons
butter, divided

1/2 cup sugar

1/4 cup brown sugar

1 tablespoon light corn syrup

3/4 teaspoon cayenne pepper

1/4 teaspoon salt

2 cups salted cashews

Line a 15-in. x 10-in. x 1-in. pan with foil and grease the foil with 2 teaspoons butter; set aside. In a large heavy saucepan, combine the sugar, brown sugar, corn syrup, cayenne, salt and remaining butter. Cook and stir until sugar is dissolved.

Add cashews and bring to a boil; cook and stir until a candy thermometer reads 280° (soft-crack stage), about 6 minutes.

Immediately pour into prepared pan; spread with a metal spatula. Cool completely. Break into pieces. Store in an airtight container. YIELD: 1-1/4 pounds.

snow flurries

(PICTURED AT RIGHT)

Star-shaped sandwich cookies look simply stunning when displayed on Christmas cookie trays or packaged as gifts. The crisp shortbread pairs perfectly with the jam filling.

Mary Ann Ludwig | *EDWARDSVILLE, IL*

1/2 cup butter, softened

1/2 cup shortening

1 cup sugar

1 tablespoon grated lemon peel

2 eggs

1 teaspoon vanilla extract

1/2 teaspoon almond extract

3-1/2 cups all-purpose flour

1/2 teaspoon baking powder

1/2 teaspoon salt

1/3 cup apricot jam

1/2 cup confectioners' sugar

In a large bowl, cream the butter, shortening, sugar and lemon peel until light and fluffy. Beat in eggs and extracts. Combine the flour, baking powder and salt; gradually add to creamed mixture and mix well. Shape into a ball; wrap in plastic wrap. Refrigerate for 1 hour or until firm.

On a lightly floured surface, roll out dough to 1/8-in. thickness. Cut with a floured 2-1/4-in. star-shaped cookie cutter. Place 1 in. apart on ungreased baking sheets. Bake at 375° for 8-10 minutes or until edges begin to brown. Remove to wire racks to cool.

To assemble, place 1/4 teaspoon apricot jam in the center of a cookie; top with another cookie, off center. Dust with the confectioners' sugar. Repeat. Store in an airtight container. **YIELD:** 6-1/2 dozen.

COOKS WHO CARE

Share the story of your charitable Christmas bake with Cooks Who Care, a program created by Taste of Home to celebrate the kind acts of home cooks and communities across the country. To read about and connect with other cooks who are making a difference, or to share your own story, be sure to visit www.CooksWhoCare.com.

chocolate-dipped orange spritz

(PICTURED ON PAGE 75)

Dipped in melted chocolate and coated in ground walnuts, this is one cookie you won't pass up.

Alissa Stehr | GAU-ODERNHEIM, GERMANY

3/4 cup butter, softened

1 cup sugar

1 egg

2 tablespoons orange juice

4 teaspoons grated orange peel

2-3/4 cups all-purpose flour

1 teaspoon baking powder

1/4 teaspoon salt

1 cup semisweet chocolate chips

1 tablespoon shortening

1/2 cup ground walnuts

In a small bowl, cream butter and sugar until light and fluffy. Beat in the egg, orange juice and peel. Combine the flour, baking powder and salt; gradually add to creamed mixture and mix well.

Using a cookie press fitted with a bar disk, form dough into long strips on ungreased baking sheets. Cut each strip into 3-in. pieces (there is no need to separate the pieces). Bake at 350° for 8-10 minutes or until set (do not brown). Cut again into individual cookies if necessary. Remove to wire racks.

In a microwave, melt chocolate and shortening; stir until smooth. Place walnuts in a small bowl. Dip a cookie halfway into chocolate and allow excess to drip off; coat with walnuts. Place on waxed paper. Repeat. Let stand until set. YIELD: 4 dozen.

CHOCOLATE-DIPPED COOKIES

When making chocolate-dipped candies or cookies, be sure to use shortening when melting the chocolate. Margarine contains some water, which will cause the chocolate to "seize" or curdle, so it can't be used to dip or coat candies.

mashed potato pecan fudge

This treasured recipe goes back to my grandmother, who loved the candy as much as I do! It's easy to make and so indulgent. Be ready to hand out the recipe.

Carolyn Hayes | JOHNSTON CITY, IL

1 teaspoon plus 1/2 cup butter, softened, divided

3 ounces unsweetened chocolate, chopped

1/2 cup mashed potatoes (without added milk and butter)

1 teaspoon vanilla extract

1/8 teaspoon salt

3-3/4 cups confectioners' sugar

1 cup chopped pecans

Line an 11-in. x 7-in. pan with foil. Grease the foil with 1 teaspoon butter; set aside. In a heavy saucepan over low heat, melt chocolate and remaining butter; set aside.

In a large bowl, combine the mashed potatoes, vanilla and salt. Gradually beat in confectioners' sugar until smooth. Stir in pecans and chocolate mixture. Spread into prepared pan. Refrigerate for 1 hour or until firm.

Using foil, lift fudge out of pan. Discard foil. Cut fudge into 1-in. squares. Store in an airtight container in the refrigerator. Remove from the refrigerator just before serving. YIELD: 1-3/4 pounds.

triple-coconut macadamia macaroons

(PICTURED AT RIGHT)

For a truly luxurious eating experience, try these slightly sweet and tender morsels. Two varieties of coconut—sweetened and unsweetened—and cream of coconut add intense flavor to every nibble.

Robin Jungers | CAMPBELLSPORT, WI

2-1/2 cups sweetened flaked coconut

2-1/2 cups finely shredded unsweetened coconut

1 cup chopped macadamia nuts

1 cup cream of coconut

4 egg whites

2 tablespoons light corn syrup

2 teaspoons vanilla extract

1/2 teaspoon salt

2 ounces semisweet chocolate, chopped

1 teaspoon shortening

In a large bowl, combine the sweetened coconut, unsweetened coconut and macadamia nuts. In a small bowl, combine the cream of coconut, egg whites, corn syrup, vanilla and salt. Stir into coconut mixture. Cover and refrigerate for 15 minutes.

Drop by tablespoonfuls 2 in. apart onto parchment paper-lined baking sheets. Shape into loose mounds. Bake at 350° for 12-16 minutes or until lightly browned. Cool for 2 minutes before removing from pans to wire racks to cool completely. In a microwave, melt chocolate and shortening; stir until smooth. Dip or drizzle cookies with chocolate mixture. Place on waxed paper; let stand until set. YIELD: 4 dozen.

EDITOR'S NOTE: Look for unsweetened coconut in the baking or health food section.

honey-nut swirls

(PICTURED ON PAGE 74)

Puff pastry creates a quick and easy "dough" for pretty, pinwheel-type cookies featuring two types of nuts. The flaky confections are hard to resist.

Sally Sibthorpe | SHELBY TOWNSHIP, MI

1 sheet frozen puff pastry, thawed

1 cup finely chopped walnuts

1 cup finely chopped pistachios

3 tablespoons brown sugar

2 tablespoons butter, softened

2 tablespoons honey

1 teaspoon ground cinnamon

1/4 teaspoon salt

2 tablespoons heavy whipping cream

2 tablespoons turbinado (washed raw) sugar or granulated sugar

On a lightly floured surface, unfold puff pastry. Roll into a 12-in. x 9-in. rectangle.

In a small bowl, combine the walnuts, pistachios, brown sugar, butter, honey, cinnamon and salt. Spread over pastry to within 1/2 in. of edges. Roll up jelly-roll style. Cut into 1/2-in. slices.

Place 2 in. apart on parchment paper-lined baking sheets. Brush with cream and sprinkle with the sugar. Bake at 375° for 10-12 minutes or until lightly browned. Remove to wire racks. YIELD: 2 dozen.

italian sesame cookies

These traditional European cookies aren't overly sweet and have a wonderful crunch from sesame seeds. They're the ideal accompaniment to a freshly brewed cup of coffee or tea.

Sarah Knoblock | HYDE PARK, NY

1/2 cup butter, softened

1 cup sugar

3 eggs

1 teaspoon vanilla extract

3 cups all-purpose flour

3 teaspoons baking powder

1/2 teaspoon salt

1-3/4 cups sesame seeds

3/4 cup 2% milk

In a large bowl, cream butter and sugar until light and fluffy. Add eggs, one at a time, beating well after each addition. Add vanilla. Combine the flour, baking powder and salt; gradually add to creamed mixture and mix well.

Turn onto a lightly floured surface, knead 10-12 times or until smooth. Divide dough into eight portions. Shape each portion into a 24-in. log. Cut logs into 2 in. pieces.

Place sesame seeds and milk in separate shallow bowls. Dip pieces in milk, then roll in sesame seeds. Place 2 in. apart on greased baking sheets. Bake at 350° for 7-9 minutes or until set and bottoms are lightly browned. Cool for 2 minutes before removing from pans to wire racks. YIELD: 8 dozen.

tiger butter candy

(PICTURED AT RIGHT)

Fans of Tiger Butter Fudge will revel in this version that's very similar to bark candy. The chocolate swirls are pleasing to the eye, and the creamy peanut flavor is a treat for the taste buds.

Philip Jones | LUBBOCK, TX

1 pound white candy coating, coarsely chopped

1/2 cup chunky peanut butter

1/2 cup semisweet chocolate chips

1/2 teaspoon shortening

Line a 15-in. x 10-in. x 1-in. pan with foil; set aside. In a microwave-safe bowl, melt candy coating and peanut butter; stir until smooth. Spread into prepared pan. In another microwave-safe bowl, melt chocolate chips and shortening; stir until smooth. Drizzle over top; cut through with a knife to swirl. Chill until firm. Break into pieces. Store in an airtight container. **YIELD:** about 1-1/4 pounds.

frosted butter cookies

*If you need to bake a lot of cookies at Christmas, this high-yield recipe is for you!
Rich, buttery and easy to make, the irresistible morsels are sure to become a holiday classic.*

Teresa Gaetzke | NORTH FREEDOM, WI

2 cups butter, softened

2 cups sugar

2 eggs

1 teaspoon vanilla extract

5 cups all-purpose flour

1 teaspoon baking soda

1/4 teaspoon salt

FROSTING:

1/2 cup butter, softened

4 ounces cream cheese, softened

1 package (2 pounds) confectioners' sugar

1/4 teaspoon salt

3 to 4 tablespoons 2% milk

Food coloring and assorted sprinkles

In a large bowl, cream butter and sugar until light and fluffy. Beat in eggs and vanilla. Combine the flour, baking soda and salt; gradually add to creamed mixture and mix well. Cover and chill for 20 minutes or until easy to handle.

On a lightly floured surface, roll out to 1/4-in. thickness. Cut with floured 3-in. cookie cutters. Place 1 in. apart on ungreased baking sheets. Bake at 350° for 10-12 minutes or until lightly browned. Cool on wire racks.

For frosting, in a large bowl, beat butter and cream cheese. Add the confectioners' sugar, salt and enough milk to achieve spreading consistency. Tint frosting with food coloring and decorate with sprinkles as desired. **YIELD:** 7 dozen.

SHORTCUTS FOR CUTE CHRISTMAS COOKIES

Even if you don't have time to bake, you and your family can still enjoy special Christmas cookies. It just takes a trip to the grocery store and a little creativity!

- Purchase several tubes of refrigerated sugar cookie dough. Slice some of the dough to make round cookies and top with colored sugars. Roll another portion into balls. You can also use some of the dough for thumbprint cookies. Bake the cookies as directed. Fill the cooled thumbprint cookies with a jam flavor of your choice.

- Dip purchased gingersnaps halfway into melted white or vanilla chips...or drizzle the melted chips over the cookies.

- Tint your favorite vanilla frosting with food coloring to pipe holiday designs on store-bought sugar cookies.

- Buy a package of chocolate-covered mint cookies; drizzle with contrasting melted white chocolate.

- Frost chocolate chip cookies with purchased or homemade chocolate frosting. Decorate with colored sugar or sprinkles.

trio of chocolate truffles

(PICTURED AT RIGHT)

Three recipes in one is a real benefit to any baker during the busy holiday season. The decadent flavor and creamy texture of these diverse and delightful treats will definitely spread holiday cheer.

Luraine MacLeod | *FEDERAL WAY, WA*

12 ounces bittersweet chocolate, chopped

1/3 cup butter, cubed

4 egg yolks, beaten

1 tablespoon rum

1-1/2 teaspoons instant coffee granules

1/3 cup raisins

1 tablespoon Cognac or brandy

4-1/2 teaspoons orange liqueur

1-1/2 teaspoons grated orange peel

COATINGS:

1 tablespoon baking cocoa

3 tablespoons grated chocolate

3 ounces bittersweet chocolate, chopped

2 teaspoons shortening

In a double boiler or metal bowl over simmering water, heat chocolate and butter until melted, stirring frequently. Whisk a small amount of mixture into egg yolks. Return all to the pan, whisking constantly. Cook and stir until mixture is thickened and coats the back of a spoon.

Remove from the heat; divide mixture among three small bowls. Into one bowl, stir rum and coffee granules until smooth. Stir raisins and Cognac into another; stir orange liqueur and peel into the third bowl.

Cool to room temperature, stirring occasionally. Refrigerate for 1 hour or until easy to handle. Shape into 1-in. balls.

Roll the coffee-flavored truffles in cocoa; roll the raisin-flavored truffles in grated chocolate.

In a microwave, melt bittersweet chocolate and shortening; stir until smooth. Dip orange-flavored truffles in melted chocolate; allow excess to drip off. Place on waxed paper-lined baking sheets.

Refrigerate truffles for 2 hours or until firm. Store in an airtight container in the refrigerator. YIELD: about 3 dozen.

toasted pecan dainties

These melt-in-your-mouth delights have an irresistible nutty taste and light, airy quality.
The dough is made ahead of time and chilled overnight, leaving just the baking to be done the next day.

Connie Wagler | CROSS HILL, SC

1 cup butter, softened

1 cup canola oil

1 cup sugar

1 cup confectioners' sugar

2 eggs

5 cups all-purpose flour

1 teaspoon baking soda

1 teaspoon cream of tartar

2 cups finely chopped pecans

In a large bowl, cream the butter, oil and sugars until light and fluffy. Add eggs, one at a time, beating well after each addition. Combine the flour, baking soda and cream of tartar; gradually add to creamed mixture and mix well. Stir in pecans. Cover and refrigerate for 30 minutes.

Shape dough into four 1-1/2-in. diameter logs; wrap each in plastic wrap. Freeze overnight.

Unwrap and cut into 1/4-in. slices. Place 2-1/2 in. apart on ungreased baking sheets. Bake at 375° for 8-12 minutes or until lightly browned. Cool for 2-3 minutes before removing to wire racks. Store in an airtight container. **YIELD:** about 11 dozen.

peppermint ribbon cookies

My daughter's favorite Christmas cookie, these mild peppermint confections add
color and variety to a platter of holiday goodies.

Virginia Strout | SHERBROOKE, QC

1 cup butter, softened

1-1/4 cups sugar

1 egg

1 teaspoon vanilla extract

1/4 teaspoon peppermint extract

2-1/4 cups all-purpose flour

1-1/4 teaspoons baking powder

1/4 teaspoon salt

7 to 9 drops each red and green food coloring

Line an 8-in. x 4-in. loaf pan with waxed paper; set aside. In a large bowl, cream butter and sugar until light and fluffy. Beat in the egg, vanilla and peppermint extract. Combine the flour, baking powder and salt; gradually add to the creamed mixture and mix well.

Divide dough into thirds. Add red food coloring to one portion; spread evenly into prepared pan. Spread second portion over first layer. Add green food coloring to third portion; spread over second layer. Cover with plastic wrap; refrigerate overnight.

Using waxed paper, lift dough out of pan. Gently peel off waxed paper. Cut dough into thirds lengthwise. Cut each portion into 1/4-in. slices.

Place 2 in. apart on ungreased baking sheets. Bake at 350° for 7-9 minutes or until set and edges are lightly browned. Cool for 1 minute before removing to wire racks. Store in an airtight container. **YIELD:** 8 dozen.

almond-pistachio dessert roll-ups

(PICTURED AT RIGHT)

With a flavor and texture similar to baklava, this classic dessert appeals to young and old alike. It's especially delicious with honey drizzled over the top.

Marie Rizzio | INTERLOCHEN, MI

1/2 cup shelled pistachios, toasted

1/4 cup unblanched whole almonds, toasted

1 tablespoon sugar

1 tablespoon butter, softened

1/2 teaspoon ground cinnamon

12 sheets phyllo dough (14 inches x 9 inches)

Butter-flavored cooking spray

1/4 cup honey, divided

Place pistachios and almonds in a food processor; cover and process until finely chopped. Add sugar, butter and cinnamon; cover and process until blended.

Place one sheet of phyllo dough on a work surface. Spray with butter-flavored cooking spray. Repeat with second layer. Keep remaining phyllo dough covered with plastic wrap and a damp towel to avoid drying out. Spread 1/3 cup nut mixture over phyllo to within 1 in. of sides; drizzle with 1 tablespoon honey. Layer with two more sheets of phyllo, spraying each layer with cooking spray.

Roll up jelly-roll style, starting from the short side. Repeat with remaining phyllo, nut mixture and honey.

With a sharp knife, cut each roll into six pieces; place seam side down on a greased baking sheet. Spray with cooking spray. Bake at 325° for 16-20 minutes or until golden; drizzle with remaining honey. **YIELD:** 1-1/2 dozen.

When winter winds are howling in many parts of the country, Mother Nature is creating little gems of citrus sunshine in other regions!

From lemons and limes to oranges and kumquats, citrus fruits bring a burst of refreshing flavor to a variety of foods.

Including citrus in desserts is a natural choice, like in the case of Fresh Mint & Grapefruit Sorbet and Lime Chiffon Cake.

But consider giving them a try in beverages (such as Kumquat Margaritas), main courses and side dishes as well.

With a bounty of brightly colored beauties, you can create aromatic, mouthwatering menus!

SEASON IN THE SUN
(PICTURED AT RIGHT)

Kumquat Margaritas (p. 88)
Fresh Mint & Grapefruit Sorbet (p. 92)
Lime Chiffon Cake (p. 88)

festive
WINTER FRUITS

lime chiffon cake

(PICTURED ON PAGE 87)

The next time you spot lovely little limes at the grocery store, pick some up and make this outstanding cake! A cool, refreshing curd peeks out from every tender slice.

Redawna Kalynchuk | *SEXSMITH, AB*

7 eggs, separated

1-3/4 cups all-purpose flour

1-3/4 cups sugar

3 teaspoons baking powder

1/2 teaspoon salt

1/2 cup water

1/2 cup canola oil

1/4 cup lime juice

4 teaspoons grated lime peel

1 teaspoon vanilla extract

1/2 teaspoon cream of tartar

LIME CURD:

4 eggs

1-1/2 cups sugar

1/2 cup lime juice

2 tablespoons grated lime peel

1/8 teaspoon salt

1/2 cup butter, cubed

1-1/2 cups heavy whipping cream

Let eggs stand at room temperature for 30 minutes.

In a large bowl, combine the flour, sugar, baking powder and salt. In another bowl, whisk the egg yolks, water, oil, lime juice, peel and vanilla. Add to the dry ingredients; beat until well blended. In another bowl, beat egg whites and cream of tartar until stiff peaks form; fold into batter.

Gently spoon into an ungreased 10-in. tube pan. Cut through the batter with a knife to remove air pockets. Bake on the lowest oven rack at 325° for 45-50 minutes or until the cake springs back when lightly touched. Immediately invert the pan; cool completely, about 1 hour. Run a knife around sides and center tube of pan; set aside.

For lime curd, in a small heavy saucepan over medium heat, whisk the eggs, sugar, lime juice, peel and salt until blended. Add butter; cook, whisking constantly, until the mixture is thickened and coats the back of a spoon. Transfer to a small bowl; cool for 10 minutes. Cover and refrigerate until chilled.

In a small bowl, beat the cream until stiff peaks form; fold in 1-1/2 cups curd.

Cut cake horizontally into two layers. Place bottom layer on a serving plate; spread with remaining curd. Top with remaining cake layer; spread whipped cream over top and sides of the cake. YIELD: 12 servings.

kumquat margaritas

(PICTURED ON PAGE 86)

These golden margaritas from our home economists bring a bit of sunshine to a winter table.

4 lime wedges

3 tablespoons kosher salt

3/4 cup tequila

1 pint kumquats (about 30)

3 tablespoons lime juice

3 cups crushed ice

1/3 cup sugar

Using lime wedges, moisten the rims of four margarita or cocktail glasses. Sprinkle salt on a plate; dip rims in salt. Set glasses aside.

Place tequila in a blender. Rinse kumquats; cut in half and remove seeds. Add to the blender; cover and process until pureed. Strain, discarding skins and pulp.

Return puree to blender. Add lime juice, ice and sugar; cover and process until blended. Pour into the prepared glasses. Serve immediately. YIELD: 4 servings.

lemon marmalade

(PICTURED AT RIGHT)

Lemons and grapefruit combine to create a tantalizing spread for English muffins, toast and even shortbread cookies. I give away jars of this marmalade every Christmas.

Barbara Carlucci | ORANGE PARK, FL

3 medium lemons

1 medium grapefruit

4 cups water

1 package (1-3/4 ounces) powdered fruit pectin

4 cups sugar

Peel rind from lemons and grapefruit; cut into thin strips, about 1 in. long. Set aside the fruit.

In a Dutch oven, combine the water and citrus peel. Bring to a boil. Reduce heat; cover and simmer for 5 minutes or until peel is softened. Remove from the heat and set aside.

Trim white pith from reserved lemons and grapefruit; discard pith. Cut lemons and grapefruit into segments, discarding membranes and seeds. Chop pulp, reserving juices; stir into reserved peel mixture.

Add pectin. Bring to a full rolling boil over high heat, stirring constantly. Stir in sugar; return to a full rolling boil. Boil for 1 minute, stirring constantly.

Remove from heat; skim off foam. Ladle hot mixture into hot half-pint jars, leaving 1/4-in. headspace. Remove air bubbles; wipe the rims and adjust lids. Process for 10 minutes in a boiling-water canner. **YIELD:** 6 half-pints.

EDITOR'S NOTE: The processing time listed is for altitudes of 1,000 feet or less. Add 1 minute to the processing time for each 1,000 feet of additional altitude.

mexican grilled salmon

(PICTURED AT FAR RIGHT)

Lime juice gives a little spark to a pesto-like mixture that coats salmon fillets. I prepare this recipe all year long.

Rosalind Pope | GREENSBORO, NC

1 cup fresh cilantro leaves

1/2 cup fresh basil leaves

1 small jalapeno pepper, halved and seeded

2 garlic cloves, minced

1/8 teaspoon salt

3 tablespoons lime juice

1 tablespoon sugar

1 tablespoon tomato sauce

1 teaspoon grated lime peel

4 salmon fillets (6 ounces each)

Salsa and lime slices, optional

Place the first five ingredients in a food processor; cover and process until finely chopped. Add the lime juice, sugar, tomato sauce and lime peel; cover and process until blended.

Transfer to a large resealable plastic bag. Add the salmon; seal bag and turn to coat. Refrigerate for 30 minutes.

Coat grill rack with cooking spray before starting the grill. Drain and discard marinade. Place salmon skin side down on grill rack. Grill, covered, over medium heat for 10-14 minutes or until fish flakes easily with a fork. Serve with salsa and lime slices if desired. **YIELD:** 4 servings.

EDITOR'S NOTE: When cutting hot peppers, disposable gloves are recommended. Avoid touching your face.

orange cream meringue cups

As a change from heavy desserts, I like to offer guests crisp meringue cups topped with creamy orange custard. The shells and filling can be made in advance; assemble just before serving.

Deirdre Dee Cox | MILWAUKEE, WI

3 egg whites

1/4 teaspoon cream of tartar

1/2 cup sugar

1/2 cup confectioners' sugar

FILLING:

3 egg yolks

3 tablespoons sugar

1/4 cup orange juice

3 tablespoons thawed orange juice concentrate

2 teaspoons grated orange peel

1 cup heavy whipping cream

Orange segments, optional

In a large bowl, beat egg whites and cream of tartar on medium speed until soft peaks form. Gradually beat in sugars, 1 tablespoon at a time, on high until stiff peaks form.

Drop the meringue into six mounds on a parchment paper-lined baking sheet. Shape into 3-in. cups with the back of a spoon.

Bake at 250° for 45 minutes or until set and dry. Turn oven off; leave meringues in oven for 1-1/2 hours.

In a small heavy saucepan over medium heat, whisk the egg yolks, sugar, orange juice, juice concentrate and peel. Cook, whisking constantly, until mixture is thickened and coats the back of a spoon. Transfer to a small bowl; cool for 10 minutes. Cover and refrigerate until chilled.

Just before serving, beat cream until stiff peaks form. Fold into egg yolk mixture just until blended. Spoon mixture into meringue cups. Garnish with orange segments if desired. **YIELD:** 6 servings.

jicama slaw with peanuts

(PICTURED AT RIGHT)

Peanuts add interest and crunch to crisp coleslaw featuring jicama and tangerines. For a creamy dressing, I sometimes stir in two heaping tablespoons of mayonnaise or yogurt.

Donna Noel | GRAY, ME

1 medium jicama, julienned

1/3 cup orange juice

1/2 teaspoon salt

1/8 to 1/4 teaspoon cayenne pepper

1/8 teaspoon pepper

3 tangerines, peeled and sectioned

1/4 cup minced fresh cilantro

1/2 cup salted peanuts

In a large bowl, combine the first five ingredients. Stir in tangerines and cilantro. Chill until serving. Just before serving, stir in peanuts. YIELD: 6 servings.

SECTIONING CITRUS FRUITS

When using citrus fruits in recipes, it's best to remove as much of the bitter pith as possible. The best way to do this is to slice off the peel and pith, and then section the fruit.

1. Cut a thin slice off the bottom and top of the fruit. Rest the fruit, with one cut side down, on a cutting board. With a sharp paring knife, cut off the peel and white pith from the fruit.

2. Holding fruit over a bowl, slice between the membrane of each section and the fruit until the knife reaches the center. Turn the knife and follow the membrane so the fruit is released. Repeat until all sections are removed.

fresh mint & grapefruit sorbet

(PICTURED ON PAGE 87)

*With a smooth, velvety texture, this pretty pink sorbet is a pleasant finish
to special-occasion meals. Mint beautifully balances the tartness of grapefruit juice.*

Lisa Speer | *PALM BEACH, FL*

2 cups sugar

2 cups water

1 cup fresh mint leaves

4 cups ruby red grapefruit juice

In a small saucepan, bring the sugar, water and mint to a boil. Reduce heat to low; cook for 5 minutes. Remove from heat; let stand for 10 minutes. Strain and discard the mint leaves. Stir in grapefruit juice. Allow mixture to cool completely.

Fill cylinder of ice cream freezer two-thirds full; freeze according to manufacturer's directions. Transfer to a freezer container; freeze for 4 hours or until firm. **YIELD:** 1-1/2 quarts.

grilled cornish hens with citrus

*A simple citrus oil wonderfully seasons moist and tender Cornish game hens.
Serving grilled grapefruit slices on the side is an innovative touch.*

Delores Moore | *FORT WORTH, TX*

1/4 cup canola oil

4 orange peel strips (3 inches)

3 lemon peel strips (2 inches)

3 lime peel strips (2 inches)

2 grapefruit peel strips (3 inches)

1/2 teaspoon ground cinnamon

1/8 teaspoon ground allspice

2/3 cup orange juice

1 tablespoon lemon juice

1 tablespoon lime juice

1 tablespoon grenadine syrup

2 Cornish game hens (20 ounces each), split lengthwise

1 medium grapefruit, cut into 1/2-inch slices

1/2 teaspoon salt

In a small skillet, heat the oil over low heat. Add the citrus peels, cinnamon and allspice; cook and stir for 1-2 minutes. Discard peels; transfer oil mixture to a small bowl.

In the same skillet, combine the juices. Bring to a boil; cook until liquid is reduced to about 3 tablespoons. Stir into oil mixture; add the grenadine.

Brush hens and grapefruit slices with oil mixture; sprinkle the hens with salt. Grill the hens, covered, over medium heat for 20-25 minutes or until juices run clear, turning occasionally.

Meanwhile, grill grapefruit slices for 2-3 minutes on each side or until heated through. Serve with hens. **YIELD:** 4 servings.

streusel-topped lemon tart

(PICTURED AT RIGHT)

A sweet streusel topping pairs well with slices of this tart. It's a spectacular spin on basic lemon bars and appears on my menus for both family and company.

Lisa Varner | *CHARLESTON, SC*

1-1/4 cups all-purpose flour

1/3 cup confectioners' sugar

1/2 teaspoon grated lemon peel

1/2 cup plus 2 tablespoons cold butter

FILLING:

4 eggs

1-1/2 cups sugar

1/4 cup lemon juice

1/4 cup all-purpose flour

1 teaspoon baking powder

1 teaspoon grated lemon peel

TOPPING:

1/3 cup all-purpose flour

1/3 cup packed brown sugar

3 tablespoons cold butter

2 tablespoons chopped pecans

Confectioners' sugar

In a small bowl, combine the flour, confectioners' sugar and lemon peel; cut in butter until crumbly. Press onto the bottom and 1/2 in. up the sides of a greased 9-in. springform pan. Bake at 350° for 10-15 minutes or until the crust is lightly browned. Cool on a wire rack.

In a small bowl, beat the eggs, sugar and lemon juice until the mixture is thick and lemon-colored. Beat in the flour, baking powder and lemon peel until blended. Pour into the crust. Bake for 20-25 minutes or until set.

For topping, in a small bowl, combine flour and brown sugar; cut in butter until crumbly. Stir in pecans. Sprinkle over filling. Bake for 20-25 minutes or until a toothpick inserted near the center comes out clean. Cool completely on a wire rack. Remove sides of pan. Dust with confectioners' sugar. Refrigerate leftovers. **YIELD:** 12 servings.

orange mocha tart

*There's just something decadent about combining orange and chocolate into
a stunning dessert. This is a showstopper every time I serve it.*

Shirley Riley | WATER VALLEY, MS

CANDIED PEEL:

3 medium navel oranges

1 cup sugar

1 cup water

Additional sugar, optional

PASTRY:

1-1/3 cups all-purpose flour

2 tablespoons sugar

1/4 teaspoon salt

1/2 cup cold butter

1 egg yolk

2 tablespoons 2% milk

FILLING:

4 ounces bittersweet chocolate, chopped

4 ounces semisweet chocolate, chopped

2/3 cup butter, cubed

1/3 cup sugar

1/4 cup all-purpose flour

1 teaspoon instant espresso powder

2 eggs

1/4 cup orange liqueur

4 teaspoons grated orange peel

1/8 teaspoon salt

GANACHE:

3 ounces bittersweet chocolate, chopped

3 ounces semisweet chocolate, chopped

1/4 teaspoon instant espresso powder

3/4 cup heavy whipping cream

CREAM:

1 cup heavy whipping cream

3 tablespoons confectioners' sugar

4-1/2 teaspoons orange liqueur

For candied peel, score oranges with a sharp knife, cutting peel into four wedge-shaped sections. Loosen peel with a spoon and remove; save fruit for another use.

Place peel in a small heavy saucepan and cover with cold water. Bring to a boil. Reduce heat; cover and simmer for 20 minutes. Drain. Cool for 5 minutes. Carefully scrape off excess pulp from peel. Cut the peel into 1/4-in. strips.

In another saucepan, combine sugar and water; cook and stir over medium heat until sugar is dissolved. Add orange peel strips; boil gently for 10-12 minutes. Using a slotted spoon, transfer strips to wire racks; let stand for 3 hours or until dry. Roll the strips in additional sugar if desired.

In a large bowl, combine the flour, sugar and salt. Cut in butter until crumbly. Add egg yolk. Gradually add milk, tossing with a fork until a ball forms.

On a lightly floured surface, roll out pastry into a 13-in. circle. Press onto bottom and up the sides of an ungreased 11-in. fluted tart pan with a removable bottom. Bake at 450° for 10 minutes. Cool on a wire rack. Reduce heat to 350°.

In a small saucepan, melt chocolates and butter over medium heat. In a large bowl, combine the sugar, flour and espresso powder. Whisk in eggs and chocolate mixture until blended. Add the liqueur, orange peel and salt; pour filling into prepared shell.

Bake at 350° for 12-15 minutes or until center is just set and top appears dull. Cool completely on a wire rack.

For ganache, place chocolates and espresso powder in a small bowl. In a small saucepan, bring cream just to a boil. Pour over the chocolate; whisk until smooth. Pour over tart; let stand at room temperature for 15 minutes or until set.

In a large bowl, beat the cream until it begins to thicken. Add confectioners' sugar and liqueur; beat until stiff peaks form. Serve with tart and candied peel. **YIELD:** 16 servings.

chocolate citrus wedges

(PICTURED AT RIGHT)

These tangy chocolate treats are a perfect anytime snack. They refresh your taste buds while satisfying a sweet tooth.

Aysha Schurman | AMMON, ID

1/2 cup orange marmalade

2 medium lemons or tangerines, peeled and separated into wedges

1/2 teaspoon ground cinnamon

4 ounces dark chocolate candy coating, coarsely chopped

2 teaspoons shortening

1/4 cup finely chopped walnuts

In a microwave, heat marmalade for 15 seconds. Dip the lemon wedges in marmalade; allow excess to drip off. Place on waxed paper; sprinkle with cinnamon. Refrigerate for 30 minutes or until set.

In a microwave, melt the chocolate and shortening; stir until smooth. Dip the wedges in chocolate; allow the excess to drip off. Place on waxed paper; sprinkle with the walnuts. Let stand until set. YIELD: about 1-1/2 dozen.

CITRUS FRUIT FACTS

- Look for citrus fruits that are firm, feel heavy for their size and have a bright color. Avoid fruits with bruises and wrinkles.
- Store unwashed kumquats in the refrigerator for about 2 weeks. Other citrus can be kept at room temperature for 3 days. For longer storage, refrigerate for 2 weeks. Juice and peel can be frozen for 1 year.
- There are three types of oranges: sweet (navel, Valencia and blood); loose skin (tangerines, Clementines and Minneolas); bitter (Seville).

- One medium grapefruit will yield 3/4 cup juice and about 1-1/2 cups segments.
- You'll get about 1/4 cup slices from three kumquats.
- A medium lemon produces 3 tablespoons juice and 2 teaspoons grated peel.
- One medium Persian lime (which is the most common variety found in stores) yields 2 tablespoons juice and 1-1/2 teaspoons grated peel.
- In one medium orange, there will be 1/3 to 1/2 cup juice. It will also yield 4 teaspoons grated peel.

ike Santa's helpers at the North Pole, you're busy during the days leading up to Christmas. But that doesn't mean there's no time to host a holiday lunch for your friends and their children.

Chase away winter chills with hot selections such as Bacon-Tomato Quesadillas, Creamy Chicken Vegetable Soup and Crusty Italian Sub Supreme. For the kid in everyone, pass a platter piled high with Elfin Banana Sandwiches.

While the adults catch up, keep the kids busy by having them assemble a festive village of Christmas Cottages.

SANTA'S WORKSHOP WONDERS
(PICTURED AT RIGHT)

Christmas Cottages (p. 100)

north pole
PARTY

holiday croutons

(PICTURED AT FAR RIGHT)

To keep my kids entertained while I was baking one Christmas, I gave them slices of bread and small cookie cutters. The baked product was so cute, I decided to season the remaining batches and turn them into croutons.

Bonnie Hawkins | ELKHORN, WI

8 bread slices

2 tablespoons butter, melted

2 tablespoons olive oil

Paprika, dill weed, minced chives or dried minced onion

Cut shapes from bread using 1-1/2 in. Christmas cookie cutters of your choice. Transfer to a large bowl.

In a small bowl, combine butter and oil; drizzle over bread and toss to coat. Divide into three batches. Sprinkle each batch with a different seasoning; toss to coat.

Arrange in a single layer on an ungreased baking sheet. Bake at 300° for 20-25 minutes or until golden brown, turning occasionally. Cool. Store in an airtight container. YIELD: 2-1/2 cups.

lime pecan bread

Lime juice is a terrific addition to ordinary quick bread. The chopped pecans add a pleasant crunch. I serve slices at breakfast and as a snack throughout the day.

Nancy Lore | ROCKLAND, MA

1 cup butter, softened

2 cups sugar

4 eggs, separated

3-1/4 cups all-purpose flour

2 teaspoons baking powder

1 teaspoon salt

1-1/4 cups milk

1 tablespoon lime juice

4 teaspoons grated lime peel

1 cup chopped pecans

GLAZE:

3/4 cup sugar

1/2 cup lime juice

In a large bowl, cream butter and sugar; beat in egg yolks. Combine the flour, baking powder and salt; add to creamed mixture alternately with milk. Add the lime juice and peel. Stir in the pecans.

In a small bowl, beat egg whites until stiff peaks form; fold into batter. Pour into two greased 8-in. x 4-in. loaf pans. Bake at 350° for 50-60 minutes or until a toothpick inserted near the center comes out clean.

Combine glaze ingredients until smooth; pour over hot loaves. Cool for 10 minutes before removing from pans to wire racks. YIELD: 2 loaves.

creamy chicken vegetable soup

(PICTURED AT RIGHT)

Children of all ages will love to eat their veggies when they taste this creamy chicken soup created in our Test Kitchen. Brie cheese adds a delightfully mild flavor.

1 small onion, finely chopped

1 celery rib, chopped

1 medium carrot, chopped

1 garlic clove, minced

1 tablespoon butter

2 cans (14-1/2 ounces each) chicken broth

1/2 teaspoon salt

1/2 teaspoon pepper

3 tablespoons all-purpose flour

1-1/2 cups half-and-half cream

2 cups cubed cooked chicken breast

1 package (10 ounces) frozen chopped spinach, thawed and squeezed dry

1 round (8 ounces) Brie cheese, rind removed and chopped

In a Dutch oven, saute the onion, celery, carrot and garlic in butter until crisp-tender. Stir in the broth, salt and pepper. Bring to a boil. Reduce the heat; simmer, uncovered, for 10 minutes.

Combine flour and cream until smooth; gradually stir into soup. Bring to a boil; cook and stir for 2 minutes. Stir in the chicken, spinach and cheese. Cook and stir for 5 minutes or until cheese is melted. **YIELD:** 5 servings.

christmas cottages

(PICTURED ON PAGE 96)

To put a simple spin on the traditional gingerbread houses, our home economists employ purchased chocolate graham crackers. Make the "houses" ahead as an edible centerpiece...or let kids assemble their own during the party.

19 whole chocolate graham crackers

1 can (16 ounces) chocolate frosting

1 can (16 ounces) vanilla frosting

Assorted candies

For roofs, break six graham crackers in half, forming 12 squares. Using a serrated knife, cut four squares diagonally in half, forming eight triangles.

Cut a small hole in the corner of pastry or plastic bag; insert a #4 round pastry tip. Fill the bag with chocolate frosting. Pipe frosting on the short edges of two triangles; attach two squares. Repeat three times. Let stand until set, about 1 hour. Frost roofs with vanilla frosting and decorate with candies as desired.

For short cottages, break four graham crackers in half, forming eight squares. Pipe chocolate frosting along one side of front of cottage and the adjoining side wall. Place walls at right angles to each other. Repeat with second side section and back. Repeat for second cottage. Let stand until set.

For tall cottages, using whole crackers, pipe chocolate frosting along a long side of front of cottage and the adjoining side wall. Place walls at right angles to each other. Repeat with second side section and back. Repeat for second cottage. Let stand until set.

Cut doors from remaining cracker. Attach roofs and doors to cottages with chocolate frosting. Decorate as desired with candies and remaining frosting. Let stand until set. **YIELD:** 4 cottages.

CREATING CHRISTMAS COTTAGES

Party guests don't have to be architects or engineers to build these adorable, edible Christmas Cottages. (And because the recipe calls for purchased graham crackers, you don't have to spend hours making homemade gingerbread cutouts!)

Before getting started, set up the work station by putting down a covering on the table, opening the graham cracker packages, placing the candies in bowls and filling bags of frosting for each child.

To make it easier for kids to carry their creations home, you may want to have them assemble the Christmas Cottages in disposable pie tins.

If the children at your party range in age, encourage older kids to help the little ones.

Any kind of candy can be used to decorate the houses. (And don't forget the flaked coconut or confectioners' sugar for a snowy scene!) To help cut costs, you can even ask each guest to bring a bag of candy to share.

When the masterpieces are complete, display them as a Christmas village (along with the North Pole Party Favors on page 105) on top of a table until the end of the party.

elfin banana sandwiches

(PICTURED AT RIGHT)

A fruity, peanut-butter filling sandwiched between slices of banana bread will have guests asking for seconds.

Carla Cook | FALCON, CO

1 package (14 ounces) banana quick bread and muffin mix

1 cup reduced-fat creamy peanut butter

4 ounces reduced-fat cream cheese

2 tablespoons honey

2 medium ripe bananas, sliced

Prepare and bake bread according to package directions, using a greased 9-in. x 5-in. loaf pan.

Cut cooled bread into 12 slices. Toast slices until golden brown. In a small bowl, beat the peanut butter, cream cheese and honey until smooth; spread 1 tablespoon over each of six toast slices. Layer with bananas. Spread remaining peanut butter mixture over remaining toast slices; place over top. **YIELD:** 6 servings.

spiced apple cider

When the temperature drops outside, I like to warm up family and friends with steaming mugs of simple spiced cider. The recipe can easily be doubled for a larger group.

Deirdre Dee Cox | MILWAUKEE, WI

6 cups apple cider or juice

8 cinnamon sticks (3 inches)

2 lemon peel strips

1/8 teaspoon ground nutmeg

8 whole cloves

4 slices red apple, cored and cut in half

In a large saucepan, combine the apple cider, cinnamon sticks, lemon peel and nutmeg. Insert a clove into each apple slice; add to the cider.

Bring to a boil over medium heat. Reduce heat; simmer, uncovered, for 1 minute. Discard the lemon peel. Ladle into mugs. **YIELD:** 8 servings.

crusty italian sub supreme

I encourage guests to grab a knife and fork before diving into hearty slices of this sandwich! Each bite is loaded with sausage, cheese, artichoke hearts and sauce.

Toni Lockhart | GILMER, TX

1 pound bulk Italian sausage

1 jar (14 ounces) spaghetti sauce

1 loaf (1 pound) unsliced Italian bread

12 slices provolone cheese

2 jars (7-1/2 ounces each) marinated quartered artichoke hearts, drained and chopped

In a large skillet, cook sausage over medium heat until no longer pink; drain. Stir in spaghetti sauce; heat through.

Cut the top third off the loaf of bread; carefully hollow out bottom, leaving a 1/2-in. shell (discard removed bread or save for another use). Line bread shell with cheese slices; top with sausage mixture and artichokes. Replace bread top. Wrap loaf in foil.

Bake at 375° for 15-20 minutes or until cheese is melted. Let stand for 5 minutes before slicing. **YIELD:** 8 servings.

savory garlic cheese spread

One day I was in the process of roasting garlic when unexpected company arrived. Having little food in the house, I grabbed the roasted garlic and some cream cheese to create a delicious dip in a dash.

Aysha Schurman | AMMON, ID

2 whole garlic bulbs

1 teaspoon olive oil

1/4 cup butter, cubed

1/4 cup unsweetened apple juice

3 tablespoons lemon juice

2 tablespoons minced fresh chives

2 tablespoons water

4 teaspoons grated lemon peel

4 teaspoons minced fresh parsley
or 1-1/2 teaspoons dried parsley flakes

2 teaspoons minced fresh rosemary
or 1/2 teaspoon dried rosemary, crushed

1/2 teaspoon salt

2 packages (8 ounces each) cream cheese, softened

Assorted fresh vegetables

Remove papery outer skin from garlic (do not peel or separate cloves). Cut tops off of garlic bulbs. Brush with oil. Wrap each bulb in heavy-duty foil. Bake at 425° for 30-35 minutes or until softened. Cool for 10-15 minutes.

In a small saucepan, melt butter. Squeeze softened garlic into pan; stir in the juices, chives, water, lemon peel, parsley, rosemary and salt; cook and stir for 2-3 minutes or until most of the liquid is absorbed. Transfer to a food processor. Add cream cheese; cover and process until blended. Serve with vegetables. **YIELD:** 2 cups.

chocolate gingerbread cookies

(PICTURED AT RIGHT)

My mother developed this recipe, and I make the cookies in her honor every Christmas. People can't get enough of the molasses and chocolate combination.

Karen Sue Garback-Pristera | ALBANY, NY

1/2 cup butter, softened

3/4 cup sugar

1 egg

1/2 cup molasses

3 cups all-purpose flour

2 tablespoons plus 1-1/2 teaspoons baking cocoa

1 teaspoon baking soda

1 teaspoon ground cinnamon

1/2 teaspoon baking powder

1/2 teaspoon salt

Icing and decorations of your choice

In a large bowl, cream butter and sugar until light and fluffy. Beat in egg and molasses. Combine the flour, cocoa, baking soda, cinnamon, baking powder and salt; gradually add to creamed mixture and mix well. Cover and refrigerate for 1 hour or until easy to handle.

On a lightly floured surface, roll dough to 1/8-in. thickness. Cut with a floured 3-1/2-in. gingerbread boy cookie cutter; place 1 in. apart on ungreased baking sheets. Repeat with remaining dough; chill and reroll scraps.

Bake at 350° for 6-8 minutes or until edges are firm. Remove to wire racks to cool. Ice and decorate as desired. YIELD: 3 dozen.

bacon-tomato quesadillas

*Kids of all ages will go crazy for these appetizers that taste like a BLT.
They're crisp on the outside...and ooey, gooey and oh-so-good on the inside!*

Virginia Warner | CARSON CITY, NV

4 medium tomatoes, seeded and finely chopped

8 bacon strips, cooked and crumbled

1 cup (4 ounces) shredded Mexican cheese blend

Cooking spray

4 flour tortillas (8 inches)

In a small bowl, combine the tomatoes, bacon and cheese. Spray cooking spray over one side of each tortilla. Place tortillas, sprayed side down, on a griddle. Spoon tomato mixture over half of each tortilla. Fold over and cook over low heat for 1-2 minutes on each side or until cheese is melted. Cut each quesadilla into three wedges. **YIELD:** 1 dozen.

nutty mini cheese balls

*Ranch salad dressing mix is the fast flavoring for these small cheese balls. If your family isn't fond of nuts,
roll the balls in minced fresh parsley, chopped ripe olives or finely shredded cheddar cheese.*

Meta West | ABILENE, KS

1 package (8 ounces) cream cheese, softened

1 cup (4 ounces) shredded cheddar cheese

1 tablespoon finely chopped onion

1 tablespoon Worcestershire sauce

2 teaspoons ranch salad dressing mix

1 cup finely chopped nuts

Assorted crackers

In a small bowl, beat cream cheese. Stir in the cheddar cheese, onion, Worcestershire sauce and salad dressing mix. Shape into 1-in. balls; roll in the nuts. Chill until serving. Serve with assorted crackers. **YIELD:** 2 dozen.

sweet apricot candy

*I first made this recipe for a ladies' Christmas luncheon, where it received rave reviews. Now it's a favorite
with my family, too. I suggest presenting the divinity-like candies in pretty paper candy cups.*

Loraieyer | BEND, OR

1 jar (7 ounces) marshmallow creme

1 tablespoon butter, softened

1/2 teaspoon vanilla extract

1/4 teaspoon salt

1/4 teaspoon grated orange peel

3 cups confectioners' sugar, divided

1/2 cup finely chopped dried apricots

1/2 cup finely chopped pecans

In a large bowl, combine the marshmallow creme, butter, vanilla, salt and orange peel; beat until well blended. Gradually add 2 cups confectioners' sugar; beat until combined (mixture will be stiff). By hand, knead in the apricots, pecans and enough remaining confectioners' sugar to make a very stiff mixture.

Press into a greased 8-in. square pan. Refrigerate for at least 4 hours. Cut into 1-in. squares. **YIELD:** 1-1/2 pounds.

north pole party favors

(PICTURED AT RIGHT)

*Create a mini workshop for the little "elves"
at your party and have them build these
cute signs that point the direction to fun!*

1 unfinished wooden wheel
(1-1/2 inch diameter)

Red and green acrylic paint

2 green and white or red and white chenille
stems (6 inch length)

1 square piece of white card stock
(1 inch x 1 inch)

2 rectangle pieces of white card stock (about
1/2 inch x 2 inch)

1 sparkle pom-pom (1/2 inch)

For the base, paint the wooden wheel red or
green; let dry.

Twist two different color chenille stems
together to make the post. Fold one end of
the twisted chenille stems up about 1/4 in.
and place in the center of painted base.

Cut both corners off one end of each
rectangle piece of card stock to create an
arrow. With a fine-line marker, write
"North Pole" on the 1-in. square of card
stock and "Santa's Workshop" and the
guest's name on the rectangle pieces. Glue
the square sign and pom-pom to top
of post. Glue the rectangle signs to front
of post. **YIELD:** 1 sign.

EDITOR'S NOTE: Unfinished wooden
wheels are available at craft stores.

EVEN MORE ELFIN FUN

Add to the fun of your North Pole Party with these other ideas:

- Stop by a discount store and pick up felt elf hats for little ones
  to wear during the party and to take home.
- Enlist a neighbor to dress up as Santa. Take pictures of each child
  telling jolly old St. Nick what they want for Christmas. Have
  Santa hand out candy canes or coloring books.
- Gather the kids around and read the book called *The Elf on
  the Shelf*.

GIVING
thanks

For folks who favor traditional Thanksgiving foods but are looking

for a tasty twist, give our Southern-style holiday dinner a try.

Cooks hosting a smaller group can rely on a mouthwatering menu

option showcasing succulent turkey breast. Enliven your usual

Thanksgiving meal with our selection of autumn side dishes.

For perfect fall finales, reach for pleasing pear desserts!

*P*ut a special spin on your traditional Thanksgiving dinner by taking your taste buds on a trip south of the Mason-Dixon Line.

Rubbed with a bounty of seasonings and infused with tangy citrus flavor, Garlic and Herb Roasted Turkey takes center stage on your table.

Then round out the holiday supper with a fabulous assortment of Southern-style fixin's.

Guests gathered around your table will be much obliged when you set out a tried-and-tried favorite like Okra & Corn Saute.

Basic white dinner rolls just won't do! Instead, pass around tender, golden Corn Muffins with Honey Butter.

DINNER IN DIXIE
(PICTURED AT RIGHT)

Garlic and Herb Roasted Turkey (p. 112)
Okra & Corn Saute (p. 112)
Corn Muffins with Honey Butter (p. 114)

southern comfort
THANKSGIVING

Thanksgiving
Dinner Agenda

A Few Weeks Before:
- Prepare two grocery lists—one for nonperishable items to purchase now and one for perishable items to purchase a few days before Thanksgiving.
- Order a fresh turkey or buy a frozen turkey; freeze.
- Bake Corn Muffins; cool and freeze in heavy-duty resealable plastic bags.

Three to Four Days Before:
- Thaw the frozen turkey in a pan in the refrigerator. (Allow 24 hours of thawing for every 5 pounds. A thawed turkey can be refrigerated for 1 to 2 days.)
- Buy remaining grocery items.

The Day Before:
- Prepare the Honey Butter; cover and refrigerate.
- For Bacon Mac & Cheese, cook the elbow macaroni according to package directions; rinse with cold water and drain. Transfer to a resealable plastic bag; refrigerate. Prepare the cheese sauce; cover and chill.
- Make Hot Cranberry Tea. Let cool, cover and refrigerate.
- For Okra & Corn Saute, cut the okra, chop the bacon and cut kernels off the corn cobs. Store in separate covered containers; chill.
- Prepare Lima Bean Okra Soup; cool and refrigerate.
- Peel and devein the shrimp for Smoky Shrimp with Creamy Grits; refrigerate in an airtight container.
- Chop the Swiss chard for the Spicy Greens; refrigerate in a resealable plastic bag.
- Assemble the Corn Casserole; cover and refrigerate.
- For Candied Sweet Potato Pies, make filling and pastry. Chill separately.
- Bake Hazelnut Pumpkin Pie; cool and refrigerate.

Thanksgiving Day:
- In the morning, thaw Corn Muffins at room temperature.
- In two separate slow cookers, reheat the Hot Cranberry Tea and Lima Bean Okra Soup on low.
- Prepare the Garlic and Herb Roasted Turkey; bake as directed.
- Assemble and bake the Bacon Mac & Cheese.
- Remove the Corn Casserole from the refrigerator 30 minutes before baking.
- Let the cooked turkey stand 15 minutes before carving. Meanwhile, make the gravy.
- Wrap the Corn Muffins in foil; reheat in the oven for 10 minutes.
- Make Jalapeno Hush Puppies and Smoky Shrimp with Creamy Grits.
- Prepare the Okra & Corn Saute and Spicy Greens.
- Serve Corn Muffins with Honey Butter.
- For dessert, fry Candied Sweet Potato Pies and serve with Hazelnut Pumpkin Pie.

lima bean okra soup

(PICTURED AT RIGHT)

This soup's unique flavor comes from the wonderful combination of allspice, okra, tomatoes, corn, pepper and cloves. Every serving is loaded with nutrition and color.

Clara Coulston | WASHINGTON COURT HOUSE, OH

1 medium green pepper, chopped

1 medium onion, chopped

1/4 teaspoon whole cloves

1 tablespoon butter

3 cups vegetable broth

3 cups chopped tomatoes

2-1/2 cups sliced fresh or frozen okra, thawed

1 cup frozen lima beans, thawed

1/2 cup fresh or frozen corn, thawed

1/2 to 1 teaspoon salt

1/4 to 1/2 teaspoon ground allspice

1/4 teaspoon pepper

1/8 teaspoon cayenne pepper

In a large saucepan, saute the green pepper, onion and cloves in butter until vegetables are tender. Discard cloves.

Stir in the remaining ingredients. Bring to a boil. Reduce heat; cover and simmer for 15-20 minutes or until beans are tender. YIELD: 7 servings.

garlic and herb roasted turkey

(PICTURED ON PAGE 109)

Our recipe specialists use an easy herb rub to turn out a moist and tender turkey with beautiful golden skin. Lemon adds a pleasant flavor to the gravy.

1 turkey (14 to 16 pounds)

1/4 cup minced fresh parsley

2 tablespoons minced fresh basil

2 tablespoons minced fresh oregano

1-1/2 teaspoons garlic powder

1-1/2 teaspoons Italian seasoning

1 teaspoon each minced fresh rosemary, tarragon and thyme

1/4 teaspoon salt

1/4 teaspoon each lemon-pepper seasoning, cayenne pepper, chili powder and paprika

2 garlic cloves, minced

1 medium lemon, cut into wedges

1 medium orange, cut into wedges

2 tablespoons all-purpose flour

Pat turkey dry. Combine the seasonings and garlic; rub over the outside and inside of turkey. Place lemon and orange wedges in cavity. Place breast side up on a rack in a roasting pan.

Bake at 325° for 3-1/2 to 4 hours or until a meat thermometer reads 180°, basting occasionally with pan drippings. Cover loosely with foil if turkey browns too quickly. Remove turkey to a serving platter; cover and let stand for 20 minutes before carving.

Pour pan drippings and loosened brown bits into a measuring cup. Skim fat, reserving 2 tablespoons. Add enough water to measure 2 cups. In a small saucepan, combine flour and fat until smooth. Gradually stir in drippings. Bring to a boil; cook and stir for 2 minutes or until thickened. Serve with turkey. **YIELD:** 14 servings (2 cups gravy).

okra & corn saute

(PICTURED ON PAGE 108)

My family loves the fresh-from-the-garden taste of this dish. The combination of the peppered bacon and the Italian seasoning adds just the right amount of zest.

Karin Christian | *PLANO, TX*

8 cups fresh or frozen okra, thawed

6 thick-sliced peppered bacon strips, chopped

2 cups fresh whole kernel corn

4 teaspoons Italian seasoning

Cut okra lengthwise; set aside. In a large skillet, cook bacon over medium heat until crisp.

Stir in the corn, Italian seasoning and reserved okra; saute until okra is tender and corn is lightly browned. **YIELD:** 12 servings (2/3 cup each).

bacon mac & cheese

(PICTURED AT RIGHT)

Bacon and jalapeno pepper update ordinary mac and cheese, giving it great grown-up taste. I serve this comforting dish throughout the year.

Shelly Boehm | *SOUTH BEND, IN*

6 cups uncooked elbow macaroni

1 pound bacon strips, chopped

1 jalapeno pepper, seeded and minced

3 cups 2% milk

2 cups (8 ounces) shredded pepper Jack cheese

1 package (8 ounces) process cheese (Velveeta), cubed

1 cup (4 ounces) shredded Colby-Monterey Jack cheese

1 cup (4 ounces) shredded cheddar cheese

1 teaspoon onion powder

1 teaspoon chili powder

1/2 teaspoon salt

1/2 teaspoon pepper

Dash hot pepper sauce

3 green onions, chopped

Cook macaroni according to package directions; drain and set aside.

Meanwhile, in a Dutch oven, cook bacon over medium heat until crisp. Using a slotted spoon, remove to paper towels; drain, reserving 1 tablespoon drippings. Saute jalapeno in reserved drippings. Add milk and cheeses to pan; cook and stir until blended. Stir in the onion powder, chili powder, salt, pepper and pepper sauce. Add the onions, cooked bacon and reserved pasta to the pan; mix well.

Transfer to a greased 13-in. x 9-in. baking dish. Cover and bake at 350° for 30 minutes. Uncover; bake 10-15 minutes longer or until heated through. **YIELD:** 16 servings (3/4 cup each).

EDITOR'S NOTE: When cutting hot peppers, disposable gloves are recommended. Avoid touching your face.

corn muffins with honey butter

(PICTURED ON PAGE 108)

I turn classic corn bread muffins into something special by serving them with delicious honey butter. I like to surprise my family with the oven-baked goodies throughout the year.
Suzanne Cleveland | LYONS, GA

1/4 cup butter, softened

1/4 cup reduced-fat cream cheese

1/2 cup sugar

2 eggs

1-1/2 cups fat-free milk

1-1/2 cups all-purpose flour

1-1/2 cups yellow cornmeal

4 teaspoons baking powder

3/4 teaspoon salt

HONEY BUTTER:

1/4 cup butter, softened

2 tablespoons honey

In a large bowl, cream the butter, cream cheese and sugar until light and fluffy. Add eggs, one at a time, beating well after each addition. Stir in the milk. Combine the flour, cornmeal, baking powder and salt; add to creamed mixture just until moistened.

Coat muffin cups with cooking spray; fill three-fourths full with batter. Bake at 400° for 18-22 minutes or until a toothpick inserted near the center comes out clean. Cool for 5 minutes before removing from pans to wire racks. Beat butter and honey until blended; serve with warm muffins. **YIELD:** 16 muffins (1/3 cup honey butter).

jalapeno hush puppies

The crunchy exterior of these Southern-style snacks from our Test Kitchen is a nice contrast to the moist corn bread. Jalapeno pepper and hot sauce add a hint of heat.

1-1/2 cups yellow cornmeal

1/2 cup all-purpose flour

1 teaspoon baking powder

1 teaspoon salt

2 eggs, lightly beaten

3/4 cup 2% milk

2 jalapeno peppers, seeded and minced

1/4 cup finely chopped onion

1 teaspoon Louisiana-style hot sauce

Oil for deep-fat frying

In a large bowl, combine the cornmeal, flour, baking powder and salt. In another bowl, beat the eggs, milk, jalapenos, onion and hot sauce. Stir into dry ingredients just until combined.

In an electric skillet or deep-fat fryer, heat oil to 375°. Drop tablespoonfuls of the batter, a few at a time, into hot oil. Fry until golden brown on both sides. Drain on paper towels. Serve warm. **YIELD:** 2-1/2 dozen.

EDITOR'S NOTE: When cutting hot peppers, disposable gloves are recommended. Avoid touching your face.

hot cranberry tea

(PICTURED AT RIGHT)

Cinnamon-infused cranberries combine with orange and lemon juices for a not-too-sweet beverage. The crimson color is perfect for the holiday season.

Sarah Dennis Scott | MURFREESBORO, TN

3 quarts water

4 cups fresh or frozen cranberries, thawed

2 cinnamon sticks (3 inches)

2 cups sugar

1/2 cup orange juice

2 tablespoons lemon juice

In a Dutch oven, combine the water, cranberries and cinnamon. Bring to a boil. Reduce the heat; cover and simmer for 12-15 minutes or until the cranberries pop, stirring occasionally.

Remove from the heat. Discard the cinnamon. Strain cranberry mixture through a cheesecloth-lined colander. Return to Dutch oven. Stir in the sugar, orange juice and lemon juice; heat through. Serve warm. YIELD: 12 servings (3 quarts).

CRAZY FOR CRANBERRIES

Ruby red cranberries are a perfect staple item when cooking around the holidays. Follow these guidelines when storing and using these beautiful berries.

- Fresh cranberries are in season from early autumn through December. Look for packages with shiny, bright red (light or dark) berries.
- Discard any berries that are bruised or shriveled or that have brown spots. Refrigerate unwashed cranberries for about 1 month.

- To freeze cranberries, place them in a single layer on a 13-inch x 9-inch baking pan. When frozen, transfer to an airtight container and freeze for up to 1 year. There's no need to defrost them before using.
- When ready to use, quickly rinse the cranberries and pluck off any stems.
- When cooking berries to make a sauce, simmer them until they crack and pop. This allows the sugar to penetrate the tart fruit.

corn casserole

Jalapenos lend a subtle spicy taste to this classic corn side. It appears on my table at Thanksgiving and Christmas, which makes my husband happy!

Anita Anderson | MESQUITE, TX

2 cans (15-1/4 ounces each) whole kernel corn, drained

1 to 2 jalapeno peppers, sliced and seeded

1 tablespoon butter

1 tablespoon all-purpose flour

1 cup milk

1 package (8 ounces) cream cheese, softened and cubed

Place half of corn in a greased 8-in. square baking dish. Top with jalapeno slices and remaining corn. In a small saucepan, melt butter. Whisk in flour until smooth. Gradually add milk. Bring to a boil; cook and stir for 1-2 minutes or until thickened and bubbly.

Stir in cream cheese just until melted. Pour over corn. Bake, uncovered, at 350° for 35-40 minutes or until lightly browned. **YIELD:** 10 servings.

EDITOR'S NOTE: When cutting hot peppers, disposable gloves are recommended. Avoid touching your face.

smoky shrimp with creamy grits

Chipotle peppers and fire-roasted tomatoes give this dish a zesty, smoky flavor, which is nicely balanced by the creamy grits. The addition of shrimp creates a special holiday side.

Jo-Anne Cooper | CAMROSE, AB

3 cups water

1 can (14-3/4 ounces) cream-style corn

1 teaspoon salt

3/4 cup quick-cooking grits

4 green onions, finely chopped

2 ounces cream cheese, softened

1/4 cup butter, cubed

1 large garlic clove, minced

1-1/2 pounds uncooked large shrimp, peeled and deveined

1 can (14-1/2 ounces) fire-roasted diced tomatoes, drained

1 teaspoon seafood seasoning

1 teaspoon minced chipotle pepper in adobo sauce

In a large saucepan, bring the water, corn and salt to a boil. Slowly stir in grits. Reduce heat; cook and stir for 5-7 minutes or until thickened. Remove from the heat; stir in onions and cream cheese.

In a large skillet, melt butter. Add garlic; saute for 1 minute. Add shrimp; cook and stir for 3-4 minutes or until shrimp turn pink. Stir in the tomatoes, seafood seasoning and chipotle pepper; heat through. Serve with grits. **YIELD:** 6 servings.

hazelnut pumpkin pie

(PICTURED AT RIGHT)

I love putting new twists on old favorites. In my version of pumpkin pie, a crunchy hazelnut topping complements a smooth pumpkin filling in a tender, flaky crust.

Marie Rizzio | INTERLOCHEN, MI

2 cups all-purpose flour

2 tablespoons confectioners' sugar

1/2 teaspoon salt

3/4 cup cold butter

5 to 6 tablespoons ice water

1 teaspoon white vinegar

FILLING:

3 eggs, lightly beaten

1 can (15 ounces) solid-pack pumpkin

3/4 cup packed brown sugar

1/2 cup sour cream

2 tablespoons all-purpose flour

2 tablespoons hazelnut liqueur, optional

2 teaspoons pumpkin pie spice

TOPPING:

1/4 cup packed brown sugar

2 tablespoons all-purpose flour

3 tablespoons cold butter

1/2 cup chopped hazelnuts

1 tablespoon hazelnut liqueur, optional

In a large bowl, combine the flour, confectioners' sugar and salt; cut in butter until crumbly. Gradually add water and vinegar, tossing with a fork until dough forms a ball. Wrap in plastic wrap. Refrigerate for 30 minutes or until easy to handle.

Roll out pastry to fit a 9-in. pie plate. Transfer pastry to pie plate. Trim pastry to 1/2 in. beyond edge of pie plate; flute edges. In a large bowl, whisk the filling ingredients until blended. Pour into pastry.

In a small bowl, combine brown sugar and flour. Cut in butter until crumbly. Stir in hazelnuts and liqueur if desired; sprinkle over filling. Cover edges loosely with foil. Bake at 375° for 50-55 minutes or until a knife inserted near the center comes out clean.

Cool on a wire rack. Refrigerate leftovers. **YIELD:** 8 servings.

candied sweet potato pies

*My grandmother made the best candied sweet potatoes and
incredible apricot fried pies. I think these treats combine the best of both recipes!*

Angela Eshelman | PHOENIX, AZ

6 cups all-purpose flour

2 teaspoons salt

2 cups shortening

2/3 cup water

2 eggs

2 tablespoons white vinegar

1 large sweet potato, peeled and cut
into 1-inch cubes

3/4 cup sugar

1/4 cup butter, cubed

1-1/2 teaspoons lemon juice

1/2 teaspoon salt

1/4 teaspoon vanilla extract

Oil for deep-fat frying

Confectioners' sugar

In a large bowl, combine the flour and salt; cut in shortening until crumbly. Combine the water, eggs and vinegar; gradually add to the dry ingredients, tossing with a fork until dough forms a ball. Wrap dough in plastic wrap. Refrigerate for 1 to 1-1/2 hours or until easy to handle.

Meanwhile, place sweet potato in a small saucepan; cover with water. Bring to a boil. Reduce heat; cover and cook for 10-15 minutes or just until tender. Drain.

In a large skillet, combine the sugar, butter and sweet potatoes; cook and stir for 15-20 minutes or until the syrup is golden brown. Remove from the heat and mash. Stir in the lemon juice, salt and vanilla. Cool to room temperature.

Roll out pastry to 1/4-in. thickness. Cut with a floured 5-1/2-in. round cookie cutter. Spoon 2 tablespoons filling onto half of each circle. Moisten edges with water; fold dough over filling and press edges with a fork to seal.

In an electric skillet or deep-fat fryer, heat oil to 375°. Fry pies in batches for 6-7 minutes or until golden brown, turning once. Drain on paper towels. Dust with confectioners' sugar. YIELD: 14 pies.

spicy greens

*Sometimes the most basic dishes are the most special. Red pepper flakes, garlic
and lemon juice simply season Swiss chard for a quick-and-easy side from our home economists.*

2 pounds Swiss chard, chopped

2 teaspoons olive oil

3 garlic cloves, minced

1 tablespoon lemon juice

1/4 to 1/2 teaspoon crushed red pepper flakes

1/8 teaspoon salt

In a Dutch oven, saute chard in oil for 3-5 minutes or just until wilted.

Stir in the garlic, lemon juice, pepper flakes and salt; cover and cook 2-3 minutes longer or until tender. YIELD: 6 servings.

indian corn centerpiece

(PICTURED AT RIGHT)

With pretty kernels in shades of red, yellow, black, brown, maroon and more, Indian corn is a classic item to use in autumn decorations.

Large glue dots

3-inch x 9-1/2-inch clear glass candle sleeve or vase

Miniature Indian corn (about 13 ears or enough to go around glass candle sleeve or vase)

1-1/2-inch wide jute ribbon in color of choice

Battery-operated candle

Place glue dots near the top and bottom on one side of an ear of corn. Press the corn onto the outside of the candle sleeve or vase. Continue to adhere ears of corn all the way around the vase, placing the tops of the ears close together. Wrap ribbon around corn just below the husks and tie ends in an overhand knot. Trim ends as desired. Place a battery-operated candle inside the sleeve or vase.

INDIAN CORN PLACE MARKER

Add festive color to each place setting at your Thanksgiving table. Wrap ribbon around an ear of miniature Indian corn. With a fine-point marker, write a guest's name on a dried bay leaf. Tuck the bay leaf under the edge of the ribbon. Set the Indian corn place card in a bowl or on a plate at each place setting.

A golden turkey...mashed potatoes...savory bread dressing. The much-anticipated Thanksgiving dinner showcases a spread of fabulous foods to please your palate and soothe your soul.

Turkey breasts are a terrific choice for folks who prefer white meat (and for those hosting a smaller group). Seasoned with a zesty rub, Chili-Roasted Turkey Breast is sure to satisfy because it turns out moist every time.

Rich and flavorful, Mushroom-Onion Bread Dressing complements the tender turkey.

With two kinds of potatoes, Golden Sweet Mashed Potatoes is a side that's twice as tasty!

Bring a refreshing crunch to the special, sit-down supper with Holiday Cranberry-Walnut Salad.

HOME FOR THE HOLIDAYS
(PICTURED AT RIGHT)

Chili-Roasted Turkey Breast (p. 126)
Golden Sweet Mashed Potatoes (p. 123)
Mushroom-Onion Bread Dressing (p. 128)
Holiday Cranberry-Walnut Salad (p. 124)

down home
THANKSGIVING DINNER

Meal Plan for
Thanksgiving

A Few Weeks Before:
- Prepare two grocery lists—one for non-perishable items to purchase now and one for perishable items to purchase a few days before Thanksgiving.
- Bake Scarborough Fair Herb Bread. Let cool; freeze in a heavy-duty resealable plastic bag.

Three Days Before:
- Buy your remaining grocery items.
- Thaw the frozen turkey breast in a pan in the refrigerator.

Two Days Before:
- Cook the squash for Winter Squash Puff; let cool. Refrigerate in a covered container.
- Prepare Maple-Honey Cranberry Sauce; cover and chill.
- For Asparagus and Green Beans with Tarragon Lemon Dip, wash and trim the asparagus and beans; refrigerate in a resealable plastic bag. Make the tarragon lemon dip; cover and chill.
- Make the cranberry sauce for the Topsy-Turvy Cranberry Cakes; cover and chill. Combine the dry cake ingredients; store in a covered container at room temperature.

The Day Before:
- Set the table.
- Thaw the Scarborough Fair Herb Bread at room temperature.
- Prepare the Pumpkin Hummus; cover and refrigerate.

- For Holiday Cranberry-Walnut Salad, cook the cranberries in port wine; drain. Cover and chill cranberries and reserved cooking liquid in separate bowls. Cook and crumble the bacon; refrigerate in a covered container. Toast the walnut halves; store at room temperature.
- For the Mushroom-Onion Bread Dressing, make mushroom mixture; cover and chill. Cube bread; place in a resealable plastic bag.

Thanksgiving Day:
- In the morning, peel and quarter the potatoes and sweet potatoes for Golden Sweet Mashed Potatoes. Cover with cold water and refrigerate.
- As guests arrive, set out the Pumpkin Hummus and pita chips.
- Bake Chili-Roasted Turkey Breast.
- Put together the Winter Squash Puff; bake as directed.
- Assemble and bake the Mushroom-Onion Bread Dressing.
- Cover the turkey breast and let stand for 15 minutes before carving.
- Wrap the bread in foil; reheat in the oven while the turkey is standing. Slice and serve with butter.
- Make Golden Sweet Mashed Potatoes.
- Prepare Asparagus and Green Beans with Tarragon Lemon Dip.
- Toss Holiday Cranberry-Walnut Salad.
- Serve Maple-Honey Cranberry Sauce.
- For dessert, bake the Topsy-Turvy Cranberry Cakes.

maple-honey cranberry sauce

(PICTURED AT RIGHT)

This recipe is simple, quick and a family favorite. I'll often make a double batch for us to use on meats, spread on toast or even garnish desserts.

Rebecca Israel | *MANSFIELD, PA*

2 cups fresh or frozen cranberries

1/2 cup maple syrup

1/2 cup honey

1 tablespoon grated orange peel

In a large saucepan, combine the cranberries, syrup, honey and orange peel. Cook over medium heat until the berries pop, about 15 minutes. Cover and store in the refrigerator. **YIELD:** 2 cups.

golden sweet mashed potatoes

(PICTURED ON PAGE 121)

Can't decide what type of spuds to serve for Thanksgiving? Make both by preparing this casserole featuring Yukon Gold and sweet potatoes. Gouda cheese provides a rich flavor.

Shelby Goddard | *BATON ROUGE, LA*

3 medium Yukon Gold potatoes, peeled and cubed

1 medium sweet potato, peeled and cubed

1/4 cup 2% milk

1/2 cup shredded Gouda cheese

1/2 teaspoon paprika

1/4 teaspoon salt

1/4 teaspoon pepper

Place potatoes in a large saucepan and cover with water. Bring to a boil. Reduce heat; cover and simmer for 10-15 minutes or until tender. Drain.

Mash potatoes with milk; stir in the cheese, paprika, salt and pepper. **YIELD:** 6 servings.

holiday cranberry-walnut salad

(PICTURED ON PAGE 120)

A warm salad is a nice change of pace at holiday dinners. Port wine infuses cranberries with flavor, while balsamic vinegar adds a bit of zip to the dressing.

Becky Walch | *MANTECA, CA*

1/2 cup dried cranberries

1/2 cup port wine

1 small red onion, finely chopped

2 tablespoons balsamic vinegar

1/2 teaspoon sugar

1/8 teaspoon salt

1/8 teaspoon pepper

3 tablespoons olive oil

1 package (6 ounces) fresh baby spinach

5 bacon strips, cooked and crumbled

1/4 cup walnut halves, toasted

1/4 cup cubed Gouda cheese

In a small saucepan, combine cranberries and wine. Bring to a boil; cook for 4-5 minutes or until plumped. Set aside to cool. Drain cranberries, reserving liquid; set cranberries aside.

Return reserved liquid to saucepan; add the onion, vinegar, sugar, salt and pepper. Bring to a boil. Reduce heat; simmer, uncovered, for 2-3 minutes or until onion is tender. Remove from the heat. Cool slightly; whisk in oil.

In a large bowl, combine the spinach, bacon, walnuts, cheese and cranberries. Drizzle with onion mixture; toss to coat. **YIELD**: 8 servings.

winter squash puff

When my grown children come home for Thanksgiving, they always ask to make sure this squash puff is on the menu. The family-favorite recipe came from my grandmother.

Diane McDuffee | *FORT PLAIN, NY*

3 cups mashed cooked winter squash

1 cup sugar

1/2 cup raisins

2 eggs, beaten

1/3 cup nonfat dry milk powder

1/3 cup orange juice

1/4 cup butter, melted

1/2 teaspoon salt

In a large bowl, combine all ingredients; spoon into a greased 1-1/2-qt. baking dish. Bake, uncovered, at 350° for 65-70 minutes or until a thermometer reads 160°. **YIELD**: 6 servings.

COOKING WINTER SQUASH

To cook the squash for Winter Squash Puff, first wash it and trim the stem. Cut the squash in half; remove the seeds and stringy portions. Place squash cut side down in a greased baking dish. Bake, uncovered, at 350° for 45-60 minutes or until tender.

Scoop the pulp from the shell and mash. A winter squash that roughly weighs 1-3/4 pounds will yield approximately 1-3/4 cups cooked and mashed.

asparagus and green beans with tarragon lemon dip

(PICTURED AT RIGHT)

Tarragon balances the tang from lemon in the creamy sauce covering colorful asparagus and green beans. I serve this as a side dish as well as an appetizer.

Bonnie Hawkins | ELKHORN, WI

1 pound fresh asparagus, trimmed

1 pound fresh green beans, trimmed

1 cup mayonnaise

1/4 cup lemon juice

1 shallot, finely chopped

2 tablespoons minced fresh tarragon or 2 teaspoons dried tarragon

2 tablespoons minced fresh parsley or 2 teaspoons dried parsley flakes

2 teaspoons grated lemon peel

Dash pepper

Place 1 in. of water in a Dutch oven; add asparagus and beans. Bring to a boil. Reduce heat; cover and simmer for 3-5 minutes or until crisp-tender.

Meanwhile, in a small bowl, combine the remaining ingredients. Drain the vegetables; transfer to a serving platter. Drizzle with dip. **YIELD:** 10 servings.

chili-roasted turkey breast

(PICTURED ON PAGE 121)

Onion soup mix is a simple way to season a tasty turkey breast, and chili powder gives gorgeous color. When weather permits, I prepare this entree on the grill.

Sara Nowacki | FRANKLIN, WI

1/4 cup canola oil

1 envelope onion soup mix

4-1/2 teaspoons lime juice

1-1/2 teaspoons chili powder

1/2 teaspoon garlic powder

1/2 teaspoon ground cumin

1/2 teaspoon dried oregano

1 bone-in turkey breast (6 to 7 pounds)

In a small bowl, combine the first seven ingredients. With fingers, carefully loosen skin from the turkey breast; rub half of mixture under the skin. Secure skin to underside of breast with toothpicks. Rub skin with remaining mixture. Place on a rack in a shallow roasting pan.

Bake, uncovered, at 325° for 1-1/2 to 2 hours or until a meat thermometer reads 170°. (Cover loosely with foil if turkey browns too quickly.) Cover and let stand for 15 minutes before slicing; discard toothpicks. YIELD: 10 servings.

NO RACK FOR ROASTING?

Don't fret if you don't have a rack for your roasting pan. Simply roll up 6 balls of aluminum foil and place them under the turkey breast to keep it upright while baking.

scarborough fair herb bread

Our dinner group hosted a meal with the theme of Parsley, Sage, Rosemary and Thyme, which are mentioned in the song "Scarborough Fair" by Simon & Garfunkel. Those herbs fabulously flavor this delightful bread.

Laurel Leslie | SONORA, CA

6 cups all-purpose flour

3 packages (1/4 ounce each) active dry yeast

2 tablespoons sugar

2 teaspoons salt

3 tablespoons minced fresh parsley

2 teaspoons each minced fresh sage, rosemary and thyme

2-1/2 cups warm water (120° to 130°)

1 tablespoon butter, melted

In a large bowl, combine 4 cups flour, yeast, sugar, salt and herbs. Add water; beat until smooth. Stir in enough remaining flour to form a soft dough (dough will be sticky).

Turn onto a floured surface; knead until smooth and elastic, about 6-8 minutes. Place in a greased bowl, turning once to grease the top. Cover and let rise in a warm place until doubled, about 1 hour.

Punch dough down. Shape into two loaves. Place in greased 9-in. x 5-in. loaf pans. Cover and let rise until nearly doubled, about 30 minutes.

Bake at 350° for 30-35 minutes or until lightly browned. Remove from pans to wire racks to cool. Brush with butter. YIELD: 2 loaves (16 slices each).

topsy-turvy cranberry cakes

(PICTURED AT RIGHT)

When planning a special dinner for company during autumn, this is the dessert recipe I reach for. The cakes are so beautiful and tasty!

Susan Bazan | SEQUIM, WA

3 tablespoons cornstarch

3/4 cup sugar, divided

1/2 cup orange juice

1 teaspoon grated orange peel, divided

1-1/2 cups fresh or frozen cranberries

1/4 cup butter, softened

1 egg

3/4 cup all-purpose flour

1/2 teaspoon baking powder

1/4 teaspoon baking soda

Dash salt

1/3 cup coconut milk

1/4 cup chopped walnuts

Vanilla ice cream, optional

In a small saucepan, combine cornstarch and 1/4 cup sugar. Stir in orange juice and 1/2 teaspoon orange peel; add cranberries. Cook over medium heat until the berries pop, about 15 minutes; set aside.

In a small bowl, cream the butter and remaining sugar until light and fluffy. Add the egg and beat well. Beat in the remaining orange peel. Combine the flour, baking powder, baking soda and salt; add to the creamed mixture alternately with the coconut milk, beating well after each addition.

Sprinkle the walnuts into four greased 4-in. fluted tube pans. Spoon the cranberry mixture over the walnuts; pour batter into pans. Bake at 350° for 25-30 minutes or until a toothpick inserted near the center comes out clean. Cool for 5 minutes before removing from the pans to a wire rack. Serve warm with ice cream if desired. **YIELD:** 4 servings.

mushroom-onion bread dressing

(PICTURED ON PAGE 121)

This savory, rustic dressing really complements tender slices of turkey.
The level of herbs is perfect. Guests won't be able to stop eating forkful after forkful!

James Hayes | RIDGECREST, CA

3/4 pound sliced baby portobello mushrooms

1 large onion, finely chopped

1 celery rib, finely chopped

3 tablespoons butter, divided

2 garlic cloves, minced

1/2 cup white wine or chicken broth

1-1/2 teaspoons minced fresh thyme
or 1/2 teaspoon dried thyme, divided

1 cup chicken broth

1/4 teaspoon salt

1/4 teaspoon pepper

10 cups cubed day-old French bread

1 cup heavy whipping cream

1 egg, beaten

2 tablespoons minced fresh parsley

In a large skillet, saute the mushrooms, onion and celery in 1 tablespoon butter until tender. Add garlic; cook 1 minute longer. Stir in wine and 3/4 teaspoon thyme; cook over medium heat until liquid is evaporated. Add the broth, salt and pepper. Bring to a boil; cook until liquid is reduced by half.

In a large bowl, combine the mushroom mixture, bread cubes, cream, egg, parsley and remaining thyme. Transfer to a greased 2-qt. baking dish (dish will be full); dot with remaining butter. Cover and bake at 325° for 50 minutes. Uncover and bake 15-20 minutes longer or until a thermometer reads 160° and top is browned. YIELD: 8 servings.

pumpkin hummus

Our home economists give traditional hummus an autumn appeal with
the addition of canned pumpkin. Hot pepper sauce lends just the right amount of heat.

2 cans (15 ounces each) garbanzo beans or chickpeas, rinsed and drained

1 can (15 ounces) solid-pack pumpkin

1/2 cup olive oil

1/3 cup tahini

5 tablespoons lemon juice

2 teaspoons hot pepper sauce

2 garlic cloves, minced

1 teaspoon salt

Baked pita chips

Place the first eight ingredients in a food processor; cover and process until blended. Serve with chips. YIELD: 4 cups.

tile table runner

(PICTURED AT RIGHT)

Tablecloths are certainly lovely at holiday dinners. But they have a formal feel and require special laundering afterwards to get out stubborn stains...like red wine!

For a more casual look, create a practical table runner using pretty, purchased natural stone or ceramic tiles.

Head out to tile shops or to discount home improvement stores. Be on the lookout for tiles that you can purchase individually. Select them in varying sizes and styles and in colors that coordinate with your decor. (You may also want to purchase some smaller tiles to use as coasters.)

At home, put felt on the back of the tiles to protect your table from scratches. (See the instructions below.)

Set the tiles down the length of your table like a runner. The tiles also serve as trivets, protecting your tabletop from hot serving dishes. In addition, large tiles can be used as chargers under dinner plates.

PROTECT YOUR TABLE WITH FELT

The bottoms of natural stone and ceramic tiles can be rough and may scratch your table. To protect your table's surface, cut craft felt the same size as each tile. Following the manufacturer's instructions, spray the back of the tiles with spray adhesive. Center the felt pieces on the back of each tile; let dry. Place the tiles right side up on a cutting mat or another protected surface. Use a craft knife to trim away any felt that shows around the edges of the tiles.

or most families, it's a given that turkey will be the star of the show at Thanksgiving dinner.

So how can cooks add a little of their own creativity to the table? It's easy with a savory assortment of spectacular side dishes!

Celebrate the finest produce of autumn by preparing Acorn Squash with Apricot Sauce. Topped with crunchy nuts and sweet fruit, it's bound to become a timeless favorite of your family.

Vegetables...biscuits...salads...pasta... potatoes...soup. You'll find a splendid selection of sides to round out formal and casual dinners throughout the season.

FALL CLASSIC
(PICTURED AT RIGHT)

Acorn Squash with Apricot Sauce (p. 132)

sensational
AUTUMN SIDES

acorn squash with apricot sauce

(PICTURED ON PAGE 131)

*With its mild flavor, acorn squash is the perfect base for crunchy walnuts
and sweet apricots. I like to double the sauce so I can serve it with my breakfast oatmeal.*

Judy Parker | MOORE, OK

2 small acorn squash

2 tablespoons brown sugar

1/4 teaspoon ground cinnamon

2 tablespoons butter

1 cup orange juice

1/2 cup dried apricots, coarsely chopped

1/2 cup chopped walnuts, optional

Cut squash in half; discard seeds. Cut a thin slice from bottom of squash with a sharp knife to allow it to sit flat. Place hollow side up in a greased 15-in. x 10-in. x 1-in. baking pan; add 1/2 in. of hot water.

Combine brown sugar and cinnamon; sprinkle over squash. Dot with butter.

Cover and bake at 375° for 55-65 minutes or until tender.

Meanwhile, in a small saucepan, combine orange juice and apricots. Bring to a boil. Reduce heat; simmer, uncovered, for 15 minutes or until apricots are tender. Transfer to a blender; cover and process until smooth. Serve with squash; sprinkle with walnuts if desired. YIELD: 4 servings.

BUYING AND STORING WINTER SQUASH

The most common varieties of winter squash are acorn, butternut, hubbard, spaghetti and turban. Look for squash which feel heavy for their size and have hard, deep-colored rinds that are free of blemishes. Unwashed winter squash can be stored in a dry, cool, well-ventilated place for up to 1 month.

spiced sweet potato wedges

*The recipe for these simply seasoned sweet potato wedges comes
from a 1900s cookbook. It's proof that tried-and-true dishes never go out of style.*

Phyllis Schmalz | KANSAS CITY, KS

3/4 cup apricot preserves

1/4 cup water

1-1/2 teaspoons lemon juice

1/4 teaspoon ground cinnamon

1/4 teaspoon ground nutmeg

4 large sweet potatoes (about 3 pounds), peeled and cut into wedges

In a small saucepan, combine preserves and water. Bring to a boil. Reduce heat; simmer, uncovered, for 5 minutes or until slightly thickened. Add the lemon juice, cinnamon and nutmeg.

Place potatoes in two greased 15-in. x 10-in. x 1-in. baking pans. Brush half of the preserve mixture over potatoes.

Bake at 400° for 35-40 minutes or until tender, basting occasionally with remaining preserve mixture. YIELD: 8 servings.

savory root vegetable soup

(PICTURED AT RIGHT)

Instead of the usual side dishes, consider serving a vegetable-laden soup at Thanksgiving or other holidays. Each spoonful will warm the body and soul.

Zan Brock | JASPER, AL

4 bacon strips

2 celery ribs, chopped

1 medium onion, chopped

1 medium green pepper, chopped

2 medium leeks (white portion only), chopped

2 cups frozen shredded hash brown potatoes

1 cup cubed peeled sweet potato

2 medium parsnips, peeled and chopped

2 medium carrots, peeled and chopped

2 small turnips, peeled and chopped

3 cans (14-1/2 ounces each) chicken broth

2 tablespoons minced fresh parsley

2 teaspoons herbes de Provence

1 garlic clove, minced

1/2 teaspoon white pepper

1/2 teaspoon ground coriander

1 cup (8 ounces) sour cream

1 cup (4 ounces) shredded Swiss cheese

In a Dutch oven, cook the bacon over medium heat until crisp. Remove to paper towels; drain, reserving drippings. Crumble bacon and set aside. Saute the celery, onion, green pepper and leeks in drippings until tender.

Add the hash browns, sweet potato, parsnips, carrots and turnips; cook and stir over medium heat for 10 minutes.

Add the broth, parsley, herbes de Provence, garlic, white pepper and coriander; bring to a boil. Reduce heat; cover and simmer for 15-20 minutes or until vegetables are tender. Ladle soup into bowls. Top each serving with sour cream, cheese and crumbled bacon. **YIELD:** 8 servings (2 quarts).

EDITOR'S NOTE: Look for herbes de Provence in the spice aisle. It is also available from Penzeys Spices. Call 1-800-741-7787 or visit *www.penzeys.com*.

butternut squash custard

My husband first tried this comforting casserole when he was still my fiance. Having enjoyed it so much, he said I needed to offer it at every Thanksgiving dinner. I was happy to oblige!

Maura Calusdian | LONDONDERRY, NH

1 medium butternut squash (2 to 3 pounds), peeled, seeded and cubed

1/2 cup all-purpose flour

1/2 cup sugar

2 cups 2% milk

3 eggs

2 tablespoons butter, melted

1/8 teaspoon salt

1/8 teaspoon ground cinnamon

1/8 teaspoon ground nutmeg

Place squash in a large saucepan and cover with water; bring to a boil. Reduce heat; cover and simmer for 8-10 minutes or until tender. Drain.

In a large bowl, mash the squash with flour and sugar until blended; beat in the milk, eggs and butter. Pour into an ungreased 2-1/2-qt. baking dish. Sprinkle with remaining ingredients.

Bake at 350° for 55-65 minutes or until center appears set. **YIELD**: 8 servings.

bacon & marinated mushroom salad

When I first served this refreshing salad more than 20 years ago, friends couldn't say enough about it. The marinated mushrooms are conveniently made the night before.

Sheila Christensen | SAN MARCOS, CA

3/4 cup olive oil

3 green onions, cut into fourths

1/4 cup lemon juice

1-1/4 teaspoons Worcestershire sauce

1 teaspoon white wine vinegar

1/2 teaspoon salt

1/2 teaspoon ground mustard

1/8 teaspoon pepper

1 pound thinly sliced fresh mushrooms

3/4 pound thick-sliced peppered bacon strips

4 cups torn romaine

4 cups torn red leaf lettuce

1/2 medium red onion, thinly sliced

Cherry tomatoes and ripe olives, optional

In a blender, combine the first eight ingredients. Cover and process until onions are finely chopped. Place the mushrooms in a large bowl; add the olive oil mixture and toss to coat. Cover and refrigerate overnight.

In a large skillet, cook bacon in batches over medium heat until crisp. Remove to paper towels to drain. Crumble bacon; stir into mushroom mixture.

Divide the romaine, leaf lettuce and onion among eight salad plates. Top each serving with 1/2 cup mushroom mixture. Garnish with tomatoes and olives if desired. **YIELD**: 8 servings.

pasta with creamy sweet potato sauce

(PICTURED AT RIGHT)

This creamy pasta dish is the result of combining two different recipes. I often turn it into a main dish by serving a green salad on the side.

Suzanne Appleyard | QUEENSBURY, NY

1 large sweet potato

2/3 cup 2% milk

2 cups uncooked penne pasta

1 tablespoon pine nuts

1 teaspoon rubbed sage

1 tablespoon butter

1 garlic clove, minced

1 teaspoon olive oil

3/4 teaspoon salt

1/4 teaspoon pepper

1/2 cup shredded Parmesan cheese

Additional shredded Parmesan cheese, optional

Scrub and pierce sweet potato; place on a microwave-safe plate. Microwave, uncovered, on high for 10-12 minutes or until tender, turning once. When cool enough to handle, remove and discard the skin. Place the potato in a large bowl and mash with the milk.

Cook pasta according to package directions. In a large skillet, saute pine nuts and sage in butter until pine nuts are toasted. Remove from pan and set aside.

In the same skillet, saute garlic in oil for 1 minute. Stir in the sweet potato mixture, salt and pepper. Drain pasta, reserving 3/4 cup cooking water; add to sweet potato mixture. Stir in cheese, pine nut mixture and reserved cooking water. Sprinkle with additional cheese if desired. **YIELD:** 5 servings.

EDITOR'S NOTE: This recipe was tested in a 1,100-watt microwave.

peppered pear celebration salad

*With sweet fruit, a tart dressing and crunchy pistachios, every forkful of this beautiful salad
is like a celebration for your taste buds! Assemble it in advance and drizzle with the vinaigrette just before serving.*

Veronica Callaghan | GLASTONBURY, CT

2-1/2 cups cubed day-old French bread

5 cups torn mixed salad greens

1 small red onion, thinly sliced

1/2 cup crumbled blue cheese

1/2 cup seedless red grapes, halved

1/4 cup pistachios

1/4 cup dried cherries

2 medium pears, peeled and thinly sliced

1 teaspoon coarsely ground pepper

VINAIGRETTE:

1/4 cup olive oil

2 tablespoons sherry vinegar

1 tablespoon seedless raspberry preserves

1 teaspoon minced fresh gingerroot

1 teaspoon finely chopped shallot

1/4 teaspoon salt

Place the bread on a baking sheet; bake at 350° for 5-8 minutes or until toasted, stirring once. Cool. Place in a salad bowl. Top with the greens, onion, cheese, grapes, pistachios and cherries.

Place pears in a small bowl; sprinkle with pepper and toss to coat. Add pears to salad.

Whisk the vinaigrette ingredients; drizzle over salad and gently toss to coat. Serve immediately. **YIELD:** 10 servings.

potato spinach gratin

Since my family loves spinach, I knew this tender potato casserole would be a hit. It accompanies many of our meaty meals.

Nellie Runne | ROCKFORD, IL

3 shallots, thinly sliced

1 tablespoon butter

2 packages (10 ounces each) frozen chopped spinach, thawed and squeezed dry

1 teaspoon salt, divided

1/2 teaspoon pepper, divided

1/8 teaspoon ground nutmeg

3 pounds medium potatoes (about 9 medium), peeled and thinly sliced

1 cup (4 ounces) shredded Gruyere or Swiss cheese

1 tablespoon cornstarch

1-1/2 cups 2% milk

1 cup heavy whipping cream

In a large skillet, saute shallots in butter until tender. Add the spinach, 1/2 teaspoon salt, 1/4 teaspoon pepper and nutmeg.

In a greased 3-qt. baking dish, layer half of the potatoes, 1/3 cup cheese and half of spinach mixture. Repeat layers. Top with remaining cheese.

In a small bowl, combine the cornstarch, milk, cream and remaining salt and pepper until smooth. Pour the milk mixture over the cheese.

Cover and bake at 350° for 1 hour. Uncover; bake 15-20 minutes longer or until potatoes are tender. **YIELD:** 12 servings (2/3 cup each).

brussels sprouts with golden raisins

(PICTURED AT RIGHT)

Take a break from ordinary steamed brussels sprouts by combining them with raisins. Thinly slicing the sprouts makes them appeal to people who normally don't like the texture.

Michaela Rosenthal | *WOODLAND HILLS, CA*

1 pound fresh brussels sprouts, thinly sliced

1 tablespoon olive oil

2 tablespoons water

1/4 teaspoon celery salt

1/8 teaspoon white pepper

1/3 cup golden raisins

1 teaspoon white balsamic vinegar

In a large skillet, saute brussels sprouts in oil until crisp-tender. Add the water, celery salt and pepper. Reduce heat; cover and cook for 4-5 minutes or until tender. Stir in raisins and vinegar. **YIELD:** 5 servings.

orange rosemary biscuits

*The appealing orange and rosemary taste of these flaky, tender biscuits
complements oven-roasted turkey. They bake up beautifully every time.*

Lorraine Caland | THUNDER BAY, ON

2 cups all-purpose flour

4 teaspoons grated orange peel

1 tablespoon baking powder

1 tablespoon minced fresh rosemary
or 1 teaspoon dried rosemary

1/2 teaspoon salt

1/2 cup cold butter, cubed

2 tablespoons orange juice

1 cup plus 1 tablespoon buttermilk, divided

Place the flour, orange peel, baking powder, rosemary and salt in a food processor; cover and pulse to blend. Add butter; cover and pulse until mixture resembles coarse crumbs. Add orange juice and 1 cup buttermilk; pulse just until moistened. Turn onto a lightly floured surface; knead 8-10 times.

Pat or roll out to 1/2-in. thickness; cut with a floured 2-1/2-in. biscuit cutter. Place 1 in. apart on a greased baking sheet. Brush with remaining buttermilk. Bake at 425° for 8-12 minutes or until golden brown. Serve warm. YIELD: 1 dozen.

FREEZING FRESH ROSEMARY

You just can't beat the aromatic flavor of fresh rosemary. You can freeze the rosemary from your garden for use in winter. Simply wrap sprigs of fresh rosemary in foil and place in a freezer bag for up to 3 months. When using, remember that frozen rosemary has a stronger flavor than fresh.

roasted vegetable medley

*When I can't decide what vegetable to serve at dinner, I turn to this mouthwatering medley
that features brussels sprouts, parsnips, carrots and butternut squash. It pleases everyone around the table.*

Betty Fulks | ONIA, AR

1 small butternut squash (about 2 pounds),
peeled, seeded and cut into 1-inch pieces

2 medium parsnips, cut into 1-inch pieces

1 cup fresh brussels sprouts, halved

1 cup fresh baby carrots

1/4 cup butter, melted

1 tablespoon minced fresh sage or 1 teaspoon
dried sage leaves

1 garlic clove, minced

In a large bowl, combine the squash, parsnips, brussels sprouts and carrots. In a small bowl, combine the remaining ingredients. Pour over vegetables; toss to coat.

Transfer to a greased 15-in. x 10-in. x 1-in. baking pan. Bake at 425° for 35-45 minutes or until tender, stirring occasionally. YIELD: 8 servings.

hoosier corn casserole

(PICTURED AT RIGHT)

This recipe combines the comforting flavors of my home state with my love of using garden-fresh herbs. From Thanksgiving turkey to grilled pork chops in summer, any entree is enhanced with this savory side.

Joyce Manier | *BEECH GROVE, IN*

1 medium green pepper, chopped

2 green onions, sliced

1 tablespoon fresh minced chives

2 teaspoons minced fresh rosemary

1 tablespoon butter

1 teaspoon canola oil

2 tablespoons bacon bits

3 eggs, lightly beaten

1/2 cup sour cream

1/2 cup half-and-half cream

1/4 cup all-purpose flour

1/2 teaspoon salt

1/4 teaspoon pepper

1/8 teaspoon cayenne pepper

4 cups frozen corn, thawed

1-1/4 cups (5 ounces) shredded cheddar cheese, divided

2 medium tomatoes, seeded and chopped

In a large skillet, saute the green pepper, onions, chives and rosemary in butter and oil until tender. Add bacon bits; cook 1 minute longer. Set aside.

In a large bowl, combine the eggs, sour cream, cream, flour, salt and peppers. Stir in the corn, 1 cup cheese and green pepper mixture until blended.

Pour into a greased 11-in. x 7-in. baking dish. Bake, uncovered, at 350° for 25 minutes. Sprinkle with tomatoes and remaining cheese. Bake 5-10 minutes longer or until cheese is melted and a knife inserted near the center comes out clean. **YIELD:** 8 servings.

*A*s the weather turns from hot and sunny and to cool and crisp, it's a terrific time to head out to a farmers market and stock up on fabulous autumn produce.

Remember to gather a peck of pretty pears so you can make a sweet selection of comforting desserts featuring one of fall's finest fruits.

In the recipe for Pear Fruit Compote, baked Boscs go from ordinary to awesome when paired with a sweet, citrus concoction.

Showcased in cakes, pies, pastries, crisps and more, sweet-and-juicy pears will appear on your table well beyond the peak picking season!

PERFECT PAIRING
(PICTURED AT RIGHT)

Pear Fruit Compote (p. 142)

pleasing
PEAR DESSERTS

pear fruit compote

(PICTURED ON PAGE 141)

This recipe pleasantly proves you can offer guests an elegant dessert with little fuss. Pop fruit-topped pears in the oven and bake...then enjoy time with family and friends while the incredible aroma fills your home.

Crystal Allen | COLLINSVILLE, TX

6 medium Bosc pears

2 medium navel oranges, peeled and sectioned

1/3 cup raisins

1 cup water

3/4 cup packed brown sugar

Dash salt

3 tablespoons butter

Place pears on their sides in a greased 13-in. x 9-in. baking dish; arrange oranges and raisins around pears. In a small bowl, combine the water, brown sugar and salt. Pour over the fruit; dot with the butter.

Cover and bake at 325° for 55-65 minutes or until pears are tender, basting occasionally. Halve and core pears; top with fruit compote. **YIELD:** 6 servings.

gingerbread trifle with pears

I originally developed this recipe for a friend's baby shower, but now it's a holiday favorite. The flavored cream cheese pairs well with the pears and gingerbread.

Nancy Cupp | LARKSPUR, CA

1 package (14-1/2 ounces) gingerbread cake mix

3 cups water

1/4 cup lemon juice

10 medium ripe pears

1 cup sugar, divided

4 tablespoons butter, divided

1/2 teaspoon ground cinnamon, divided

1/2 teaspoon ground ginger, divided

TRIFLE CREAM:

2 packages (8 ounces each) cream cheese, softened

1/4 cup packed brown sugar

2 tablespoons orange juice

1 tablespoon grated orange peel

1/4 to 1/2 teaspoon rum extract

1 cup heavy whipping cream, whipped

Prepare and bake cake mix according to package directions. Cool completely on a wire rack.

In a large bowl, combine water and lemon juice. Peel pears, one at a time, quarter and cut into 1 to 1-1/2-in. chunks. Place in water mixture to prevent browning.

Drain the pears. In a large skillet, combine 1/2 cup sugar, 2 tablespoons butter and 1/4 teaspoon each cinnamon and ginger. Add half the pears. Cook and stir over medium-high heat for 4-5 minutes or until syrup is golden brown. Reduce heat to medium-low; cover and cook 10 minutes longer, stirring occasionally. Transfer to a bowl.

Repeat with remaining sugar, butter, cinnamon, ginger and pears. Cool completely.

Meanwhile, for trifle cream, in a large bowl, beat the cream cheese, brown sugar, orange juice, orange peel and extract until blended. Gently fold in whipped cream.

To assemble, cut cake into 1/4-in. slices. Place a third in a 3-qt. trifle dish or glass serving bowl; top with a third of pears and a third of cream cheese mixture. Repeat layers twice. Cover and refrigerate for several hours or overnight. **YIELD:** 14-16 servings.

sugar and spice pear pie

(PICTURED AT RIGHT)

My family loves pear pie because it's a little less tart than apple pie. Chopped pecans enhance the flaky, buttery crust.

Kristina Pontier | HILLSBORO, OR

5 large pears, peeled and sliced

3/4 cup sugar

1/4 cup orange juice

4-1/2 teaspoons quick-cooking tapioca

1 tablespoon grated lemon peel

1 teaspoon lemon juice

1/2 teaspoon ground nutmeg

1/4 teaspoon salt

1/4 teaspoon minced fresh gingerroot

Pastry for double-crust pie (9 inches)

1/2 cup chopped pecans

1/4 cup packed brown sugar

3 tablespoons butter

In a large bowl, combine the first nine ingredients.

Line a 9-in. pie plate with bottom crust; trim pastry even with edge. Sprinkle with pecans and brown sugar; fill with pear mixture. Dot with butter. Roll out remaining pastry to fit top of pie; place over filling. Trim, seal and flute edges. Cut slits in pastry.

Bake at 400° for 40-45 minutes or until the crust is golden brown and the filling is bubbly. Cover the edges with foil during the last 15 minutes to prevent overbrowning if necessary. Cool on a wire rack. **YIELD:** 8 servings.

WHAT TYPE OF PEAR TO USE?

When a dessert in this chapter can be made with any kind of cooking pear (like Anjou, Bartlett, Bosc or Seckel), the recipe will generically say "pears." But for dishes where it's important for the pear to hold its shape, the recipe will specifically call for Bosc pears in order to yield the best results.

fig pear strudels

Filled with pears, figs and nuts, these pastries are a delightful dessert.

Cheryl Perry | HERTFORD, NC

2 medium pears, peeled and chopped

1/4 cup pear nectar

2 tablespoons brown sugar

1-1/2 teaspoons butter

1/2 teaspoon grated lemon peel

1/8 teaspoon ground allspice

Dash salt

1-1/2 teaspoons cornstarch

1-1/2 teaspoons water

1/2 cup chopped dried figs

1/2 cup Mascarpone cheese

1 tablespoon heavy whipping cream

1/2 teaspoon vanilla extract

16 sheets frozen phyllo dough, thawed (14-inch x 9-inch sheet size)

1 cup butter, melted

1 cup finely chopped black walnuts, divided

2 tablespoons coarse sugar

In a large saucepan, bring the pears, pear nectar, brown sugar, butter, lemon peel, allspice and salt to a boil. Reduce heat, simmer, uncovered, for 8-10 minutes. Combine cornstarch and water until smooth. Gradually stir into pear mixture. Bring to a boil; cook and stir for 2 minutes or until thickened. Remove from the heat; stir in figs. Cover and let stand for 10 minutes.

In a small bowl, combine the cheese, cream and vanilla. Place one sheet of phyllo dough on a work surface; brush with butter. (Keep remaining phyllo covered with plastic wrap and a damp towel to prevent it from drying out.) Repeat with two more sheets of phyllo, brushing each layer with butter. Sprinkle with 1/4 cup walnuts. Repeat. Top with two sheets of phyllo, brushing each layer with butter.

Spread half of cheese mixture over phyllo to within 1/4 in. of edges. Spread half of pear mixture widthwise over half of cheese mixture. Roll up jelly-roll style, starting with the short side spread with pear mixture.

Place seam side down on a greased 15-in. x 10-in. x 1-in. baking pan. Using a sharp knife, cut slits in top. Brush with butter and sprinkle with coarse sugar. Repeat with remaining phyllo, melted butter, walnuts, cheese mixture and pear mixture. Bake at 350° for 40-45 minutes or until golden brown. Cool to room temperature. Cut into slices. **YIELD:** 2 strudels (4 slices each).

PEAR POINTERS

Although pears are readily available year-round, the peak season is July through January. Purchase pears that are plump and free of bruises, soft spots and cuts.

To ripen pears, place in a paper bag and store at room temperature for 2 to 3 days. Store unwashed, ripe pears in the refrigerator for 3 to 5 days.

One pound of pears (about 3 medium) yields roughly 3 cups sliced.

From sunny yellow to regal red, colorful pears come in many varieties, including the following:

ANJOU. Has a sweet, spicy flavor and tender texture. Good for eating, cooking and using in salads.

BARTLETT. Has a sweet flavor and tender texture. Good for eating, cooking and using in salads.

BOSC. Has a sweet, spicy flavor and dense texture. Good for eating, cooking, baking and poaching.

COMICE. Has a sweet flavor, fruity aroma and smooth texture. Good for eating.

SECKEL. Has a sweet, spicy flavor and firm, grainy texture. Good for cooking.

old-fashioned almond pear cake

(PICTURED AT RIGHT)

Pear lovers will find it hard to resist going back for seconds (and maybe even thirds) of this old-fashioned cake. Almond extract beautifully complements the pears.

Roxanne Chan | ALBANY, CA

4 cups sliced peeled fresh pears

1/4 cup finely chopped crystallized ginger

1/4 cup lemon juice

4 eggs

3/4 cup confectioners' sugar

1/2 cup butter, melted

1/2 teaspoon almond extract

1-1/4 cups all-purpose flour

1 teaspoon baking powder

1/4 cup sliced almonds

In a large bowl, combine the pears, ginger and lemon juice; set aside.

In another bowl, beat eggs, confectioners' sugar, butter and extract until blended. Combine flour and baking powder; gradually beat into the egg mixture until blended. Stir in pear mixture.

Transfer to a greased 9-in. springform pan; sprinkle with almonds. Bake at 350° for 35-40 minutes or until a toothpick inserted near the center comes out clean. Cool on a wire rack for 10 minutes before cutting. Serve warm. **YIELD:** 8 servings.

toffee-pear crisp bread pudding

My son asked me to make two desserts one day so I combined them into this one dish. It's absolutely fantastic!

Kurt Wait | *REDWOOD CITY, CA*

1-3/4 cups 2% milk

1 cup butterscotch-caramel ice cream topping

1/4 cup butter, cubed

1 teaspoon ground cinnamon

1/2 teaspoon ground ginger

2 eggs, beaten

4 cups cubed day-old French bread

2 cups sliced peeled fresh pears

TOPPING:

1/2 cup all-purpose flour

1/2 cup packed brown sugar

1/3 cup cold butter

1/3 cup English toffee bits

In a small saucepan, combine the milk, caramel topping and butter. Cook and stir over medium-low heat until butter is melted; add cinnamon and ginger. Stir a small amount of mixture into eggs; return all to the pan, stirring constantly.

Place bread cubes in a large bowl; gently stir in milk mixture. Let stand for 10 minutes. Gently stir in pears; transfer to a greased 11-in. x 7-in. baking dish. Bake, uncovered, at 350° for 20 minutes.

In a small bowl, combine flour and brown sugar; cut in butter until crumbly. Stir in toffee bits.

Sprinkle flour mixture over dish. Bake 20-25 minutes longer or until a knife inserted near the center comes out clean and pears are tender. Cool for 10 minutes before serving. Refrigerate leftovers. **YIELD:** 12 servings.

upside-down pear spice cake

Our Test Kitchen infuses spice cake with cocoa for a deliciously different flavor.

1/4 cup butter, cubed

1/2 cup chopped walnuts

1/3 cup packed brown sugar

2 tablespoons maple syrup

1/4 teaspoon ground cinnamon

2 medium ripe pears, peeled and thinly sliced

CAKE:

3/4 cup butter, softened

1-1/2 cups sugar

3 eggs, separated

3/4 teaspoon vanilla extract

2 cups all-purpose flour

2 tablespoons baking cocoa

3/4 teaspoon salt

3/4 teaspoon baking powder

3/4 teaspoon baking soda

3/4 teaspoon ground cinnamon

1/8 teaspoon ground nutmeg

3/4 cup buttermilk

In a small saucepan, melt butter. Stir in the walnuts, brown sugar, maple syrup and cinnamon until blended. Pour into a greased 9-in. round baking pan. Arrange the pear slices in a single layer over walnut mixture.

In a large bowl, cream butter and sugar until light and fluffy. Add egg yolks; beat well. Stir in vanilla. Combine the flour, cocoa, salt, baking powder, baking soda, cinnamon and nutmeg. Add dry ingredients to the creamed mixture alternately with buttermilk, beating well after each addition.

In a small bowl with clean beaters, beat egg whites on medium speed until soft peaks form. Gradually fold into batter. Spoon over the pears. Bake at 350° for 50-60 minutes or until a toothpick comes out clean. Cool for 10 minutes before inverting onto a serving plate. Serve warm. **YIELD:** 8 servings.

pear-adise spice twists

(PICTURED AT RIGHT)

Flaky, buttery pear dumplings bake on top of sweet caramel syrup for a fabulous fall finale. I also like to serve them alongside cinnamon ice cream.

Wendy Nickel | KIESTER, MN

1-1/2 cups all-purpose flour

1/2 teaspoon salt

1/4 cup cold butter

1/4 cup shortening

4 to 5 tablespoons cold water

2 large Bosc pears

SAUCE:

1/3 cup packed brown sugar

1 teaspoon ground cinnamon

1/4 teaspoon ground nutmeg

1/8 teaspoon ground cloves

1/2 cup water

1/4 cup butter, cubed

Vanilla ice cream, optional

In a large bowl, combine flour and salt; cut in butter and shortening until crumbly. Gradually add water, tossing with a fork until dough forms a ball. Divide in half; wrap each portion in plastic wrap. Refrigerate for 1 to 1-1/2 hours or until easy to handle.

Peel pears and cut each into eight wedges. Roll out each portion of dough into a 10-in. x 8-in. rectangle. Cut each into eight 1-in.-wide strips. Wrap each strip around a pear wedge.

Place wrapped pears in an ungreased 11-in. x 7-in. baking dish. Combine brown sugar and spices; sprinkle over the top. In a small saucepan, bring water and butter to a boil; pour mixture over pear twists. Bake, uncovered, at 425° for 25-30 minutes or until golden brown. Serve warm with ice cream if desired. YIELD: 8 servings.

cranberry pear tart with gingerbread crust

Three fabulous flavors of fall—pears, cranberries and gingerbread—come together in one delectable dessert. It can be served warm, but my family prefers it chilled.

Sarah Badding | *LANGDON, ND*

4 cups cranberry juice

1/2 cup sugar

2 tablespoons lemon juice

1 cinnamon stick (3 inches)

4 medium pears, peeled, halved and cored

1/3 cup dried cranberries

CRUST:

1-1/2 cups all-purpose flour

3 tablespoons brown sugar

2-1/2 teaspoons ground cinnamon

2 teaspoons ground ginger

3/4 teaspoon ground allspice

1/2 teaspoon salt

1/2 cup cold butter

1 egg

2 tablespoons molasses

CUSTARD:

3 eggs

1/2 cup sour cream

1/3 cup sugar

1/4 cup 2% milk

1 teaspoon grated orange peel

1/4 teaspoon vanilla extract

Dash salt

In a large saucepan, bring the cranberry juice, sugar, lemon juice and cinnamon stick to a boil; add pears. Reduce heat, simmer, uncovered, for 10-15 minutes or until pears are tender. Remove from the heat; stir in cranberries. Cool to room temperature.

Meanwhile, in a food processor, combine the flour, brown sugar, cinnamon, ginger, allspice and salt; cover and pulse to blend. Add butter; cover and pulse until mixture resembles coarse crumbs. Add egg and molasses; pulse just until moistened. Press onto the bottom and 1 in. up the sides of a greased 11-in. fluted tart pan with removable bottom. Bake at 375° for 15 minutes. Cool completely on a wire rack. Reduce heat to 325°.

Drain pears and cranberries, reserving juice. Pat the pears and cranberries dry; discard cinnamon stick.

In a small bowl, whisk the eggs, sour cream, sugar, milk, orange peel, vanilla and salt. Stir in half of the cranberries; spoon half of mixture into tart. Slice pear halves; arrange over custard. Top with remaining custard. Bake for 45-50 minutes or until custard is set. Cool completely on a wire rack.

Place reserved juice in a large saucepan. Bring to a boil. Cook until liquid is reduced to 1 cup; brush over pears. Arrange remaining cranberries around tart. Chill until serving. **YIELD:** 12 servings.

poached pears in lace cookie cups

(PICTURED AT RIGHT)

Growing up in a German household, I often enjoyed an assortment of sweet treats. I carry on that tradition with my own family by making these molasses cookie cups, which we use to hold pretty poached pears as well as ice cream.

Petra Maria | OAKLAND, CA

1/4 cup butter, cubed

1/4 cup sugar

3 tablespoons molasses

1/3 cup ground walnuts

1/4 cup all-purpose flour

1/4 teaspoon ground ginger

PEARS:

4 medium Bosc pears

5 cups water

1 cup sugar

3 tablespoons grated orange peel

4 teaspoons vanilla extract

In a small saucepan, combine the butter, sugar and molasses. Bring to a boil. Remove from the heat; stir in the walnuts, flour and ginger. Spoon 3 tablespoonfuls of the batter 7 in. apart onto parchment paper-lined baking sheets.

Bake at 350° for 8-10 minutes or until golden brown and lacy. Cool for 2 minutes before removing from pans. Drape each cookie over an inverted glass with a 2-in.-diameter bottom, forming four cups. Cool completely.

Core pears from the bottom, leaving stems intact; peel pears. Place pears on their sides in a large saucepan. Add the water, sugar, orange peel and vanilla. Bring to a boil. Reduce heat; cover and simmer for 8-10 minutes or until pears are almost tender, turning once.

Remove pears with a slotted spoon; cool to room temperature. Discard cooking liquid. Place pears in cookie cups. **YIELD:** 4 servings.

EASTER
gatherings

Easter often signals the arrival of spring...and a turn towards lighter, fresher fare. Hop to it and host an early-day brunch featuring Tomato-Herb Frittata, Cilantro-Lime Fruit Salad and Lemon-Poppy Seed Doughnut Holes. If playing the Easter Bunny has left you "eggs-hausted," serve a delightful dinner later in the day. Two deliciously different glaze recipes will dress up ordinary baked ham.

*I*f the idea of hosting an elaborate Easter dinner has you wanting to hide along with those colored eggs, why not invite friends and family over for a casual brunch instead?

Gather around the table for a scrumptious morning feast featuring spring's finest flavors.

Ripe tomatoes, gooey cheese and savory herbs highlight every bite of Tomato Herb Frittata. Pair the hearty egg bake with succulent Breakfast Sausage Patties and refreshing Cilantro-Lime Fruit Salad.

Then watch as guests sneak "just one more" of the irresistible Lemon-Poppy Seed Doughnut Holes.

RISE AND SHINE!
(PICTURED AT RIGHT)

Tomato Herb Frittata (p. 154)
Breakfast Sausage Patties (p. 154)
Cilantro-Lime Fruit Salad (p. 156)
Lemon-Poppy Seed Doughnut Holes (p. 156)

a memorable
EASTER BRUNCH

breakfast sausage patties

(PICTURED ON PAGE 153)

*Buttermilk is the "secret" ingredient that keeps these pork patties moist,
while a blend of seasonings creates a wonderful, slightly spicy taste.*

Harvey Keeney | MANDAN, ND

3/4 cup buttermilk

2-1/4 teaspoons kosher salt

1-1/2 teaspoons rubbed sage

1-1/2 teaspoons brown sugar

1-1/2 teaspoons pepper

3/4 teaspoon dried marjoram

3/4 teaspoon dried savory

3/4 teaspoon cayenne pepper

1/4 teaspoon ground nutmeg

2-1/2 pounds ground boneless pork butt roast

In a large bowl, combine the buttermilk and seasonings. Crumble pork over mixture; mix well. Shape into twenty-one 3-in. patties. In a large skillet coated with cooking spray, cook patties in batches over medium heat for 5-6 minutes on each side or until meat is no longer pink. Drain if necessary on paper towels. **YIELD:** 21 sausage patties.

tomato herb frittata

(PICTURED ON PAGE 153)

*Fresh herbs and garlic really add to the flavor of this hearty and savory early-day dish.
Every slice is brimming with cheesy eggs and bright tomatoes.*

Candy Summerhill | ALEXANDER, AR

9 eggs

1-1/4 cups (5 ounces) shredded part-skim mozzarella cheese, divided

1/2 cup 2% milk

1 tablespoon minced fresh basil or 1 teaspoon dried basil

1 tablespoon minced fresh oregano or 1 teaspoon dried oregano

1 teaspoon minced fresh thyme or 1/4 teaspoon dried thyme

1/2 teaspoon salt

1/4 teaspoon pepper

1-1/2 cups grape tomatoes

2 tablespoons olive oil

2 garlic cloves, minced

Thinly sliced fresh basil, optional

In a small bowl, whisk the eggs, 3/4 cup cheese, milk, herbs, salt and pepper; set aside.

In a 10-in. ovenproof skillet, saute tomatoes in oil until tender. Add garlic; cook 1 minute longer. Pour egg mixture into pan; sprinkle with remaining cheese.

Bake at 400° for 12-15 minutes or until eggs are completely set. Let stand for 5 minutes. Cut into wedges. Garnish with sliced basil if desired. **YIELD:** 6 servings.

italian sausage & egg croissants

(PICTURED AT RIGHT)

Wake up your taste buds with eye-opening breakfast sandwiches featuring zesty sausage, fluffy egg and creamy avocado piled high on a flaky croissant.

Emory Doty | JASPER, GA

1 cup (4 ounces) crumbled blue cheese

1 jalapeno pepper, seeded and minced

1 teaspoon each dried basil, oregano and parsley flakes

1 pound bulk Italian sausage

8 eggs

3 tablespoons 2% milk

1/8 teaspoon salt

1/8 teaspoon pepper

3 tablespoons butter, divided

1/2 cup mayonnaise

8 croissants, split

8 slices tomato

1 medium ripe avocado, peeled and sliced

In a large bowl, combine the cheese, jalapeno and herbs. Crumble sausage over the mixture and mix well. Shape into eight patties.

In a large nonstick skillet over medium heat, cook patties for 4-5 minutes on each side or until no longer pink. Set aside and keep warm.

Whisk the eggs, milk, salt and pepper. In another large nonstick skillet, melt half of the butter over medium-high heat. Add half of the egg mixture to the skillet (mixture should set immediately at edges).

As eggs set, push cooked edges toward the center, letting uncooked portion flow underneath. Cover and cook 1-2 minutes longer or until top is set. Slide eggs onto a plate; cut into four wedges. Repeat with remaining butter and egg mixture.

Spread mayonnaise over croissants; top with sausage patties, eggs, tomato and avocado. **YIELD:** 8 servings.

EDITOR'S NOTE: When cutting hot peppers, disposable gloves are recommended. Avoid touching your face.

lemon-poppy seed doughnut holes

(PICTURED ON PAGE 152)

*The tender texture and light lemon flavor of these irresistible gems
make them a hit at breakfasts and brunches—or even as snacks.*

Lee Elrod | NEWNAN, GA

1-1/2 cups all-purpose flour

3 tablespoons poppy seeds

1-1/2 teaspoons baking powder

1/2 teaspoon salt

2 eggs

1/2 cup sugar

1/4 cup buttermilk

3 tablespoons butter, melted

1 tablespoon grated lemon peel

1 teaspoon vanilla extract

Oil for deep-fat frying

GLAZE:

2 cups confectioners' sugar

5 tablespoons lemon juice

In a large bowl, combine the flour, poppy seeds, baking powder and salt. In a small bowl, combine the eggs, sugar, buttermilk, butter, lemon peel and vanilla; stir into dry ingredients just until combined. Cover and refrigerate for at least 1 hour.

In an electric skillet or deep-fat fryer, heat oil to 375°. Drop tablespoonfuls of batter, a few at a time, into hot oil. Fry until golden brown on both sides. Drain on paper towels.

For glaze, in a small bowl, combine confectioners' sugar and lemon juice. Drizzle over doughnut holes. **YIELD:** about 2 dozen.

cilantro-lime fruit salad

(PICTURED ON PAGE 153)

Cilantro, when blended with lime juice and honey, creates a deliciously different spin on ordinary fruit salad.

Denette Brents | PORTERVILLE, CA

2-1/2 cups cantaloupe balls

2 medium mangoes, peeled and finely chopped

3 medium kiwifruit, peeled, halved and sliced

2 medium ripe bananas, sliced

1/4 cup minced fresh cilantro

2 tablespoons lime juice

1 tablespoon honey

1/4 teaspoon salt

In a large bowl, combine the fruits. In a small bowl, combine the remaining ingredients. Drizzle over salad; toss to coat. Chill until serving. **YIELD:** 8 servings.

PEELING KIWI

Peel kiwifruit quickly and easily—and without any special gadgets! First, cut off both ends of the kiwi. Then slip a teaspoon just under the skin, matching the spoon's curve to the curve of the fruit. Slide the spoon around the kiwi to separate the fruit from the skin. The fruit will slip out of the skin in one smooth piece.

rhubarb popover pie

(PICTURED AT RIGHT)

This fabulous spring breakfast "pie" is also scrumptious when pineapple or even fresh strawberries are mixed in with the rhubarb filling. Yum!

Patricia Kile | ELIZABETHTOWN, PA

1/2 cup all-purpose flour

1/4 teaspoon salt

2 eggs

1/2 cup 2% milk

2 tablespoons butter

FILLING:

1-1/2 cups sliced fresh or frozen rhubarb, thawed

1/2 cup canned pineapple chunks

1/3 cup butter, cubed

1/2 cup packed brown sugar

Whipped cream or vanilla ice cream, optional

In a large bowl, combine flour and salt. In another bowl, whisk eggs and milk.

Place butter in a 9-in. pie plate; heat in a 425° oven for 3-5 minutes or until butter is melted. Meanwhile, stir egg mixture into dry ingredients just until moistened.

Carefully swirl the butter in the pan to coat the sides and bottom of pan; add batter. Bake at 425° for 16-20 minutes or until puffed and golden brown.

Meanwhile, in a large skillet, saute rhubarb and pineapple in butter until rhubarb is tender. Stir in brown sugar; bring to a boil over medium heat, stirring constantly. Pour into the center of puffed pancake; cut into six wedges. Serve immediately with whipped cream if desired.

YIELD: 6 servings.

EDITOR'S NOTE: If using frozen rhubarb, measure rhubarb while still frozen, then thaw completely. Drain in a colander, but do not press liquid out.

so-easy cheese danish

A brunch menu just isn't the same without this tender, flaky Danish. The warm cream cheese center is a delightful surprise. Convenient refrigerated crescent roll dough means I can make it in a snap.

Cathleen Bushman | GENEVA, IL

2 packages (8 ounces each) cream cheese, softened

1 cup sugar

1 egg yolk

1 teaspoon vanilla extract

2 tubes (8 ounces each) refrigerated crescent rolls

1 egg white, lightly beaten

TOPPING:

1/2 cup sugar

1/2 cup chopped pecans

1/4 teaspoon ground cinnamon

In a large bowl, beat cream cheese and sugar until fluffy. Add egg yolk and vanilla; beat on low speed until blended.

Unroll one tube of crescent roll dough into one long rectangle; seal seams and perforations. Press onto the bottom of an ungreased 13-in. x 9-in. baking dish. Spread with cream cheese mixture. On a lightly floured surface, press or roll out remaining dough into a 13-in. x 9-in. rectangle. Place over filling; brush with egg white.

In a small bowl, combine the sugar, pecans and cinnamon; sprinkle over top. Bake at 350° for 25-30 minutes or until golden brown. Cool slightly on a wire rack; serve warm. Refrigerate leftovers. **YIELD:** 15 servings.

strawberry-rhubarb applesauce

The slightly sweet, slightly tart flavors of fresh rhubarb, strawberries and a hint of citrus shine through in every bite of this springtime spin on traditional applesauce.

Samantha Shupe | OGDEN, UT

4 large Golden Delicious apples, peeled and cut into chunks

2 tablespoons water

2 cups sliced fresh or frozen rhubarb

1 cup sliced fresh strawberries

2/3 cup orange juice

1/2 cup sugar

4 teaspoons grated orange peel

Combine apples and water in a large saucepan. Cook over medium heat for 5 minutes, stirring occasionally. Stir in the rhubarb, strawberries, orange juice, sugar and orange peel. Bring to a boil. Reduce heat; cover and simmer for 12-16 minutes or until desired consistency. **YIELD:** 4 cups.

EDITOR'S NOTE: If using frozen rhubarb, measure rhubarb while still frozen, then thaw completely. Drain in a colander, but do not press liquid out.

chocolate-covered eggs

(PICTURED AT RIGHT)

These pretty little candies beat any store-bought variety. They take some effort, but the look of delight on the faces of those who try them make every minute worth it.

Louise Oberfoell | BOWMAN, ND

1/4 cup butter, softened

1 jar (7 ounces) marshmallow creme

1 teaspoon vanilla extract

3 cups plus 1 tablespoon confectioners' sugar, divided

3 to 4 drops yellow food coloring, optional

2 cups (12 ounces) white baking chips or semisweet chocolate chips

2 tablespoons shortening

Icing of your choice

Assorted decorating candies

In a large bowl, beat the butter, marshmallow creme and vanilla until smooth. Gradually beat in 3 cups confectioners' sugar. Place 1/4 cup creamed mixture in a bowl; add yellow food coloring if desired and mix well. Shape into 24 small balls; cover and chill for 30 minutes. Wrap plain mixture in plastic wrap; chill for 30 minutes.

Dust work surface with remaining confectioners' sugar. Divide plain dough into 24 pieces. Wrap one piece of plain dough around each yellow ball and form into an egg shape. Place on a waxed paper-lined baking sheet; cover with plastic wrap. Freeze for 15 minutes or until firm.

In a microwave, melt chips and shortening; stir until smooth. Dip eggs in mixture; allow excess to drip off. Return eggs to waxed paper. Refrigerate for 30 minutes or until set. Decorate with icing and decorating candies as desired. Store in an airtight container in the refrigerator. **YIELD:** 2 dozen.

almond-crusted french toast

This elegant version of French toast is ideal for special occasions. It seems so simple, but the sliced almonds and dusting of powdered sugar make such a difference.

Judith Austic | KIRKSVILLE, MO

8 eggs

1/2 cup 2% milk

3 tablespoons sugar

1 teaspoon almond extract

1/2 teaspoon vanilla extract

10 slices Italian bread (1 inch thick)

1/2 cup sliced almonds

Confectioners' sugar and maple syrup

In a large bowl, combine the first five ingredients. Dip each slice of bread into egg mixture; place on waxed paper. Press almonds onto tops of bread slices.

Cook on a greased hot griddle for 3-4 minutes on each side or until golden brown. Sprinkle with confectioners' sugar and serve with syrup. **YIELD:** 5 servings.

creamy smoked salmon spread

With its mild herb and salmon flavor, this creamy spread is wonderful on miniature bagels as part of a spring brunch.

Faith Agnew | SPOTSWOOD, NJ

1/2 pound smoked salmon fillet

1 package (8 ounces) garlic-herb cheese spread

1/4 cup minced fresh parsley

Miniature bagels, split and toasted

Flake salmon into small pieces. In a small bowl, combine the cheese spread, parsley and salmon. Serve on bagels. **YIELD:** 1-1/2 cups.

BLOWN EGG PLACE CARD

Set the stage for a delightful Easter brunch by welcoming guests to the table with these whimsical blown egg place cards.

Blow out a brown egg as directed in the Blown Egg Ornament Tree instructions at right. Use a very small pointed scissors to turn each of the holes into a small slit. With a permanent marker, write words of encouragement near the ends of an 8-in. long narrow ribbon. Insert the ribbon through one end of the egg and out the other end; center the ribbon. Slip a pony bead over each end of the ribbon; slide beads close to the egg to hide the holes and glue in place if desired. Write a guest's name on each egg with a white paint pen.

blown egg ornament tree

(PICTURED AT RIGHT)

Ordinary brown eggs are transformed into stunning ornaments for this whimsical spring centerpiece. Hung from delicate pussy willow branches, the blown egg ornaments make a dazzling focal point for your Easter celebration.

Desired number of brown eggs

Long needle

Small drinking straw

12-inch length of craft wire

22-inch length of sheer ribbon for each egg

Decorative beads strung onto thread or fine wire

Pussy willow branches

TO BLOW OUT EGGS: Use a push pin to make holes in opposite ends of each egg. Carefully break away a bit more of the shell to make 1/8-inch holes.

Insert a long needle or wire into one hole; swirl it around to break up the yolk.

Hold the egg over a small container with a hole facing downward. Insert a small drinking straw into the top hole. Blow into the straw, forcing out the contents of egg. Repeat until egg is completely empty.

Run cold water into the eggshell; gently shake. Blow out the water with the straw. Repeat until water runs clear.

Dry eggshells in the microwave on high for 15 to 30 seconds, bake in a 300° oven for 10 minutes or let air-dry with one of the holes facing downward for 2-3 days.

TO MAKE THE EGG TREE: Bend craft wire in half. Center the ribbon in the fold of the wire, letting the ends hang down. Feed the ends of the wire through the bottom hole (wide end) of the egg and out the top hole (narrow end) so that a 6-inch loop of ribbon extends from the top. Remove the wire. Tie an overhand knot in the ribbon at the top of the egg, covering the hole and forming a hanging loop.

At the bottom of the egg, tie the ribbon ends together with a square or double knot, tying the beaded wire into the knot and covering the hole. Trim ribbon ends if desired. Repeat with the remaining eggs.

Place pussy willow branches into a sturdy container. Hang eggs by the top loops onto branches.

*I*f you think the Easter meal means the same ol' ham dinner, one bite of this scrumptious Easter feast will quickly change your mind.

With its crisp, sugary crust, Bourbon Baked Ham is as pleasing to the eye as it is to the palate. Even those who aren't usually fond of ham won't pass up servings of this marvelous main dish that's really quite simple to prepare.

Strawberry-Arugula Salad adds a splash of color to the menu with its fresh medley of tender arugula, sweet strawberries, tangy feta cheese and crunchy slivered almonds.

SUCCULENT HAM DINNER
(PICTURED AT RIGHT)

Bourbon Baked Ham (p. 166)
Strawberry Arugula Salad (p. 166)

simply elegant
EASTER FEAST

Easter Dinner
Timeline

A Few Weeks Before:
- Prepare two grocery lists—one for nonperishable items to purchase now and one for the perishable items to purchase a few days before Easter.
- Order a ham or buy and freeze a ham.
- For Mini Carrot Cake Tortes, bake the cake, cool and cut into layers. Freeze in heavy-duty resealable plastic bags.

Two to Three Days Before:
- Buy your remaining grocery items, including ham if you ordered one.

The Day Before:
- Set the table.
- For the Strawberry Arugula Salad, wash and slice the strawberries, tear the salad greens and make the dressing; chill in separate containers.
- For Mini Carrot Cake Tortes, thaw the cakes at room temperature and toast the walnuts. Make the frosting; cover and refrigerate.
- Make the Savory Mushroom Bread; let cool and wrap tightly in plastic wrap.
- Thinly slice the fennel bulbs for Fennel Au Gratin. Cook, drain and pat dry. Cool and refrigerate in a covered container.
- Peel and cut the cucumbers for Cucumbers with Tapenade Mousse; chill in a covered container. Combine the cream cheese, tapenade and salt, but do not add whipping cream. Cover and store in the refrigerator.
- For Mediterranean Penne Salad, cook, rinse and drain the pasta; chill in a covered container. Prepare dressing; cover and refrigerate.
- Bake the Almond, Strawberry & Rhubarb Pie; cool. Store loosely covered at room temperature.

Easter Day:
- In the morning, assemble the Mini Carrot Cake Tortes; refrigerate until serving.
- Make the Mediterranean Penne Salad; cover and chill.
- Put together the Fennel Au Gratin; bake.
- Shortly before guests arrive, whip the whipping cream for the Cucumbers with Tapenade Mousse and add to the cream cheese mixture. Assemble the appetizer.
- Roast the Bourbon Baked Ham, Plum & Chutney Glazed Ham or Root Beer Glazed Ham as directed. (The ham can also be prepared and sliced the day before and then served cold or reheated on Easter day.)
- If desired, wrap Savory Mushroom Bread in foil and reheat in a 350° oven for 10 minutes. Serve with butter.
- Make the Strawberry Arugula Salad.
- For dessert, serve the Almond, Strawberry & Rhubarb Pie and Mini Carrot Cake Tortes.

fennel au gratin

(PICTURED AT RIGHT)

Here's a lovely variation on traditional potatoes au gratin. Rich and buttery, this baked side dish has just the right amount of fennel flavor.

Sue Kauffman | COLUMBIA CITY, IN

2 large fennel bulbs, thinly sliced

1/4 cup butter, cubed

3 tablespoons all-purpose flour

1/2 teaspoon salt

1/4 teaspoon coarsely ground pepper

1 cup heavy whipping cream

1/2 cup shredded Gruyere or Swiss cheese

2 tablespoons grated Parmesan cheese

In a large saucepan, bring 1 in. of water to a boil. Add fennel; cover and cook for 6-8 minutes or until crisp-tender. Drain and pat dry; place in a greased 11-in. x 7-in. baking dish.

In a small saucepan, melt butter. Stir in flour, salt and pepper until smooth; gradually add cream. Bring to a boil; cook and stir for 1-2 minutes or until thickened.

Stir in Gruyere cheese. Pour over fennel and sprinkle with Parmesan cheese.

Cover and bake at 375° for 15 minutes. Uncover and bake 15-20 minutes longer or until the casserole is golden brown and bubbly. YIELD: 8 servings.

cucumbers with tapenade mousse

Crisp cucumber rounds act as the base for this deliciously different appetizer. Piping the savory mousse-like filling onto each cucumber creates a stunning presentation.

Mary Brinkhaus | BLOOMINGTON, MN

1 English cucumber

4 ounces cream cheese, softened

1/3 cup tapenade or ripe olive bruschetta topping

1/4 teaspoon salt

1/2 cup heavy whipping cream

Pitted Greek olives, optional

Peel strips from cucumber to create a decorative edge; cut cucumber into 1/4-in. slices. Blot with paper towels to remove excess moisture; set aside.

In a small bowl, combine the cream cheese, tapenade and salt. In another bowl, beat cream until stiff peaks form. Fold into cream cheese mixture.

Pipe or dollop mousse onto cucumber slices. Garnish with olives if desired. YIELD: about 4 dozen.

bourbon baked ham

(PICTURED ON PAGE 163)

Because of its simple ingredient list, easy preparation and unbeatable flavor, this baked ham is one you'll come to rely on often. The honey-bourbon glaze not only looks lovely, but also helps to seal in the meat's juices.

Jean Adams | WAYCROSS, GA

1 bone-in fully cooked spiral-sliced ham (7 to 9 pounds)

1 cup honey

1/2 cup bourbon

1/2 cup molasses

1/4 cup orange juice

2 tablespoons Dijon mustard

Place ham on a rack in a shallow roasting pan. Score the surface of the ham, making diamond shapes 1/2 in. deep. Bake at 325° for 2 hours.

In a small saucepan, combine the remaining ingredients; cook and stir until smooth.

Brush ham with some of the glaze; bake 30-60 minutes longer or until a meat thermometer reads 140°, brushing occasionally with remaining glaze. YIELD: 15 servings.

strawberry arugula salad

(PICTURED ON PAGE 163)

The combination of peppery arugula, sweet strawberries and robust feta cheese may sound unusual, but one bite wins over taste buds.

Carla Horne | MERIDIAN, MS

6 cups fresh arugula or baby spinach

1-1/2 cups sliced fresh strawberries

1/2 cup slivered almonds or pine nuts

1/2 cup crumbled garlic and herb feta cheese

4 green onions, chopped

VINAIGRETTE:

1/3 cup olive oil

1 tablespoon Dijon mustard

1 tablespoon red wine vinegar

2 teaspoons lemon juice

1-1/2 teaspoons balsamic vinegar

1 teaspoon minced fresh rosemary or 1/4 teaspoon dried rosemary, crushed

1 teaspoon fresh sage or 1/4 teaspoon dried sage leaves

1/2 teaspoon celery seed

1/8 teaspoon pepper

In a salad bowl, combine the first five ingredients. In a small bowl, whisk the vinaigrette ingredients. Drizzle over salad; toss to coat. Serve immediately. YIELD: 12 servings (3/4 cup each).

A LESSON IN ARUGULA

Before using arugula, swish the leaves in a bowl of cold water to remove any dirt or sand. Lift out the greens, allowing the sand and grit to sink to the bottom. Repeat in clean water if needed. Pat leaves dry with paper towels. Refrigerate in a resealable plastic bag with a piece of paper towel and use within a week.

savory mushroom bread

(PICTURED AT RIGHT)

The hearty texture, rustic appearance and scrumptious flavor make this yeast bread a winner with dinner guests time and time again. Nothing can compare to the heavenly aroma while it bakes.

Denice Hageli | ELMHURST, IL

1/4 cup butter, cubed

1 pound fresh mushrooms, chopped

1 medium onion, finely chopped

3 tablespoons soy sauce

2 packages (1/4 ounce each) active dry yeast

1 cup warm water (110° to 115°)

2 tablespoons plain yogurt

2 tablespoons honey

1 teaspoon salt

4-3/4 to 5-1/4 cups all-purpose flour

In a large skillet, melt the butter. Add mushrooms and onion; saute until tender. Add soy sauce; cook and stir 2 minutes longer. Cool to room temperature.

In a large bowl, dissolve yeast in warm water. Add the yogurt, honey, salt, mushroom mixture and 2-1/2 cups flour. Beat until smooth. Stir in enough remaining flour to form a soft dough (dough will be sticky).

Turn onto a floured surface; knead until smooth and elastic, about 6-8 minutes. Place in a greased bowl, turning once to grease the top. Cover and let rise in a warm place until doubled, about 1 hour.

Divide dough in half; shape into loaves. Place in two greased 9-in. x 5-in. loaf pans. Cover and let rise until doubled, about 45 minutes. Bake at 400° for 20-25 minutes or until golden brown. **YIELD:** 2 loaves (16 slices each).

mediterranean penne salad

If you're looking for a dish that adds color and flavor to your menu, you've found it! In this chilled delight, tender pasta, tomatoes, artichokes, fresh basil and olives are tossed with a tangy vinaigrette.

Sharon Lowe | JUNEAU, AK

2 cups uncooked penne pasta

1 can (14-1/2 ounces) diced tomatoes, drained

1 jar (7-1/2 ounces) marinated quartered artichoke hearts, drained

1 can (2-1/4 ounces) sliced ripe olives, drained

1/4 cup chopped pitted Greek olives

3 tablespoons minced fresh basil

2 tablespoons grated Parmesan cheese

1/2 teaspoon pepper

VINAIGRETTE:

1/4 cup olive oil

2 tablespoons minced fresh parsley

2 tablespoons minced fresh basil
or 2 teaspoons dried basil

2 tablespoons chopped oil-packed sun-dried tomatoes

2 tablespoons red wine vinegar

1 tablespoon capers, drained

1/4 teaspoon salt

1/8 teaspoon crushed red pepper flakes

Cook pasta according to package directions; drain and rinse in cold water. Transfer to a large bowl; add the tomatoes, artichokes, olives, basil, cheese and pepper.

Combine the vinaigrette ingredients; drizzle over the pasta mixture and toss to coat. Refrigerate the salad for at least 1 hour. **YIELD:** 10 servings.

plum & chutney glazed ham

I first saw this ham in a magazine more than 30 years ago, and knew I had to serve it for Easter dinner. Over the years, I've tweaked it here and there to make it my own.

Arletta Slocum | VENICE, FL

1 bone-in fully cooked spiral-sliced ham
(7 to 9 pounds)

1 cup plum jam

1/2 cup mango chutney

2 tablespoons Dijon mustard

2 garlic cloves, minced

2 teaspoons white wine vinegar

1 teaspoon hot pepper sauce

1 cup packed brown sugar

Place ham on a rack in a shallow roasting pan. Bake at 325° for 2 hours.

In a small saucepan, combine the jam, chutney, mustard, garlic, vinegar and pepper sauce. Cook and stir over medium heat until jam and chutney are melted; brush over ham. Press brown sugar onto ham.

Bake 30-60 minutes longer or until a meat thermometer reads 140°. **YIELD:** 15 servings.

mini carrot cake tortes

(PICTURED AT RIGHT)

"How cute!" is what you'll hear from guests when they spy these individual tortes. A rich cream cheese frosting is sandwiched between layers of moist cake.

Beatriz Marciano | *ROCKVILLE, MD*

2 English Breakfast or other black tea bags

1 cup boiling water

1-1/2 cups sugar

1 cup canola oil

4 eggs

1/2 cup honey

1 tablespoon maple syrup

2 teaspoons vanilla extract

3 cups all-purpose flour

2 teaspoons ground cinnamon

1 teaspoon baking powder

1 teaspoon baking soda

1/4 teaspoon ground cloves

2 cups shredded carrots

1 cup chopped walnuts

1 cup raisins

FROSTING:

1 package (8 ounces) cream cheese, softened

1/2 cup butter, softened

1 teaspoon vanilla extract

3-3/4 cups confectioners' sugar

Toasted chopped walnuts, optional

Place tea bags in a small bowl; add boiling water. Cover and steep for 3-5 minutes. Discard tea bags; set tea aside. Line a 15-in. x 10-in. x 1-in. baking pan with parchment paper and coat the paper with cooking spray; set aside.

In a large bowl, beat the sugar, oil, eggs, tea, honey, syrup and vanilla until well blended. Combine the flour, cinnamon, baking powder, baking soda and cloves; gradually beat into sugar mixture until blended. Stir in the carrots, walnuts and raisins. Transfer to prepared pan (pan will be full).

Bake at 350° for 25-30 minutes or until a toothpick inserted near the center comes out clean. Cool in pan on a wire rack; remove from pan and discard paper.

For frosting, in a large bowl, beat cream cheese and butter until light and fluffy. Beat in vanilla. Gradually beat in confectioners' sugar until smooth.

Using a metal 3-in. round cutter, cut 15 circles from cake. Cut each circle in half horizontally; place cake bottoms on a parchment paper-lined baking sheet. Pipe frosting over each. Top with remaining cake layers and frosting; sprinkle with walnuts if desired. Store in the refrigerator. **YIELD:** 15 mini tortes.

almond, strawberry & rhubarb pie

Every bite of this delicious pie bursts with fresh spring flavor.
The filling's subtle almond taste sets it apart from other strawberry-rhubarb pies.

Patricia Kile | ELIZABETHTOWN, PA

2/3 cup sugar

1/2 cup almond cake and pastry filling

1/4 cup cornstarch

1 tablespoon lemon juice

1/2 teaspoon ground nutmeg

1/4 teaspoon salt

3 cups sliced fresh or frozen rhubarb

2-1/2 cups sliced fresh or frozen strawberries

1 package (15 ounces) refrigerated pie pastry

1 tablespoon butter

1 egg white, beaten

2 tablespoons sliced almonds

In a large bowl, combine the first six ingredients; stir in the rhubarb and strawberries.

On a lightly floured surface, unroll pastry. Transfer to a 9-in. pie plate. Trim pastry to 1/2 in. beyond edge of plate. Fill with fruit mixture and dot with butter. Top with remaining pastry. Trim, seal and flute edges. Cut slits in the top; brush with egg white and sprinkle with almonds.

Bake at 425° for 20 minutes. Reduce the heat to 375°; bake 35-45 minutes longer or until the crust is golden brown and the filling is bubbly. Cover the edges with foil during the last 20 minutes to prevent overbrowning if necessary. Cool on a wire rack. **YIELD:** 8 servings.

EDITOR'S NOTE: This recipe was tested with Solo brand cake and pastry filling. Look for it in the baking aisle. If using frozen fruit, measure fruit while still frozen, then thaw completely. Drain in a colander, but do not press liquid out.

root beer glazed ham

For a unique spin on the traditional glazed ham recipe, try this Southern specialty
from our Test Kitchen where the secret ingredient is root beer!

1 bone-in fully cooked spiral-sliced ham (7 to 9 pounds)

3 cups root beer

3/4 cup packed brown sugar

1/2 cup ketchup

1/4 cup white wine vinegar

3 tablespoons steak sauce

1 tablespoon Dijon mustard

1/2 teaspoon crushed red pepper flakes

1/4 teaspoon ground cloves

Place ham on a rack in a shallow roasting pan. Score the surface of the ham, making diamond shapes 1/2 in. deep. Bake at 325° for 2 hours.

In a large saucepan, combine the remaining ingredients. Bring to a boil; cook until liquid is reduced by half, about 30 minutes.

Brush ham with some of the glaze; bake 30-60 minutes longer or until a meat thermometer reads 140°, brushing occasionally with remaining glaze. **YIELD:** 15 servings.

fresh-as-a-daisy table toppers

(PICTURED AT RIGHT)

Wonderfully bright and cheery, these Gerbera daisy centerpieces are sure to add a touch of whimsy to your Easter table.

The look is easy to achieve, too. All you need are Gerbera daisies in the color of your choice, a few simple craft supplies and clear glass footed containers. Using containers of various heights will add depth and interest to your display.

Apply double-sided transparent tape around the top of a clear glass footed container.

Wrap grosgrain or sheer ribbon over the tape. If using grosgrain ribbon, allow the ends of the ribbon to just meet and press against the tape to secure. If using sheer ribbon, press the ribbon against the tape to secure, and then tie the ends in a knot, allowing streamers of the ribbon to trail onto the table.

Fill the containers with water. Snip the stems from the flowers and place them in the container.

Place a tea light candle in the center of some of the flowers if desired.

SPECIAL *celebrations*

Elegant hors d'oeuvres are the main attraction at a Hollywood gala, while down-home dishes shine during family events such as a day in the kitchen canning and preserving or in the woods creating maple syrup from sap. Toast the new couple at a bridal barbecue...soak in the summer heat with a New England clam bake or Cuban-themed dinner...and then scare up food and fun with a Halloween bash.

You may not be able to head to Hollywood, don a designer gown and walk the red carpet to take part in Hollywood's award season this spring.

But you can invite fellow movie buffs to your home to watch the televised events.

Starring an assortment of elegant hors d'oeuvres, your menu is a shoe-in to win over even finicky food critics.

With their showstopping flavors and textures, Asian Bacon-Wrapped Scallops, Steak Salad Baskets and Lemon-Marinated Antipasto earn top billing on your table.

Cheese Straws and Sun-Dried Tomato Pesto take on supporting roles that are just as award-worthy.

AND THE WINNER IS...
(PICTURED AT RIGHT)

star studded
MOTION PICTURE GALA

asian bacon-wrapped scallops

(PICTURED ON PAGE 175)

Crunchy chow mein noodles and water chestnuts complement tender scallops in this elegant appetizer. Chili sauce gives the mayonnaise a bit of zip.

Thomas Kolek | CHICAGO, IL

9 bacon strips

18 sea scallops (1-1/2 pounds)

1 tablespoon olive oil

1/2 teaspoon salt

1/2 teaspoon pepper

1/2 cup mayonnaise

1 tablespoon sriracha Asian hot chili sauce or 1-1/2 teaspoons hot pepper sauce

1 tablespoon lime juice

1/2 cup canned sliced water chestnuts

1 can (3 ounces) chow mein noodles

Cut bacon strips in half widthwise. In a large skillet, cook bacon over medium heat until partially cooked but not crisp. Remove to paper towels to drain.

Wrap a bacon piece around each scallop; secure with toothpicks. Place on a greased baking sheet. Drizzle with oil; sprinkle with salt and pepper. Broil 6 in. from the heat for 4-5 minutes on each side or until scallops are firm and opaque.

In a small bowl, combine the mayonnaise, chili sauce and juice. Remove toothpicks from scallops. Top each with a slice of water chestnut; drizzle with mayonnaise mixture. Sprinkle with chow mein noodles. YIELD: 18 appetizers.

lemon-marinated antipasto

(PICTURED ON PAGE 175)

When I found this make-ahead recipe, it spoke to my Italian heritage. I like to serve crusty bread on the side to soak up the incredible dressing.

Nancy Beckman | HELENA, MT

1 package (19-1/2 ounces) Italian turkey sausage links

1 jar (12 ounces) roasted sweet red peppers, drained and thinly sliced

1 cup pitted Greek olives

1/3 cup olive oil

1/3 cup lemon juice

2 tablespoons minced fresh basil

2 teaspoons Italian seasoning

2 teaspoons grated lemon peel

3 garlic cloves, minced

1 pound fresh mozzarella cheese, cut into 1/2-inch cubes

In a large skillet, cook sausage over medium heat until no longer pink, about 15 minutes, turning occasionally. Let cool; cut into 1/4-in. slices.

In a large bowl, combine the sausage, peppers and olives. In a small bowl, whisk the oil, lemon juice, basil, Italian seasoning, lemon peel and garlic. Pour over the sausage mixture; toss to coat. Cover and refrigerate overnight.

Remove from the refrigerator and stir in cheese 30 minutes before serving. Arrange on a serving platter. YIELD: 15 servings (1/2 cup each).

steak salad baskets

(PICTURED AT RIGHT AND ON PAGE 175)

Our Test Kitchen created homemade cheese baskets to hold a satisfying salad packed with tender steak, fresh veggies and flavorful olives.

2-1/2 cups shredded Asiago cheese

3/4 pound beef ribeye steak, thinly sliced

1/2 teaspoon salt, divided

1/2 teaspoon pepper, divided

2 cups julienned peeled cucumbers

1 cup shredded carrots

1/3 cup pitted Greek olives, halved

2 tablespoons olive oil

4 teaspoons red wine vinegar

1 tablespoon minced fresh oregano

Heat a small nonstick skillet over medium-high heat. Sprinkle 2 tablespoons cheese over the bottom of the skillet. Cook for 1-2 minutes or until edges are golden brown and cheese is bubbly. Remove from the heat and let stand for 30 seconds.

Using a spatula, carefully remove cheese mixture and immediately drape over an inverted shot glass or miniature muffin cup; cool completely. Repeat with remaining cheese, forming 20 baskets.

Sprinkle steak with 1/4 teaspoon salt and 1/4 teaspoon pepper. In a large skillet, cook steak over medium-high heat until no longer pink. Cool and drain, discarding pan juices; place in a large bowl. Add the cucumbers, carrots and olives.

Combine the oil, vinegar, oregano, and remaining salt and pepper; add to steak mixture and toss to coat. Place about 3 tablespoons salad in each basket. Serve immediately. **YIELD:** 20 appetizers.

sun-dried tomato pesto

(PICTURED ON PAGE 174)

*Sun-dried tomatoes add a rich, smoky taste to always-pleasing pesto.
I also like to serve it as a main dish tossed with pasta alongside a green salad and French bread.*

Catherine Chintala | ROBBINSVILLE, NJ

1 jar (8-1/2 ounces) oil-packed sun-dried tomatoes, undrained

1 cup loosely packed basil leaves

1 small garlic clove

1/4 teaspoon salt

1/4 teaspoon pepper

1/4 cup grated Parmesan cheese

French bread baguette slices, toasted

In a food processor, combine the tomatoes, basil, garlic, salt and pepper. Cover and process until finely chopped. Stir in cheese. Serve with toasted baguette slices. **YIELD:** 1-1/4 cups.

EDITOR'S NOTE: To use as a pasta sauce, combine 1/3 cup pesto and 2 tablespoons olive oil. Toss with hot cooked pasta.

lemon artichoke bottoms

*While most people have had artichoke dip, they've never experienced artichoke bottoms.
Whenever I serve these buttery, bite-size snacks, I'm asked for the recipe.*

Kelly Lindner | WEATHERFORD, TX

2 cans (14 ounces each) artichoke bottoms, drained

1/2 cup grated Parmesan cheese

1/2 cup mayonnaise

2 tablespoons lemon juice

1 garlic clove, minced

Cut 1/4 in. from the bottom of the artichokes to level if necessary. Place on a greased 15-in. x 10-in. x 1-in. baking pan. In a small bowl, combine the remaining ingredients. Spoon into the artichokes. Bake at 375° for 18-22 minutes or until golden brown. **YIELD:** about 16 appetizers.

ALL ABOUT ARTICHOKE BOTTOMS

Artichoke bottoms are the fleshy base of the artichoke. The cup shape makes them perfect for holding a filling. The number of artichoke bottoms varies by can and brand. But typically, there are 8 bottoms in a 14-ounce can.

red carpet-tini

(PICTURED AT RIGHT)

Our recipe specialists give bubbly Champagne a fruity punch with pomegranate juice and raspberry and orange liqueurs.

Ice cubes

1 ounce raspberry liqueur

1/2 ounce orange liqueur

1/2 ounce pomegranate juice

3 fresh raspberries

1/2 cup chilled Champagne

Fill a mixing glass or tumbler one-third full with ice. Add the raspberry liqueur, orange liqueur and pomegranate juice; stir until condensation forms on outside of glass.

Place raspberries in a chilled champagne flute or cocktail glass; strain liqueur mixture into glass. Top with Champagne. **YIELD:** 1 serving.

cappuccino tarts

These tarts from our Test Kitchen staff may be tiny, but they're packed with flavor. Coffee connoisseurs will be in heaven!

1/4 cup sugar

4-1/2 teaspoons cornstarch

1-1/2 teaspoons instant coffee granules

1-3/4 teaspoons ground cinnamon, divided

1-1/4 cups whole milk

2 tablespoons coffee liqueur

2 packages (1.9 ounces each) frozen miniature phyllo tart shells

In a small saucepan, combine the sugar, cornstarch, coffee granules and 1-1/2 teaspoons cinnamon. Add the milk and coffee liqueur; stir until smooth. Cook and stir over medium heat until the mixture comes to a boil. Cook and stir 1-2 minutes longer or until thickened. Remove from the heat. Cool to room temperature, stirring occasionally.

Spoon into tart shells. Sprinkle with remaining cinnamon. Refrigerate until chilled. **YIELD:** 2-1/2 dozen.

cheese straws

(PICTURED ON PAGE 174)

I transform five ingredients into long, crisp cracker sticks. The handheld snacks make for easy mingling at parties.
Elizabeth Robinson | CONROE, TX

1/2 cup butter, softened

2 cups (8 ounces) shredded sharp cheddar cheese

1-1/4 cups all-purpose flour

1/2 teaspoon salt

1/4 teaspoon cayenne pepper

In a large bowl, beat butter until light and fluffy. Beat in cheese until blended. Combine the flour, salt and cayenne; stir into cheese mixture until a dough forms. Roll into a 15-in. x 6-in. rectangle. Cut into thirty 6-in. strips. Gently place strips 1 in. apart on ungreased baking sheets.

Bake at 350° for 15-20 minutes or until lightly browned. Cool for 5 minutes before removing from pans to wire racks to cool completely. Store in an airtight container. YIELD: 2-1/2 dozen.

pistachio fig tartlets

Our family and friends love figs, pistachios and blue cheese. So one day I decided to combine those ingredients in simple-to-prepare bites. The results were delicious!
Kathleen Boulanger | WILLISTON, VT

1/3 cup chopped dried figs

1/4 cup packed brown sugar

3 bacon strips, cooked and crumbled

2 tablespoons butter, melted

1 package (1.9 ounces) frozen miniature phyllo tart shells

2 ounces cream cheese, softened

2 tablespoons crumbled blue cheese

1 tablespoon confectioners' sugar

1 tablespoon thawed apple juice concentrate

3 tablespoons finely chopped pistachios

Additional pistachios, optional

In a small bowl, combine the figs, brown sugar, bacon and butter. Spoon into tart shells.

In another bowl, beat the cheeses, confectioners' sugar and apple juice concentrate until blended. Stir in chopped pistachios; dollop over tartlets. Sprinkle with additional pistachios if desired. Chill until serving. YIELD: 15 appetizers.

clams casino

(PICTURED AT RIGHT)

Your guests will be impressed with our home economists' version of a classic, upscale appetizer. Cayenne pepper nicely seasons the bread crumb topping.

1 pound kosher salt

1 dozen fresh cherrystone clams

1/3 cup soft bread crumbs

3 tablespoons minced fresh parsley, divided

2 tablespoons olive oil

1 garlic clove, minced

1/8 teaspoon cayenne pepper

1/8 teaspoon coarsely ground pepper

Spread salt into a metal oven-safe serving platter or a 15-in. x 10-in. x 1-in. baking pan. Shuck clams, reserving bottom shells; drain liquid (save for another use). Arrange clams in salt-lined pan.

Combine the bread crumbs, 2 tablespoons parsley, oil, garlic, cayenne and pepper; spoon over clams.

Bake at 450° for 15-18 minutes or until clams are firm and bread crumb mixture is crisp and golden brown. Sprinkle with remaining parsley. Serve immediately. **YIELD:** 1 dozen.

SHUCKING HARD-SHELL CLAMS

1. Scrub under cold running water with a stiff brush. Place on a tray and refrigerate for 30 minutes. They will be easier to open. Protect your hand by placing the clam in a clean kitchen towel with the hinge facing out. Insert clam knife next to the hinge. Slide the knife around to loosen the shells.
2. Open the top shell and cut the muscle from the top shell. Discard the top shell.
3. Use the knife to release clam from bottom shell. If desired, pour clam juice into a strainer and reserve for another use.

mediterranean palmiers

My mother shared this recipe with me a few years ago...it quickly became a family favorite for any occasion. I often assemble and freeze them. When ready to serve, bake until golden.

Christine Farnsworth | FLAGSTAFF, AZ

1 package (17.3 ounces) frozen puff pastry, thawed

1/4 cup prepared pesto

1/2 cup crumbled feta cheese

1/4 cup chopped oil-packed sun-dried tomatoes, patted dry

1/4 cup finely chopped walnuts

Unfold one sheet of the puff pastry. Spread 2 tablespoons of the pesto to within 1/2 in. of edges. Sprinkle with half of the cheese, tomatoes and walnuts.

Working from the left and right sides, roll edges of pastry jelly-roll style toward the center. Roll at 1-in. intervals so that rolls meet in the center. Repeat with remaining ingredients. Cut each pastry sheet into 20 slices.

Place cut side down 2 in. apart on parchment paper-lined baking sheets. Bake at 400° for 10-12 minutes or until golden brown. Serve warm. **YIELD:** 40 appetizers.

NEW FILLING FOR PALMIERS

Instead of making Mediterranean Palmiers with prepared pesto, sun-dried tomatoes and walnuts, whip up Sun-Dried Tomato Pesto on page 178. Spread 6 tablespoons on one sheet of puff pastry; sprinkle with the feta cheese. Continue with the recipe as directed.

cucumber tuna appetizers

When my grandmother emigrated from Italy, she brought along her love of cooking, which she then passed on to me. Using cucumber slices instead of bread adds crunch as well as nutrition.

Lisa DiVito | PITTSBURGH, PA

2 cans (5 ounces each) light water-packed tuna, drained and flaked

1/4 cup ricotta cheese

2 tablespoons minced fresh basil

2 tablespoons lemon juice

1 tablespoon olive oil

1 tablespoon capers, drained

1 teaspoon grated lemon peel

1 garlic clove, minced

1/8 teaspoon salt

Dash pepper

1 medium cucumber, sliced

In a large bowl, combine the first ten ingredients. Cover; chill until serving. Serve on cucumber slices. **YIELD:** 20 appetizers.

apple-raisin egg rolls

(PICTURED AT RIGHT)

Tender apples are rolled inside crisp egg roll wrappers for a deliciously different dessert. As fancy as these treats look, they're really quite simple to make.

Karen Orvis | *PLAINVILLE, CT*

4 medium tart apples, peeled and sliced

1/4 cup raisins

1/2 teaspoon ground cinnamon

2 tablespoons butter

1 tablespoon cornstarch

1 cup unsweetened apple juice

3 tablespoons honey

16 egg roll wrappers

Oil for deep-fat frying

Vanilla ice cream

In a large skillet, saute the apples, raisins and cinnamon in butter until tender. Combine the cornstarch, juice and honey until smooth; stir into apple mixture. Bring to a boil over medium heat. Cook and stir for 1-2 minutes or until thickened. Remove from the heat; cool.

Place 1/4 cupful of apple mixture in the center of one egg roll wrapper. Fold bottom corner over filling. Fold sides toward center over filling. Moisten remaining corner with water; roll up tightly to seal. Repeat with remaining apple mixture and wrappers. Let stand for 15 minutes.

In an electric skillet, heat 1 in. of oil to 375°. Fry turnovers, a few at a time, for 1-2 minutes on each side or until golden brown. Drain on paper towels. Serve with ice cream. **YIELD:** 16 servings.

parmesan appetizer puffs

Fresh-from-the-oven appetizers are always well received at get-togethers throughout the year. The flaky, rich pastry holds a savory olive filling.

Betty Fulks | ONIA, AR

1-1/2 cups all-purpose flour

1 teaspoon salt

1 cup cold butter

1/2 cup sour cream

1/4 cup grated Parmesan cheese

1/4 cup each finely chopped green onions, fresh mushrooms and ripe olives

In a large bowl, combine flour and salt. Cut in butter until crumbly. Stir in sour cream until a dough forms. Divide dough into fourths. Wrap in plastic wrap and refrigerate for 2 hours or until easy to handle.

Combine the cheese, onions, mushrooms and olives. On a floured surface, roll one portion of dough into a 12-in. x 6-in. rectangle. Sprinkle a fourth of the cheese mixture over half of the dough; fold dough in half to form a 6-in. square. Cut into 2-in. squares; press edges to seal. Repeat with the remaining dough and filling.

Place squares 2 in. apart on ungreased baking sheets. Bake at 350° for 20-25 minutes or until golden brown. Serve warm. **YIELD:** 3 dozen.

salmon mousse endive leaves

I recently made this simple but elegant appetizer to rave reviews. The thick mousse has a lovely presentation well suited for special occasions.

Doreen Matthew | SAN MARCOS, CA

2 packages (3 ounces each) smoked salmon or lox

2 packages (3 ounces each) cream cheese, softened

1 tablespoon dill weed

1 tablespoon lemon juice

1/2 teaspoon onion powder

1/2 teaspoon prepared horseradish

24 endive leaves

Watercress and diced pimientos, optional

Place the first six ingredients in a food processor; cover and process until smooth. Pipe or spoon about 1 tablespoon filling onto each endive leaf. Garnish with watercress and pimientos if desired. **YIELD:** 2 dozen.

silver screen swag bags

(PICTURED AT RIGHT)

When the final credits roll on the enchanted evening, award your glamorous girlfriends with goodie bags...just like the ones A-list celebrities receive!

IT'S IN THE BAG. Purchase star-studded cellophane bags online or at a party store. For an even more formal feel, look for velvet drawstring bags.

BEAUTY LOOT. Pamper your VIPs (Very Important Partygoers) in style with a lovely lipstick case and lipstick in each of your friends' favorite shades. You may also want to tuck in nail polish, emery boards and assorted bath soaps or lotions.

SILVER SCREEN SNACKS. Even Tinseltown's appearance-conscious actresses indulge in main attraction treats! Special confections include gourmet chocolate bars and small bottles of bubbly.

BRING THE BLING. Department stores often offer discounts on upscale costume jewelry. Look at the clearance bin for super savings on cocktail rings, earrings, bracelets and necklaces. Or do you make jewelry? Fashion a few homemade baubles for your best friends.

FLICK FUN. For the die-hard cinema enthusiasts, tuck in some movie passes or a DVD of your favorite nominated film.

When signs of spring are just around the corner, but the nights are chilly and the trees still bare, it's time for a "maple sugaring party."

A common gathering throughout areas of Vermont, Wisconsin and even Canada, a "sugaring party" is when friends and family get together to tap maple trees, collect the sap and make fresh maple syrup.

After all that work, you'll hardly be able to wait to use that rich, golden syrup in a mouthwatering dinner featuring savory Maple Pork Chops, crisp Apple Salad with Maple Vinaigrette and sweet-tangy Asparagus, Mushrooms and Peas.

MARVELOUS MAPLE!

(PICTURED AT RIGHT)

Apple Salad with Maple Vinaigrette (p. 188)
Asparagus, Mushrooms and Peas (p. 195)
Maple Pork Chops (p. 188)

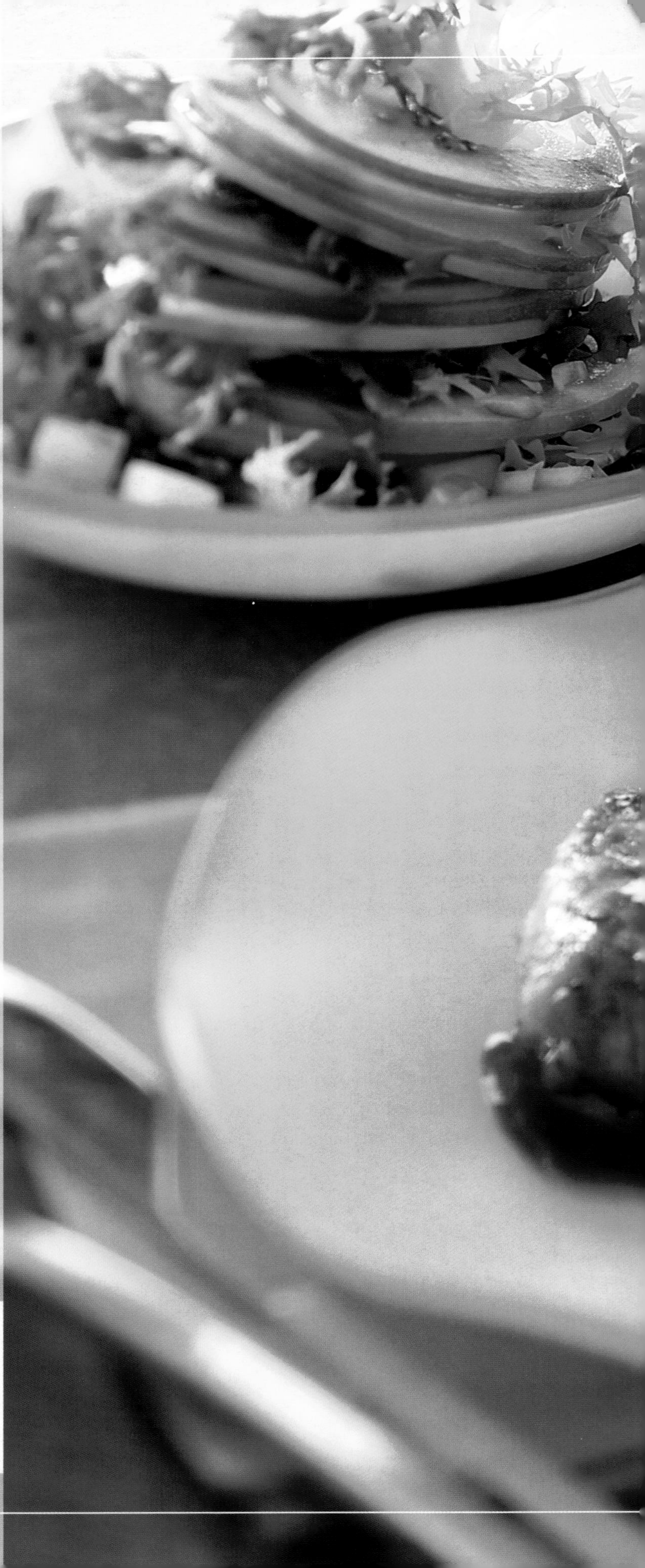

tap into
MAPLE SYRUP FUN

maple pork chops

(PICTURED ON PAGE 187)

Tender pork chops are cooked in a maple glaze that makes every bite absolutely succulent.
This hearty entree from our Test Kitchen delivers big flavor without a lot of fuss.

4 boneless pork loin chops
(1 inch thick and 6 ounces each)

1 teaspoon minced fresh thyme
or 1/4 teaspoon dried thyme

1/2 teaspoon salt

1/2 teaspoon pepper

1 tablespoon olive oil

1/2 cup brewed coffee

1/4 cup maple syrup

1 tablespoon Dijon mustard

2 teaspoons Worcestershire sauce

Sprinkle pork chops with thyme, salt and pepper. In a large skillet, brown chops in oil. Remove and keep warm.

Add remaining ingredients to skillet. Bring to a boil; cook until liquid is reduced by half.

Return pork chops to skillet. Reduce heat; cover and simmer for 10-12 minutes or until meat is tender, turning once. Serve with sauce. **YIELD:** 4 servings.

apple salad with maple vinaigrette

(PICTURED ON PAGE 186)

This delightful salad brings so many compliments. The balsamic vinegar dressing
has a pleasant taste and nicely coats the apples, endive and other salad ingredients.

Marie Rizzio | INTERLOCHEN, MI

1/2 cup walnut oil

1/4 cup balsamic vinegar

1/4 cup maple syrup

1 tablespoon Dijon mustard

1/4 teaspoon ground nutmeg

Salt and pepper to taste

2 medium red apples, thinly sliced

2 medium green apples, thinly sliced

2 cups endive

1 block (4 ounces) brick cheese, cubed

2/3 cup chopped pecans, toasted

2 tablespoons finely chopped red onion

In a small bowl, whisk the oil, vinegar, syrup, mustard and nutmeg; season with salt and pepper. In a salad bowl, combine the apples, endive, cheese, pecans and onion. Drizzle desired amount of vinaigrette over salad; toss to coat. Refrigerate leftover vinaigrette. **YIELD:** 8 servings. (1 cup vinaigrette).

vermont baked beans

(PICTURED AT RIGHT)

These baked beans are nothing like the canned variety you may be used to. The rich sauce has wonderful smokiness from chopped bacon and a subtle sweetness from maple syrup.

Elizabeth Horton | BRATTLEBORO, VT

1 pound dried navy beans

4 cups water

1/2 pound thick-sliced bacon strips, chopped

1 large onion, chopped

2/3 cup maple syrup

2 teaspoons salt

1 teaspoon ground mustard

1/2 teaspoon coarsely ground pepper

Soak beans according to package directions. Drain and rinse beans, discarding liquid. Return beans to Dutch oven; add water. Bring to a boil.

Meanwhile, in a large skillet, cook bacon over medium heat until crisp; drain. Stir the onion, syrup, salt, mustard, pepper and bacon into the beans.

Cover and bake at 300° for 3 to 3-1/2 hours or until beans are tender and reach the desired consistency, stirring every 30 minutes. **YIELD:** 8 servings.

NOT JUST FOR BREAKFAST!

Maple is for more than just pancakes and waffles. Try drizzling the sweet, sticky syrup on halved grapefruit, cooked carrots or even squash. And for a delicious twist on the ice cream sundae, use it in place of chocolate syrup for an irresistible treat.

maple oatmeal wheat bread

This is our favorite toasting bread. While it's especially good fresh out of the oven and slathered with butter, its subtle sweet flavor means it's equally delicious on its own.

Judy Wilson | SUN CITY WEST, AZ

1-3/4 cups boiling water

1 cup old-fashioned oats

1/2 cup maple syrup

1/3 cup sugar

1/3 cup shortening

2 teaspoons salt

2 packages (1/4 ounce each) active dry yeast

1/4 cup warm water (110° to 115°)

2 eggs

3 cups whole wheat flour

3 cups all-purpose flour

In a large bowl, pour boiling water over oats. Add the syrup, sugar, shortening and salt. Let stand until mixture cools to 110°-115°, stirring occasionally.

In a small bowl, dissolve yeast in warm water. Add the yeast mixture, eggs, whole wheat flour and 1 cup all-purpose flour to oat mixture. Beat until smooth. Stir in enough remaining all-purpose flour to form a soft dough.

Turn onto a floured surface; knead until smooth and elastic, about 8-10 minutes. Place in a greased bowl, turning once to grease the top. Cover and let rise in a warm place until doubled, about 1 hour.

Punch dough down. Turn onto a lightly floured surface; divide in half. Shape into loaves. Place in two greased 9-in. x 5-in. loaf pans. Cover and let rise until doubled, about 45 minutes.

Bake at 350° for 35-40 minutes or until golden brown. Remove from pans to wire racks to cool. **YIELD:** 2 loaves (16 slices each).

maple-pecan granola

For a quick breakfast or healthy munching, nothing hits the spot like crunchy granola. Good-for-you ingredients like oats, flaxseed and pecans—plus brown sugar and maple syrup—make it a truly addictive treat.

Serena DiRienzo | AUBURN HILLS, MI

7 cups quick-cooking oats

1 cup chopped pecans

1/2 cup flaxseed

1 teaspoon salt

1 cup packed brown sugar

1/2 cup maple syrup

1/4 cup water

3 tablespoons canola oil

In a large bowl, combine the oats, pecans, flaxseed and salt; set aside. In a small saucepan, combine brown sugar, syrup, water and oil. Cook and stir over medium heat for 2-3 minutes or until heated through. Pour over oat mixture and toss to coat.

Transfer to two greased 15-in. x 10-in. x 1-in. baking pans. Bake at 300° for 30-35 minutes or until golden brown, stirring once. Cool completely on a wire rack. Store in an airtight container. **YIELD:** 12 cups.

maple butter tarts

(PICTURED AT RIGHT)

These individual tarts are so scrumptious and syrupy that I often double the recipe so I have enough for guests to take home. They're a little slice of heaven alongside a cup of coffee.

Lorraine Caland | *THUNDER BAY, ON*

1 package (15 ounces) refrigerated pie pastry

1-1/2 cups raisins

2 cups boiling water

1-3/4 cups packed brown sugar

3 eggs

1/2 cup butter, melted

1/4 cup maple syrup

1 teaspoon maple flavoring

Butter pecan or vanilla ice cream, optional

Cut each pastry sheet into quarters; roll each quarter into a 6-in. circle. Transfer pastry to eight ungreased 4-in. fluted tart pans with removable bottoms. Trim pastry even with edges. Place on baking sheets. Bake at 450° for 5-6 minutes or until golden brown. Cool on wire racks. Reduce heat to 350°.

Place raisins in a large bowl. Cover with boiling water; let stand for 5 minutes. Drain. In another bowl, beat the brown sugar, eggs, butter, syrup and flavoring; stir in raisins. Divide filling among tart shells.

Bake for 16-20 minutes or until centers are just set (mixture will jiggle). Cool on a wire rack. Serve with ice cream if desired. **YIELD:** 8 tarts.

A SWEET ALTERNATIVE

When baking, maple syrup can replace the sugar used in the recipe. Use 3/4 cup maple syrup for every 1 cup of sugar, reduce the liquid in the recipe by 2 to 4 tablespoons and add 1/4 teaspoon baking soda. To prevent overbrowning, reduce the oven temperature by 25 degrees.

peach-maple ice cream

Maple and peach? The combination may sound unusual, but in this unique homemade ice cream, it's absolutely decadent! It's the definition of refreshment.

Arline Hofland | *DEER LODGE, MT*

4 cups sliced peeled peaches or frozen unsweetened sliced peaches (about 3 pounds)

3 tablespoons lemon juice

3 cups 2% milk

1 cup sugar

3/4 cup maple syrup

1/8 teaspoon salt

6 egg yolks, lightly beaten

3 cups heavy whipping cream

2 tablespoons vanilla extract

Additional maple syrup, optional

Place peaches in a blender; cover and process until smooth. Stir in lemon juice; set aside.

In a large saucepan, heat milk to 175°. Stir in the sugar, syrup and salt until dissolved. Whisk a small amount of the hot mixture into the egg yolks. Return all to the pan, whisking constantly. Cook and stir over low heat until mixture is thickened and coats the back of a spoon.

Remove from the heat. Cool quickly by placing pan in a bowl of ice water; stir for 2 minutes. Stir in the cream, vanilla and peach mixture. Transfer to a large bowl; press waxed paper onto the surface of ice cream. Refrigerate for several hours or overnight.

Fill cylinder of ice cream freezer two-thirds full; freeze according to the manufacturer's directions. Refrigerate remaining mixture until ready to freeze. When ice cream is frozen, transfer to a freezer container; freeze for at least 4 hours before serving.

Serve in dessert dishes; drizzle with additional syrup if desired.
YIELD: 3 quarts.

delicious maple flan

Here's a deliciously different spin on traditional flan that's also quick and easy to prepare. Its smooth, creamy texture simply melts in your mouth.

Ruby Thomas | *GURNEE, IL*

1/2 cup maple syrup

3 eggs

1 can (14 ounces) sweetened condensed milk

1 can (12 ounces) evaporated milk

Pour syrup into an ungreased 10-in. round baking dish, tilting to coat the bottom of dish; set aside.

In a large bowl, beat the eggs, condensed milk and evaporated milk. Slowly pour into prepared dish. Place dish in a large baking pan. Add 1 in. hot water to large baking pan.

Bake at 350° for 50-60 minutes or until center is just set (mixture will jiggle). Remove flan to a wire rack; cool for 1 hour. Chill overnight.

Carefully run a knife around edge to loosen; invert onto a rimmed serving platter. **YIELD:** 12 servings.

maple crunch popcorn

(PICTURED AT RIGHT)

For a snack that's sure to bring smiles, try this medley of popcorn and pecans covered in a sweet and buttery coating.

Elmira Trombetti | PADUCAH, KY

10 cups popped popcorn

1-1/2 cups pecan halves, toasted

1-1/3 cups sugar

1 cup butter, cubed

1/4 cup maple syrup

1/4 cup corn syrup

1/2 teaspoon salt

1 teaspoon maple flavoring

Place popcorn and pecans in a large bowl; set aside. In a large heavy saucepan, combine the sugar, butter, maple syrup, corn syrup and salt. Cook and stir over medium heat until a candy thermometer reads 300° (hard-crack stage). Remove from the heat; stir in the maple flavoring. Quickly pour over the popcorn mixture and mix well.

Transfer to baking sheets lined with waxed paper to cool. Break into clusters. Store in airtight containers. **YIELD:** 3-1/2 quarts.

EDITOR'S NOTE: We recommend that you test your candy thermometer before each use by bringing water to a boil; the thermometer should read 212°. Adjust your recipe temperature up or down based on your test.

MAPLE SYRUP KNOW-HOW

For a 4- to 6-week period each spring—when the daytime temperatures reach into the 40s and the nighttime temps dip back down into the 20s—the sugaring season is in full force across many northern and northeastern states and into Canada.

A small drill is used to make a hole in sugar maple and black maple trees that are at least 40 years old. A tool called a spile is placed into each hole, allowing sap to drip out.

After the sap is collected, it's boiled down in a maple sugar evaporator, which removes the water and leaves behind syrup to be filtered and bottled. Between 35 and 50 gallons of sap are needed to make one gallon of syrup.

Because pure maple syrup is labor-intensive to make during a short season, it's more expensive than pancake syrup, which is made mostly from corn syrup and which contains only about 2% pure maple syrup.

You can store unopened bottles of pure maple syrup in a cool, dark place for up to 2 years. Refrigerate the syrup after opening and use within 1 year.

maple-glazed squash and parsnips

I can remember my mom offering this family-favorite side dish for special occasions. But because it requires so few ingredients and comes together quickly, you'll likely make it for everyday dinners, too.

Nella Parker | *HERSEY, MI*

2 medium acorn squash

1-1/2 pounds medium parsnips, peeled, quartered and cut into 3-inch pieces

1-1/4 cups maple syrup

2 tablespoons butter, melted

1 tablespoon minced fresh parsley

Wash squash. Cut in half lengthwise; discard seeds and membranes. Cut squash halves widthwise into 1/2-in. slices; discard ends. Place in a large skillet with parsnips; cover with water. Bring to a boil. Reduce heat; cover and simmer for 10 minutes or until crisp-tender. Drain.

In a small bowl, combine maple syrup and butter; pour over squash and parsnips. Cook for 12-15 minutes or until tender, basting occasionally. Using a slotted spoon, remove squash and arrange in a circle on a serving plate. Spoon parsnips into center; drizzle with cooking juices. Sprinkle with parsley. **YIELD:** 10 servings.

maple blueberry crisp

With sweet blueberries and a tender crumb topping, this yummy crisp is a wonderful treat following a brunch or evening meal. I sometimes top servings with a scoop of vanilla ice cream.

Mona Wright | *VILLA RICA, GA*

4 cups fresh or frozen blueberries

1/2 cup maple syrup

2 tablespoons cornstarch

1 teaspoon ground cinnamon

1-1/4 cups all-purpose flour

3/4 cup packed brown sugar

1/2 cup cold butter

1 teaspoon almond extract

In a large bowl, combine the blueberries, syrup, cornstarch and cinnamon. Transfer to a greased 8-in square baking dish. In a small bowl, combine flour and brown sugar. Cut in butter until mixture resembles coarse crumbs; stir in extract. Sprinkle over top.

Bake at 375° for 35-40 minutes or until filling is bubbly and topping is golden brown. **YIELD:** 9 servings.

spicy lamb kabobs

(PICTURED AT RIGHT AND ON PAGE 197)

This hearty meal-in-one is spicy, sweet and savory all at the same time. The combination of grilled lamb, crisp salad and honey pita wedges is wonderful.

Melinda Winner | GULFPORT, MS

1 large cucumber

2 cups (8 ounces) sour cream or plain yogurt

2 teaspoons lemon juice

1/2 teaspoon salt

1/8 teaspoon garlic powder

1/8 teaspoon dill weed

1/8 teaspoon pepper

KABOBS:

2 cups buttermilk

2 teaspoons ground turmeric

2 teaspoons curry powder

1 teaspoon coarsely ground pepper

1 teaspoon chili powder

1 teaspoon minced fresh sage

1/2 teaspoon salt

2-1/2 pounds lean boneless lamb, cut into 1-inch cubes

16 cubes fresh pineapple (1 inch)

16 cherry tomatoes

SALAD:

8 cups torn leaf lettuce

2 cups torn romaine

2 cups torn Bibb or Boston lettuce

1/2 large sweet onion, sliced

1/2 medium red onion, finely chopped

1 medium tomato, chopped

1/2 cup fresh bean sprouts

1/2 cup green grapes, quartered

1/2 cup chopped walnuts

1/2 cup crumbled feta cheese

1/4 cup butter, softened

2 tablespoons honey

4 pita breads (6 inches), halved and warmed

Peel cucumber and remove seeds. Place cucumber in a food processor; cover and process until finely chopped. Remove half of cucumber; set aside. Process remaining cucumber until pureed. Combine pureed cucumber and reserved cucumber; stir in the sour cream, lemon juice and seasonings. Refrigerate for at least 1 hour.

In a small bowl, combine the first seven kabob ingredients. Pour 1-1/2 cups marinade into a large resealable plastic bag; add the lamb. Seal bag and turn to coat; refrigerate for at least 1 hour. Cover and refrigerate remaining marinade for basting.

Drain and discard marinade. On each of eight metal or soaked wooden skewers, alternately thread lamb, pineapple and tomatoes.

In a large bowl, combine the lettuces, onions, tomato, sprouts, grapes and walnuts; sprinkle with cheese. Set aside.

Grill kabobs, covered, over medium heat for 5-6 minutes on each side or until lamb reaches desired doneness (for medium-rare, a meat thermometer should read 145°; medium, 160°; well-done, 170°), basting frequently with reserved marinade. Beat butter and honey until blended; brush over pitas. Serve with kabobs, salad and sauce. **YIELD:** 8 servings.

summertime fruit trifles

(PICTURED AT RIGHT)

Eye-catching trifles are easy to prepare when you use purchased pound cake, instant pudding and frozen whipped topping. Letting guests assemble their own makes it fun—and saves you time!

Darlene Brenden | SALEM, OR

1/3 cup sugar

1/4 cup all-purpose flour

1-1/2 cups whole milk

1 egg, beaten

1/2 cup orange juice

1 tablespoon butter

1 teaspoon grated orange peel

1 can (20 ounces) crushed pineapple, undrained

1 package (3.4 ounces) instant vanilla pudding mix

1 cup whipped topping

2 cups sliced peeled fresh or frozen peaches, thawed

1 cup sliced fresh strawberries

1 cup fresh raspberries

1/2 cup fresh blueberries

2 loaves (10-3/4 ounces each) frozen pound cake, thawed and cut into 1/2-inch cubes

In a large saucepan, combine sugar and flour; stir in milk until smooth. Cook and stir over medium-high heat until thickened and bubbly. Reduce heat to low; cook and stir 2 minutes longer. Remove from the heat.

Stir a small amount of hot mixture into egg; return all to pan. Bring to a gentle boil, stirring constantly; cook and stir for 2 minutes. Remove from the heat. Gently stir in the orange juice, butter and orange peel. Transfer to a small bowl; refrigerate custard until chilled.

In large bowl, combine the pineapple and pudding mix; fold in the whipped topping. In another bowl, combine the peaches and berries.

In individual parfait glasses or a 3-qt. trifle bowl, layer a third of the cake cubes, fruit and pineapple mixture. Repeat layers twice. Refrigerate until serving. **YIELD:** 12 servings.

smoked salmon rolls

Even though I've been serving these rich roll-ups for more than 30 years, they're always the first appetizers to disappear at parties. The recipe comes from my grandmother.

Radelle Knappenberger | OVIEDO, FL

2 cups all-purpose flour

1 package (8 ounces) reduced-fat cream cheese

1/2 cup cold butter

2 to 3 tablespoons cold water

3 packages (3 ounces each) smoked salmon or lox, chopped

1/2 cup finely chopped red onion

1 egg, beaten

Place flour in a large bowl; cut in cream cheese and butter until crumbly. Gradually add water, tossing with a fork until dough forms a ball.

Divide dough in half. Between two sheets of waxed paper, roll each portion into a 9-in. circle. Chill for 10 minutes or until firm. Sprinkle salmon and onion to within 1/2 in. of edges. Cut each circle into 16 wedges. Roll up wedges from the wide ends and place point side down 2 in. apart on greased baking sheets. Brush with egg.

Bake at 425° for 15-18 minutes or until golden brown. Serve warm. **YIELD:** 32 appetizers.

tasty trifle bar

(PICTURED ABOVE)

With lovely layers of sweet fixings such as creamy pudding, tender cake and refreshing fruit, it's no wonder that trifles have been popular for generations.

Add a little fun to your next gathering by having guests assemble their own made-to-order treats.

In addition to offering the ingredients from Summertime Fruit Trifles (recipe on opposite page), set out bowls of other confections.

FRUIT. Turn to nature for unbeatable flavor! Ideas include assorted berries, mandarin oranges, kiwi, pineapple, mango and even dried fruit.

FILLINGS. Along with pudding, separate the layers with other creamy items such as whipped cream, lemon or lime curd, mousse, gelatin, cream cheese and pie filling.

CAKES AND COOKIES. From pound, angel and sponge cakes to quick breads, macaroons and sandwich cookies, the palate-pleasing possibilities are endless!

EXTRAS. Entice the taste buds with other sweet surprises. Options include toasted coconut, chopped nuts, chopped candy bars, miniature marshmallows, granola, chocolate-covered coffee beans, hot fudge, cocoa powder and caramel sauce.

*R*emember when mom and grandma would gather in the kitchen on a sweltering summer day to "put up" their best garden-fresh fruits and vegetables?

Prepping the produce...filling the empty vessels...processing the jars... it was an all-day event, which they performed with ease. Now you can carry on that homespun tradition with these easy recipes.

Brimming with Old-Fashioned Garlic Dill Pickles, Over-the-Top Cherry Jam, Tomato Bounty Salsa, Garden's Harvest Pickles and Iowa Corn Relish, the glistening jars resting on the countertop contain tastes of summer that family, friends and neighbors will enjoy long into the winter.

WELL-PRESERVED PRODUCE
(PICTURED AT RIGHT)

it's time for
CANNING & PRESERVING

tomato bounty salsa

(PICTURED ON PAGE 206)

I like to make this mild-tasting salsa with yellow tomatoes, but feel free to try other varieties.
Use the salsa as a dip for chips or as a condiment for meats.

Joanne Surfus | *STURGEON BAY, WI*

9 pounds yellow tomatoes (25 to 30 medium)

4 medium onions, finely chopped

2 cans (6 ounces each) tomato paste

1 large sweet red pepper, finely chopped

3/4 cup white vinegar

4 jalapeno peppers, seeded and chopped

4 garlic cloves, minced

3 teaspoons salt

1/2 teaspoon pepper

In a large saucepan, bring 8 cups water to a boil. Add tomatoes, a few at a time; boil for 30 seconds. Drain and immediately place tomatoes in ice water. Drain and pat dry; peel and finely chop.

In a stockpot, combine remaining ingredients. Stir in tomatoes. Bring to a boil over medium-high heat. Reduce the heat; simmer, uncovered, for 20 minutes or until desired thickness. Carefully ladle hot mixture into hot 1-pint jars, leaving 1/2-in. headspace. Remove air bubbles; wipe the rims and adjust lids. Process for 20 minutes in a boiling-water canner. **YIELD:** 9 pints.

EDITOR'S NOTE: When cutting hot peppers, disposable gloves are recommended. Avoid touching your face. Processing time listed is for altitudes of 1,000 feet or less. For altitudes up to 3,000 feet, add 5 minutes; 6,000 feet, add 10 minutes; 8,000 feet, add 15 minutes; 10,000 feet, add 20 minutes.

SECRETS FOR SUCCESSFUL CANNING

• Select fruits and vegetables at the peak of quality and flavor. Wash thoroughly before using.

• Follow directions for each recipe exactly without substituting ingredients or changing processing times. Prepare only one recipe at a time—do not double.

• Only use white vinegar when pickling.

• You can use any deep pot for a boiling-water canner; just make sure the pot is at least 3 inches deeper than the height of the jars.

• Use a cake cooling rack if you don't have a rack specifically made for canning. Or tie extra screw bands together to cover the bottom of the pot.

• Canning funnels have wide openings and sit on the inside of the mouth of the jar, making them ideal for filling jars cleanly and easily. Wipe the threads and rim of each jar to remove any food that may have spilled.

• Use non-metallic utensils when filling and cleaning jars; metal can easily damage canning jars, resulting in seal failure or breakage.

• Because the headspace can affect sealing and the preservation of the contents, each filled jar should be measured accurately. A clear plastic ruler—kept solely for kitchen use—will help determine the correct headspace.

• If a small amount of product is left over that would not fill a full jar, refrigerate it and use within several days.

• The lid is not reusable, but the screw band can be reused if it isn't warped or rusty.

• Home-canned foods can be stored in your cupboard for up to 1 year.

raspberry lemonade concentrate

(PICTURED AT RIGHT)

Our home economists created a concentrate so you can enjoy a refreshing summer beverage any time of year. Sweet raspberries balance the tartness of lemons.

4 pounds fresh raspberries (about 14 cups)

6 cups sugar

4 cups lemon juice

Chilled tonic water or ginger ale

Ice cubes

Place raspberries in a food processor; cover and process until blended. Strain raspberries, reserving juice. Discard seeds. Place juice in a Dutch oven; stir in sugar and lemon juice. Heat over medium-high heat to 190°. Do not boil. Remove from the heat; skim off foam.

Carefully ladle hot mixture into hot 1-pint jars, leaving 1/4-in. headspace. Remove air bubbles; wipe rims and adjust lids. Process for 10 minutes in a boiling-water canner.

TO USE CONCENTRATE: Mix 1 pint concentrate with 1 pint tonic water. Serve over ice. **YIELD:** 5 pints (4 servings each).

EDITOR'S NOTE: The processing time listed is for altitudes of 1,000 feet or less. Add 1 minute to the processing time for each 1,000 feet of additional altitude.

over-the-top cherry jam

(PICTURED ON PAGE 206)

We live in Door County, Wisconsin—an area known for its wonderful tart cherries. This beautiful, sweet jam tastes great on toast and English muffins.

Karen Haen | STURGEON BAY, WI

2-1/2 pounds fresh tart cherries, pitted

1 package (1-3/4 ounces) powdered fruit pectin

1/2 teaspoon butter

4-3/4 cups sugar

In a food processor, cover and process cherries in batches until finely chopped. Transfer to a Dutch oven; stir in pectin and butter. Bring to a full rolling boil over high heat, stirring constantly. Stir in sugar; return to a full rolling boil. Boil for 1 minute, stirring constantly.

Remove from the heat; skim off foam. Ladle hot mixture into hot sterilized half-pint jars, leaving 1/4-in. headspace. Remove air bubbles; wipe rims and adjust lids. Process for 5 minutes in a boiling-water canner. **YIELD:** 6 half-pints.

EDITOR'S NOTE: The processing time listed is for altitudes of 1,000 feet or less. Add 1 minute to the processing time for each 1,000 feet of additional altitude.

HOT JARS VS. HOT STERLIZED JARS

Some canning recipes call for hot sterilized jars, while others simply call for hot jars.

If the mixture will be processed in the boiling-water canner for longer than 10 minutes, the jars just need to be hot.

If the processing time is less than 10 minutes, the jars need to be sterilized in the kettle of hot water for 10 minutes. (Boil 1 more minute for each 1,000 feet of additional altitude.)

spicy pickled green beans

(PICTURED AT FAR RIGHT)

A coworker brought these pickled beans into work one day...I was hooked after one bite. And I was thrilled when a jar of my beans won first place at the local county fair!

Jill Darin | GENESEO, IL

1-3/4 pounds fresh green beans, trimmed

1 teaspoon cayenne pepper

4 garlic cloves, peeled

4 teaspoons dill seed or 4 fresh dill heads

2-1/2 cups water

2-1/2 cups white vinegar

1/4 cup canning salt

Pack beans into four hot 1-pint jars to within 1/2 in. of the top. Add the cayenne, garlic and dill seed to jars.

In a large saucepan, bring the water, vinegar and salt to a boil. Carefully ladle hot mixture over beans, leaving 1/2-in. headspace. Remove air bubbles; wipe the rims and adjust lids. Process for 10 minutes in a boiling-water canner. **YIELD:** 4 pints.

EDITOR'S NOTE: The processing time listed is for altitudes of 1,000 feet or less. For altitudes up to 3,000 feet, add 5 minutes; 6,000 feet, add 10 minutes; 8,000 feet, add 15 minutes; 10,000 feet, add 20 minutes.

garden's harvest pickles

(PICTURED AT RIGHT AND ON PAGE 207)

This relish recipe from a friend is similar to giardiniera only sweeter. I have a certain sense of pride when giving jars as gifts knowing all the vegetables were grown in my own garden.

Linda Chapman | MERIDEN, IA

3 large onions, cut into wedges

3 medium green peppers, cut into 1-inch pieces

3 medium sweet red peppers, cut into 1-inch pieces

1/4 cup canning salt

6 celery ribs, cut into 2-inch lengths

6 medium carrots, cut into 1/2-inch slices

3 cups cauliflower florets

3 cups cut fresh green beans (2-inch lengths)

3 medium zucchini, cut into 1-inch slices

6 cups sugar

6 cups white vinegar

1/4 cup mustard seed

1/4 cup celery seed

In a large bowl, combine the onions, peppers and canning salt. Cover and refrigerate overnight.

Drain; place in a stockpot. Add the remaining ingredients. Bring to a boil. Reduce heat; simmer, uncovered, for 15-20 minutes or until tender. Carefully ladle hot mixture into hot 1-pint jars, leaving 1/2-in. headspace. Remove air bubbles; wipe the rims and adjust lids. Process for 20 minutes in a boiling-water canner. **YIELD:** 11 pints.

EDITOR'S NOTE: The processing time listed is for altitudes of 1,000 feet or less. For altitudes up to 3,000 feet, add 5 minutes; 6,000 feet, add 10 minutes; 8,000 feet, add 15 minutes; 10,000 feet, add 20 minutes.

BOILING-WATER BATH BASICS

Before beginning, inspect the glass canning (mason) jars carefully for any chips, cracks or breaks. Discard any imperfect jars. Wash the jars, screw bands and lids in hot soapy water; rinse thoroughly in hot water. (A dishwasher can also be used.)

Just before preparing your recipe, place the jars and screw bands in a large kettle. Fill the jars and kettle with hot (not boiling) water over low heat, covering the jars by 1 inch. Place the lids in a small saucepan of hot water over low heat. Keep the jars, screw bands and lids in the hot water until ready to use.

When ready to fill the jars, remove them with a jar lifter, emptying the water from the jars back into the kettle. Set the jars, screw bands and lids on a clean kitchen towel.

1. Put the rack in your canner. Add several inches of water; bring to a simmer. Prepare the recipe as directed. Ladle or pour the hot mixture into hot sterilized jars. Use a ruler to make sure you're leaving the recommended headspace for expansion during processing.

2. Wipe the threads and rim of the jar with a clean, damp cloth. Place a warm lid on top of each jar with the sealing compound next to the glass.

3. Screw a band onto the jar just until resistance is met.

4. Immediately after filling each jar, use a jar lifter to place the jar onto the rack in the canner, making sure the jars are not touching. Lower the rack when filled. If necessary, add enough boiling water to the canner to cover jars by 1 to 2 inches. Cover the canner. Adjust heat to hold a steady rolling boil. Start counting the processing time when the water returns to a boil. If the water level decreases while processing, add additional boiling water.

5. When the processing time has ended, remove the jars from the canner with a jar lifter. Stand upright on a towel; keep away from drafts.

blueberry preserves

(PICTURED AT RIGHT)

Juicy blueberries swimming in a sweet jelly taste terrific spooned over vanilla ice cream. But we also enjoy it on top of waffles and pancakes.

Shannon Arthur | PORTSMOUTH, OH

5 cups fresh blueberries

2-1/4 cups sugar

2 teaspoons cider vinegar

1/2 teaspoon ground allspice

1/2 teaspoon ground cinnamon

1/4 teaspoon ground cloves

In a large saucepan, combine all ingredients. Bring to a boil; cook for 15-18 minutes or until thickened, stirring frequently.

Remove from the heat; skim off foam. Ladle hot mixture into hot sterilized half-pint jars, leaving 1/4-in. headspace. Remove air bubbles; wipe rims and adjust lids. Process for 5 minutes in a boiling-water canner. **YIELD:** 3 half-pints.

EDITOR'S NOTE: The processing time listed is for altitudes of 1,000 feet or less. Add 1 minute to the processing time for each 1,000 feet of additional altitude.

sweet-hot asian dipping sauce

Created in our Test Kitchen, this Asian-inspired sauce is a delicious dip for egg rolls or veggies. Or use it to make a flavorful vinaigrette.

3 cups sugar

3 cups cider vinegar

1/4 cup crushed red pepper flakes

6 garlic cloves, minced

2 tablespoons minced fresh gingerroot

1-1/2 teaspoons canning salt

In a Dutch oven, bring sugar and vinegar to a boil. Reduce heat; simmer, uncovered, for 5 minutes. Remove from the heat; stir in the remaining ingredients. Ladle hot mixture into hot half-pint jars, leaving 1/4-in. headspace. Remove air bubbles; wipe rims and adjust lids. Process for 20 minutes in a boiling-water canner. Serve dipping sauce with assorted fresh vegetables or your favorite hot appetizers. **YIELD:** 6 half-pints.

TO MAKE A VINAIGRETTE: Combine 1 part dipping sauce with 2 parts oil and toss with fresh torn lettuce.

EDITOR'S NOTE: The processing time listed is for altitudes of 1,000 feet or less. Add 1 minute to the processing time for each 1,000 feet of additional altitude.

bill's apple butter

I came up with this old-fashioned apple butter after some trial and error. The red-hot candies make it unique.

Bill Elliott | URBANA, MO

15 pounds early-season apples (Gala, Jonathan and/or Cortland), peeled and quartered

3/4 cup cider vinegar

5-1/3 cups packed brown sugar

4 cups sugar

2 tablespoons ground cinnamon

1 teaspoon salt

1 teaspoon cinnamon extract

1/2 teaspoon ground cloves

1/2 teaspoon ground allspice

1 cup red-hot candies

1 cup boiling water

Place apples and vinegar in a stockpot; cover and cook over medium heat for 30-40 minutes or until tender, stirring occasionally. Cool slightly. In a food processor, process mixture in batches until blended. Return all to the pan.

Add the brown sugar, sugar, cinnamon, salt, extract, cloves and allspice. Dissolve red-hots in boiling water; stir into apple mixture.

Bring to a boil. Reduce heat; simmer, uncovered, for 2 hours or until mixture reaches a thick, spreadable consistency. Carefully ladle the hot mixture into hot sterilized 1-pint jars, leaving 1/4-in. headspace. Remove air bubbles; wipe the rims and adjust lids. Process for 5 minutes in a boiling-water canner. **YIELD:** 8 pints.

EDITOR'S NOTE: The processing time listed is for altitudes of 1,000 feet or less. Add 1 minute to the processing time for each 1,000 feet of additional altitude.

TESTING APPLE BUTTER FOR DONENESS

To test doneness of apple butter, spoon a small quantity of cooked mixture onto a chilled plate. The butter is ready to ladle into jars and process when the mixture does not separate and holds its shape and when the texture is of spreading consistency.

strawberry-basil vinegar

The recipe for this robust vinegar comes from our recipe specialists. The mild, fruity flavor of the vinaigrette complements any tossed salad.

4 cups fresh strawberries, hulled

4 cups white wine vinegar

1 tablespoon grated lemon peel

1 cup loosely packed basil leaves

Place strawberries in a food processor; cover and process until pureed. Transfer to a large glass bowl; add vinegar and lemon peel. Place 1/4 cup basil in a small bowl. With a mortar or a wooden spoon, crush basil until aromas are released. Repeat with remaining basil; stir into strawberry mixture. Cover and let stand in a cool dark place for up to 3 days, stirring once daily.

Line a strainer with four layers of cheesecloth or one coffee filter and place over a large saucepan. Strain vinegar into pan (do not press out solids). Discard solids. Heat vinegar to 180° over medium heat. Carefully ladle hot mixture into hot half-pint jars, leaving 1/4-in. headspace. Wipe rims and adjust lids. Process for 10 minutes in a boiling-water canner. **YIELD:** 5 half-pints.

TO MAKE A VINAIGRETTE: Combine 1 part vinegar with 1 part oil. Toss with fresh spinach, sliced fresh strawberries and toasted walnuts.

EDITOR'S NOTE: The processing time listed is for altitudes of 1,000 feet or less. Add 1 minute to the processing time for each 1,000 feet of additional altitude.

iowa corn relish

(PICTURED AT RIGHT AND ON PAGE 207)

I've been making colorful, crunchy corn relish for more than 30 years, and my family never tires of it. It's excellent served with grilled sausages and roasted turkey, pork or ham.

Deanna Ogle | BELLINGHAM, WA

20 medium ears sweet corn

2-2/3 cups white vinegar

2 cups water

1-1/2 cups sugar

2 medium onions, chopped

2 celery ribs, chopped

1 large green pepper, chopped

1 large sweet red pepper, chopped

4-1/2 teaspoons mustard seed

1 tablespoon canning salt

1 teaspoon celery seed

1/2 teaspoon ground turmeric

Place corn in a stockpot; cover with water. Bring to a boil; cover and cook for 3 minutes or until tender. Drain. Cut corn from cobs, making about 10 cups. Return corn to the pan; add remaining ingredients. Bring to a boil. Reduce heat; simmer for 20 minutes.

Carefully ladle hot mixture into hot 1-pint jars, leaving 1/2-in. headspace. Remove the air bubbles; wipe rims and adjust the lids. Process for 20 minutes in a boiling-water canner.
YIELD: 5 pints.

EDITOR'S NOTE: The processing time listed is for altitudes of 1,000 feet or less. For altitudes up to 3,000 feet, add 5 minutes; 6,000 feet, add 10 minutes; 8,000 feet, add 15 minutes; 10,000 feet, add 20 minutes.

old-fashioned garlic dill pickles

(PICTURED ON PAGE 206)

When I was raising my big family, I'd make dill pickles toward the end of the growing season for winter's keeping. Crushed red pepper flakes provide a bit of bite.

Lillian Julow | GAINESVILLE, FL

15 garlic cloves, peeled and halved, divided

15 fresh dill heads

4 pounds small cucumbers (3 to 4 inches long)

6 cups water

4-1/2 cups white vinegar

6 tablespoons canning salt

3/4 teaspoon crushed red pepper flakes

Place five garlic clove halves and five dill heads in each of three hot 1-qt. jars. Pack cucumbers into jars to within 1/2 in. of the top.

In a large saucepan, bring the water, vinegar, salt and pepper flakes to a boil. Carefully ladle hot liquid over cucumbers, leaving 1/2-in. headspace. Add remaining five garlic clove halves to each jar. Remove air bubbles; wipe rims and adjust lids. Process for 15 minutes in a boiling-water canner. **YIELD:** 3 quarts.

EDITOR'S NOTE: The processing time listed is for altitudes of 1,000 feet or less. For altitudes up to 3,000 feet, add 5 minutes; 6,000 feet, add 10 minutes; 8,000 feet, add 15 minutes; 10,000 feet, add 20 minutes.

chipotle sauce

I plant a huge garden every year to help feed my family of seven. My sister shared this recipe with me as a way to use up my bounty of tomatoes. We enjoy it with tacos, chips and sandwiches.

Jean Kennedy | WALTON, OR

4 pounds plum tomatoes (about 12 medium)

1 cup packed brown sugar

3/4 cup cider vinegar

1/4 cup minced chipotle peppers in adobo sauce

2 teaspoons salt

In a large saucepan, bring 8 cups water to a boil. Add tomatoes, a few at a time; boil for 30 seconds. Drain and immediately place tomatoes in ice water. Drain and pat dry; peel.

In a food processor, cover and process tomatoes in batches until finely chopped. Transfer to a Dutch oven. Add the brown sugar, vinegar, chipotle peppers and salt. Bring to a boil. Reduce heat; simmer, uncovered, for 20-25 minutes or until most of the liquid is evaporated, stirring constantly.

Carefully ladle sauce into hot half-pint jars, leaving 1/2-in. headspace. Remove air bubbles; wipe rims and adjust lids. Process for 15 minutes in a boiling-water canner. **YIELD:** 6 half-pints.

EDITOR'S NOTE: The processing time listed is for altitudes of 1,000 feet or less. For altitudes up to 3,000 feet, add 5 minutes; 6,000 feet, add 10 minutes; 8,000 feet, add 15 minutes; 10,000 feet, add 20 minutes.

raspberry-onion jalapeno chutney

(PICTURED AT RIGHT)

Sweet raspberries and spicy jalapenos come together to create a chutney that tastes terrific on top of cream cheese or over grilled chicken.

Jo-Anne Cooper | ALBERTA, CANADA

4 large onions, chopped

2 large red onions, chopped

1-1/2 cups packed brown sugar

1 cup raisins

1-1/4 cups cider vinegar

1 cup balsamic vinegar

1/2 cup sugar

2 jalapeno peppers, seeded and chopped

2 tablespoons grated orange peel

2 teaspoons canning salt

4 cups fresh raspberries

In a Dutch oven, bring first 10 ingredients to a boil. Reduce heat; simmer, uncovered, for 25-30 minutes or until thickened, stirring occasionally. Stir in the raspberries; heat through.

Remove from the heat. Ladle hot mixture into hot half-pint jars, leaving 1/2-in. headspace. Remove air bubbles; wipe rims and adjust lids. Process for 15 minutes in a boiling-water canner. **YIELD:** 7 half-pints.

EDITOR'S NOTE: When cutting hot peppers, disposable gloves are recommended. Avoid touching your face. The processing time listed is for altitudes of 1,000 feet or less. For altitudes up to 3,000 feet, add 5 minutes; 6,000 feet, add 10 minutes; 8,000 feet, add 15 minutes; 10,000 feet, add 20 minutes.

TESTING SEALS ON PROCESSED JARS

After 12 to 24 hours, test each of the lids to determine if they have sealed by pressing the center of the lid. If the lid is indented, remove the band and try to lift the lid. If the lid is secure, the jar is vacuum-sealed. Wipe the jars to remove any food. Label and date the jars.

If the lid is not sealed, do not reprocess. Store the jar in the refrigerator and eat the contents within several days.

*I*n New England, clam bakes are as much a part of summer as sultry temperatures and family vacations.

While not all of us are fortunate enough to live near the shoreline, that doesn't mean you can't experience the fantastic flavors of a classic clam bake.

Instead of making a fire in the sand, ignite the grill in your backyard and prepare Grilled Clam Bake. It features the traditional tastes of clams, crab, corn and potatoes.

New England Iced Tea—an adult beverage with a bit of a kick—will help beat the summer heat.

Forego the usual French bread and pass a basket brimming with Cheddar Drop Biscuits.

FROM-THE-SEA FARE
(PICTURED AT RIGHT)

New England Iced Tea (p. 220)
Grilled Clam Bake (p. 220)
Cheddar Drop Biscuits (p. 222)

new england
CLAM BAKE

grilled clam bake

(PICTURED ON PAGE 219)

With clams and crab legs, this entree from our home economists looks impressive
but is quite easy to prepare on the grill. The addition of corn and potatoes makes it a meal in one.

18 fresh littleneck clams

4 medium ears sweet corn, husks removed and cut into thirds

8 medium red potatoes, cut into 1/2-inch cubes

2 medium onions, cut into 2-inch pieces

1 cup white wine or chicken broth

1 cup minced fresh parsley

1/4 cup minced fresh basil

1/2 cup olive oil

2 garlic cloves, minced

1 teaspoon coarsely ground pepper

1 teaspoon hot pepper sauce

1/2 teaspoon salt

3 bay leaves

3 pounds uncooked snow crab legs

1/4 cup butter, cubed

French bread, optional

Tap clams; discard any that do not close. In a large disposable roasting pan, layer the clams, corn, potatoes, onions, wine, herbs, oil, garlic, pepper, pepper sauce, salt and bay leaves. Grill, covered, over medium heat for 15 minutes.

Add crab; cook until potatoes are tender, about 25-30 minutes. Discard bay leaves; stir in butter. Serve with bread if desired. **YIELD:** 6 servings.

new england iced tea

(PICTURED ON PAGE 218)

While growing up in Massachusetts, my family spent summers at our cottage.
The clam bakes on the beach would also include these cocktails for the adults.

Ann Liebergen | BROOKFIELD, WI

2 tablespoons sugar

1 ounce vodka

1 ounce light rum

1 ounce gin

1 ounce Triple Sec

1 ounce lime juice

1 ounce tequila

1 to 1-1/2 cups ice cubes

2 ounces cranberry juice

Lemon slice, optional

In a mixing glass or tumbler, combine the sugar, vodka, rum, gin, Triple Sec, lime juice and tequila; stir until sugar is dissolved. Place ice in a highball glass; pour in the sugar mixture. Top with cranberry juice. Garnish with lemon if desired. **YIELD:** 1 serving.

lobster rolls

(PICTURED AT RIGHT)

Mayonnaise infused with dill and lemon lends refreshing flavor to our Test Kitchen's super sandwiches. Try toasting the buns for something a little more special.

1 cup chopped celery

1/3 cup mayonnaise

2 tablespoons lemon juice

1/2 teaspoon dill weed

5 cups cubed cooked lobster meat (about 4 small lobsters)

8 hoagie rolls, split and toasted

In a large bowl, combine the celery, mayonnaise, lemon juice and dill weed. Gently stir in the lobster. Serve on rolls. **YIELD:** 8 servings.

colorful coleslaw

(PICTURED ABOVE)

Although raspberry vinegar may seem like an odd ingredient in coleslaw, it adds a unique, fruity taste. The recipe can easily be doubled for a larger gathering.

Kathy Rairigh | MILFORD, IN

7 cups shredded cabbage

1 cup cherry tomatoes, halved

1/2 cup chopped fresh broccoli

1/2 cup chopped zucchini

1/4 cup chopped red onion

1/4 cup chopped sweet red pepper

1/2 cup white wine vinegar

1/2 cup canola oil

1/3 cup sugar

2 teaspoons Dijon mustard

1 teaspoon salt

1 teaspoon celery seed

1 teaspoon mustard seed

1 teaspoon raspberry vinegar

In a large bowl, combine the first six ingredients. In a small bowl, whisk the remaining ingredients; pour over salad and toss to coat. Cover and refrigerate for at least 4 hours, stirring occasionally. **YIELD:** 9 servings.

cheddar drop biscuits

(PICTURED AT FAR RIGHT AND ON PAGE 219)

Bakers of any skill level can make these savory biscuits because there's no rolling and cutting.
The heavenly bundles are filled with the fabulous flavor of cheese, butter and garlic.

Marlana Barousse | *CARRIERE, MS*

1-1/4 cups self-rising flour

3/4 cup cake flour

1 tablespoon sugar

3/4 teaspoon baking powder

1/2 teaspoon salt

1/4 teaspoon garlic powder

1/8 teaspoon baking soda

1/4 cup cold butter

1-1/4 cups heavy whipping cream

1 cup (4 ounces) shredded sharp cheddar cheese

OIL MIXTURE:

1/3 cup olive oil

1 teaspoon garlic powder

1 teaspoon dried parsley flakes

1/4 teaspoon salt

In a small bowl, combine the first seven ingredients. Cut in butter until mixture resembles coarse crumbs. Stir in cream and cheese just until moistened.

Drop dough by 1/8 cupfuls 2 in. apart onto a greased 15-in. x 10-in. x 1-in. baking pan. In a small bowl, combine the remaining ingredients. Brush half of oil mixture over biscuits.

Bake at 450° for 8-10 minutes or until golden brown. Brush with remaining oil mixture. Serve warm. **YIELD:** 1-1/2 dozen.

EDITOR'S NOTE: As a substitute for each cup of self-rising flour, place 1-1/2 teaspoons baking powder and 1/2 teaspoon salt in a measuring cup. Add all-purpose flour to measure 1 cup.

chocolate peanut butter pie

The classic combination of peanut butter and chocolate never fails to satisfy...and this indulgent pie from our recipe specialists is no exception. It can also be kept in the freezer for dessert at a moment's notice.

3 cups crushed cream-filled chocolate sandwich cookies (about 30 cookies)

1-1/2 cups creamy peanut butter, divided

1 package (8 ounces) cream cheese, softened

1-1/4 cups confectioners' sugar

2 tablespoons chopped salted peanuts

2 tablespoons 2% milk

2-2/3 cups heavy whipping cream, divided

6 ounces semisweet chocolate, chopped

In a small bowl, combine cookie crumbs and 1/2 cup peanut butter. Press onto the bottom and 1 in. up the sides of an ungreased 9-in. springform pan; set aside. Place pan on a baking sheet. Bake at 350° for 10 minutes or until set. Cool on a wire rack.

In a large bowl, beat cream cheese and confectioners' sugar until smooth. Beat in the peanuts, milk and remaining peanut butter. In a small bowl with clean beaters, beat 2 cups cream until stiff peaks form. With a spatula, stir a fourth of the whipped cream into peanut butter mixture. Fold in remaining whipped cream. Spoon into crust. Refrigerate for at least 1 hour.

Place chocolate in a small bowl. In a small saucepan, bring remaining cream just to a boil. Pour over chocolate; whisk until smooth. Cool slightly, stirring occasionally. Pour chocolate mixture over cake. Refrigerate until set. **YIELD:** 12 servings.

EDITOR'S NOTE: Reduced-fat or generic brands of peanut butter are not recommended for this recipe.

seafood chowder

(PICTURED AT RIGHT)

Chock-full of fish, shrimp and scallops, this comforting chowder has been pleasing my family for many years. The seasoned oyster crackers add a bit of spice.

Virginia Anthony | *JACKSONVILLE, FL*

1 tablespoon unsalted butter, melted

1 tablespoon Worcestershire sauce for chicken

1 teaspoon hot pepper sauce

1/4 teaspoon curry powder

1/4 teaspoon paprika

1-1/4 cups oyster crackers

CHOWDER:

8 bacon strips, chopped

1-1/2 pounds red potatoes, cut into 1/2-inch cubes

2 cups thinly sliced leeks (white portion only)

1/4 cup all-purpose flour

3/4 teaspoon dried thyme

1 carton (32 ounces) reduced-sodium chicken broth

4 cups clam juice

1 package (12 ounces) frozen corn

1-1/2 cups diced zucchini

1 pound grouper or tilapia fillets, cut into 1-inch cubes

3/4 pound uncooked medium shrimp, peeled and deveined

1/2 pound bay scallops

1 cup half-and-half cream

1 teaspoon salt

1/4 teaspoon white pepper

In a small bowl, combine the butter, Worcestershire sauce, pepper sauce, curry and paprika. Add the crackers; toss to coat.

Transfer to a greased 15-in. x 10-in. x 1-in. baking pan. Bake at 350° for 8-10 minutes or until golden brown, stirring twice. Set aside.

Meanwhile, in a stockpot, cook bacon over medium heat until crisp. Using a slotted spoon, remove to paper towels to drain.

Saute potatoes and leeks in drippings; stir in flour and thyme until blended. Gradually whisk in broth and clam juice. Bring to a boil, stirring constantly. Cook and stir 1-2 minutes longer. Reduce heat; cover and simmer for 10 minutes or until potatoes are tender.

Add the corn, zucchini, grouper, shrimp and scallops; cook for 2-4 minutes or until fish flakes easily with a fork. Stir in the cream, salt and pepper; heat through. Serve with the crackers and bacon. **YIELD:** 12 servings (4-1/2 quarts).

spiced grilled corn

The wonderful spice mixture from our Test Kitchen doesn't add heat...just great flavor.
This just may be the best corn you've ever had!

2 teaspoons ground cumin

2 teaspoons ground coriander

1 teaspoon salt

1 teaspoon dried oregano

1/2 teaspoon ground ginger

1/4 teaspoon ground cinnamon

1/4 teaspoon pepper

1/8 teaspoon ground cloves

2 tablespoons olive oil

8 medium ears sweet corn, husks removed

In a small bowl, combine the first eight ingredients. Brush oil over corn; sprinkle with spice mixture. Place each on a double thickness of heavy-duty foil (about 14 in. x 12. in.). Fold foil over corn and seal tightly.

Grill corn, covered, over medium heat for 15-20 minutes or until tender, turning occasionally. Open foil carefully to allow steam to escape. **YIELD:** 8 servings.

maine blueberry pie with crumb topping

I make this delicious, fruity pie with small Maine berries, but any variety can be used.
The shortbread topping provides crunch and sweetness.

Jessie Grearson-Sapat | *FALMOUTH, ME*

1 sheet refrigerated pie pastry

6 cups fresh or frozen blueberries

3/4 cup sugar

3 tablespoons all-purpose flour

1/8 teaspoon ground cinnamon

1 teaspoon minced fresh thyme, optional

1 tablespoon butter, cubed

TOPPING:

12 shortbread cookies

3 tablespoons quick-cooking oats

3 tablespoons brown sugar

3 tablespoons butter, cubed

2 tablespoons all-purpose flour

1/4 teaspoon ground cinnamon

Dash salt

Whipped cream

Unroll pastry into a 9-in. deep-dish pie plate; flute edges.

In a large bowl, combine the blueberries, sugar, flour, cinnamon and thyme if desired; toss gently. Spoon into crust; dot with butter.

In a food processor, cover and process cookies until coarsely chopped. Add remaining topping ingredients; process until crumbly. Sprinkle over berry mixture.

Bake at 400° for 45-55 minutes or until crust is golden brown and filling is bubbly. Cover edges with foil during the last 15 minutes to prevent overbrowning if necessary. Cool on a wire rack. Serve with whipped cream. **YIELD:** 8 servings.

white sands centerpiece

(PICTURED AT RIGHT)

Whether you're hosting a clam bake at the shore, at a park or at your own home, bring a bit of the beach to the table.

With some simple ocean items—and possibly a quick trip to your local craft store—it's a breeze to assemble an eye-catching coastal centerpiece.

First, fish around your cupboards for clear vases in varying sizes and shapes. Then place some sand inside. There are many kinds of sand available, including beach, playground and craft.

Stick a sprig of fresh or artificial ornamental grass into the sand, building up the sand around the base. (The photo at right shows lily grass.)

Do you have a collection of shells from beachcombing while on vacation? Tuck some inside the vases. (Or stop at a craft store to purchase a few inexpensive items.)

Other seaside additions to your centerpiece could include bits of coral, starfish, sea glass, pebbles and small pieces of driftwood.

SAND DOLLAR PLACE CARD

You don't have to spend a lot of cash to create attractive place cards for your clam bake. Look for sand dollars about 2 to 4 inches in circumference at the beach or a craft store. Write the name of each guest on the front of the sand dollar with a felt-tipped pen. If desired, tuck the sand dollar inside a folded napkin or simply set on the plate.

Has Mother Nature turned up the heat in your part of the world? Or maybe winter has rolled in and you're longing for warmer days.

No matter the season, you can add a little spice to your next dinner party with friends by preparing an assortment of Cuban foods.

Unlike Mexican cooking, which is mainly influenced by Spain and Aztec traditions, Cuban cuisine is inspired by a blend of cultures, including the Caribbean, Spain and Africa.

Start the evening by offering each guest an ice-cold Refreshing Mojito. Then pass a basket of crunchy Plantain Chips with Citrus Guacamole.

Zesty servings of Yellow Rice & Black Bean Salad complement traditional Cuban Roasted Pork Sandwiches.

CUBAN CUISINE
(PICTURED AT RIGHT)

havana nights
DINNER PARTY

cuban roasted pork sandwiches

(PICTURED ON PAGE 227)

*Our home economists slowly roast pork in a seasoned citrus marinade,
then layer slices with pickles, zippy mustard, ham and cheese for an incredible hot sandwich.*

5 to 6 pounds boneless pork shoulder roast

4 garlic cloves, sliced

2 large onions, sliced

1 cup orange juice

1 cup lime juice

2 tablespoons dried oregano

2 teaspoons ground cumin

1 teaspoon salt

1 teaspoon pepper

SANDWICHES:

4 loaves (1 pound each) French bread

3/4 cup butter, softened

Yellow mustard, optional

24 thin sandwich pickle slices

2-1/4 pounds sliced deli ham

2-1/4 pounds Swiss cheese, sliced

Cut sixteen 1-in. slits in roast; insert garlic slices.

In a large bowl, combine the onions, orange juice, lime juice and seasonings. Pour 1-1/2 cups marinade into a large resealable plastic bag; add the pork. Seal bag and turn to coat; refrigerate for at least 8 hours or overnight. Cover and refrigerate remaining marinade.

Drain and discard marinade. Place roast and reserved marinade in a shallow roasting pan. Bake at 350° for 2-3/4 to 3-1/4 hours or until a meat thermometer reaches 160°, basting occasionally. Let stand for 10 minutes.

Meanwhile, cut each loaf of bread in half lengthwise. Spread butter and mustard if desired over cut sides of bread. Thinly slice pork across the grain. Layer bottom halves of bread with pickles, pork, ham and cheese. Replace tops. Cut each loaf into sixths.

Cook in batches on a panini maker or indoor grill for 4-5 minutes or until bread is browned and cheese is melted. **YIELD:** 24 servings.

PREPARING PANINIS ON THE GRILL

You can make many Cuban Roasted Pork Sandwiches at the same time on an outdoor grill. Assemble the sandwiches as directed. Place on grill grates coated with cooking spray over medium heat. Lay a clean brick wrapped in foil over one or two sandwiches. Grill until the bread is browned and the cheese is melted. Be sure to handle the hot bricks with oven mitts.

picadillo
(PICTURED AT RIGHT)

Like most traditional recipes, there are numerous variations...and this is my version of a Cuban classic. For added convenience, I adapted it for the slow cooker.

Sanford Brown | BIG PINE KEY, FL

2 large onions, chopped

2 tablespoons olive oil

3/4 cup white wine or beef broth

2 pounds lean ground beef (90% lean)

1-1/4 cups crushed tomatoes

1 can (8 ounces) tomato sauce

1/3 cup tomato paste

4 garlic cloves, minced

2 teaspoons dried oregano

1/2 teaspoon salt

1/2 teaspoon ground cinnamon

1/2 teaspoon ground cloves

1/2 teaspoon pepper

1 cup raisins

1 medium green pepper, chopped

3/4 cup pimiento-stuffed olives, cut into thirds

2 tablespoons chopped seeded jalapeno pepper

Hot cooked brown rice

In a large skillet, cook onions in oil over low heat for 15-20 minutes or until onions are golden brown, stirring occasionally. Add wine; cook and stir 2 minutes longer. Transfer to a 3- or 4-qt. slow cooker.

In the same skillet, cook the beef over medium heat until no longer pink. Add to the slow cooker. Combine the tomatoes, tomato sauce, tomato paste, garlic and seasonings; pour over top. Cover and cook on low for 4-6 hours or until heated through.

Place raisins in a small bowl. Cover with boiling water; let stand for 5 minutes. Drain. Stir the green pepper, olives, jalapeno and raisins into the slow cooker. Cover and cook 30 minutes longer. Serve with rice. **YIELD:** 8 servings.

EDITOR'S NOTE: When cutting hot peppers, disposable gloves are recommended. Avoid touching your face.

yellow rice & black bean salad

(PICTURED ON PAGE 226)

Chipotle peppers turn up the heat on a colorful rice dish brimming with black beans. It can be served hot or cold.

Rose Rodwell | BERGEN, NY

4 teaspoons ground cumin, divided

1/4 cup lime juice

2 tablespoons plus 1-1/2 teaspoons canola oil

1/2 teaspoon ground turmeric

1-1/2 cups water

1 cup uncooked basmati rice

1 teaspoon salt

4 green onions, sliced

1 can (15 ounces) black beans, rinsed and drained

1 small green pepper, chopped

1/2 cup chopped roasted sweet red peppers

1/3 cup minced fresh cilantro

1-1/2 teaspoons chopped chipotle pepper in adobo sauce

Place three teaspoons cumin in a small skillet; cook over medium heat for 1 minute or until aromas are released. Stir in lime juice and oil; set aside.

In a large saucepan, combine turmeric and remaining cumin. Cook over medium heat for 1 minute or until aromatic. Add the water, rice and salt; bring to a boil. Reduce heat to low; cover and simmer 15 minutes or until water is absorbed. Cool. Stir in onions and half of the lime juice mixture.

In a large bowl, combine the remaining ingredients. Add the rice mixture and remaining lime juice mixture; toss to coat. YIELD: 12 servings (1/2 cup each).

mini chicken empanadas

Refrigerated pie pastry makes quick work of assembling these bite-sized appetizers loaded with chicken and cheese. I've made them several times since receiving the recipe from a friend.

Betty Fulks | ONIA, AR

1 cup finely chopped cooked chicken

2/3 cup shredded Colby-Monterey Jack cheese

3 tablespoons cream cheese, softened

4 teaspoons chopped sweet red pepper

2 teaspoons chopped seeded jalapeno pepper

1 teaspoon ground cumin

1/2 teaspoon salt

1/8 teaspoon pepper

1 package (15 ounces) refrigerated pie pastry

In a small bowl, combine the first eight ingredients. On a lightly floured surface, roll each pastry into a 15-inch circle. Cut pastry with a floured 3-in. round biscuit cutter. Place a heaping teaspoonful of filling on one side of each circle. Brush edges of pastry with water; fold circles in half.

Place on greased baking sheets. With a fork, press edges to seal. Bake at 400° for 12-15 minutes or until golden brown. Serve warm. YIELD: about 2-1/2 dozen.

EDITOR'S NOTE: When cutting hot peppers, disposable gloves are recommended. Avoid touching your face.

orange shrimp mojo

(PICTURED AT RIGHT)

With jalapeno, orange and avocado, every bite of this enticing entree is spicy, tangy and fresh. The sauce beautifully glazes the shrimp.

Don Thompson | HOUSTON, OH

1 tablespoon cumin seeds

1 tablespoon whole peppercorns

1 tablespoon grated orange or tangerine peel

1/2 teaspoon dried oregano

1/2 teaspoon salt

1 pound uncooked jumbo shrimp, peeled and deveined

4 teaspoons olive oil

3 cups orange juice

3 tablespoons rum or chicken broth

1 garlic clove, minced

1 large navel orange, peeled, sectioned and chopped

1/2 large sweet onion, chopped

1 cup cubed avocado

1/2 cup minced fresh cilantro, divided

1 teaspoon chopped seeded jalapeno pepper

In a small skillet over medium heat, toast the cumin seeds and peppercorns until aromatic, about 1-2 minutes. Remove from the skillet. Crush the seeds using a spice mill or blender.

In a small bowl, combine the orange peel, oregano, salt and crushed cumin and peppercorns. Sprinkle 1 tablespoon spice mixture over shrimp.

In a large skillet, cook shrimp in oil over medium-high heat for 1 minute; turn shrimp. Add the orange juice, rum, garlic and 1 tablespoon spice mixture. Cook and stir 1-2 minutes longer or until shrimp turn pink; remove and keep warm. Bring liquid in skillet to a boil. Cook until reduced to 2/3 cup, about 35 minutes.

Meanwhile, for salsa, combine the orange, onion, avocado, 1/4 cup cilantro, jalapeno and remaining spice mixture in a small bowl.

Stir remaining cilantro into sauce. Serve with shrimp and salsa.
YIELD: 8 servings.

EDITOR'S NOTE: When cutting hot peppers, disposable gloves are recommended. Avoid touching your face.

KNOW YOUR MOJO

Mojo refers to several kinds of sauces varying in spiciness that originated in the Canary Islands. In Cuban cooking, mojo applies to any sauce made with garlic, olive oil and citrus juice.

plantain chips with citrus guacamole

(PICTURED ON PAGE 227)

Our recipe specialists offer their version of plantain chips, a popular side dish in Cuba. They're not only great tasting but are more nutritious than potato chips.

3 medium ripe avocados, peeled

1 tablespoon each lemon, lime and orange juice

1 jalapeno pepper, seeded and minced

1-1/2 teaspoons salt, divided

3 green plantains

Oil for deep-fat frying

1/2 teaspoon ground cumin

1/8 teaspoon cayenne pepper

In a small bowl, mash avocados with juices, jalapeno and 1/2 teaspoon salt; set aside.

Peel plantains. With a mandoline or vegetable peeler, cut plantains lengthwise into thin slices. In an electric skillet or deep-fat fryer, heat oil to 375°. Add plantains, a few at a time, and cook for 30-60 seconds or until golden brown, turning often. Drain on paper towels.

Combine the cumin, cayenne and remaining salt; sprinkle over chips. Serve with guacamole. **YIELD:** 9 cups chips (2 cups guacamole).

EDITOR'S NOTE: If plantains are not available, substitute green bananas and use a mandoline for slicing rather than a vegetable peeler. When cutting the hot peppers, disposable gloves are recommended. Avoid touching your face.

PLANTAIN POINTERS

Plantains (sometimes called "cooking bananas") are a popular tropical fruit in Latin American cooking. Because they're somewhat starchy, plantains are often used more as a vegetable (like potatoes) than as a fruit.

Purchase plantains that are firm, not mushy or cracked; store at room temperature. Before using, rinse and trim both ends. With a sharp knife, cut a lengthwise slit down the fruit through the thick, stiff peel. Remove the peel.

refreshing mojito

(PICTURED ON PAGE 226)

The great minty flavor of mojitos helps balance the spiciness of Cuban food. My easy recipe calls for apple rum and a purchased mix.

Eric Brill | WAUWATOSA, WI

2 ounces Mojito mix, divided

1 mint sprig

1/2 teaspoon sugar

1 to 1-1/2 cups ice cubes

2 ounces apple rum or light rum

1 ounce club soda

Place 1 ounce Mojito mix, mint and sugar in a highball glass; muddle. Add ice. Pour rum, club soda and remaining Mojito mix into glass; stir. Serve immediately. **YIELD:** 1 serving.

ham and black bean soup

(PICTURED AT RIGHT)

I originally made this slightly spicy soup for my husband, who enjoys black beans. But I ended up loving it, too! Even more compliments came from our neighbors who stopped by and stayed for supper.

Laura Meurer | GREEN BAY, WI

3 cans (15 ounces each) black beans, rinsed and drained

2 cans (14-1/2 ounces each) beef broth

1 can (14-1/2 ounces) diced tomatoes, undrained

1-1/2 cups cubed fully cooked ham

1 can (4 ounces) chopped green chilies

1/4 cup red wine vinegar

1 large onion, chopped

3 garlic cloves, minced

1 teaspoon dried oregano

1 teaspoon dried thyme

1 teaspoon pepper

In a 3-qt. slow cooker, combine all of the ingredients. Cover and cook on high for 4-5 hours or until onion is tender. **YIELD:** 8 servings (about 2 quarts).

ham croquettes with mustard sauce

Any leftover ham is set aside for these crispy croquettes. I shape them early in the day, and then simply fry them at dinnertime. The mustard sauce is mild and pairs well with ham.

Kathy Vincek | TOMS RIVER, NJ

2 cups finely chopped fully cooked ham

1 tablespoon finely chopped onion

1 teaspoon minced fresh parsley

1/4 cup butter, cubed

1/4 cup all-purpose flour

1/4 teaspoon salt

1/8 teaspoon pepper

1 cup milk

1 egg

2 tablespoons water

3/4 cup dry bread crumbs

Oil for deep-fat frying

SAUCE:

1-1/2 teaspoons butter

1-1/2 teaspoons all-purpose flour

1/4 teaspoon salt

Dash pepper

1/2 cup milk

4-1/2 teaspoons yellow mustard

In a small bowl, combine the ham, onion and parsley; set aside.

In a small saucepan, melt butter. Stir in the flour, salt and pepper until smooth; gradually add milk. Bring to a boil; cook and stir for 1 minute or until thickened. Stir into ham mixture.

Spread into an 8-in. square baking dish; cover and refrigerate for at least 2 hours.

In a shallow bowl, combine egg and water. Place bread crumbs in a separate shallow bowl. Shape the ham mixture into 12 balls (mixture will be soft); roll each ball into egg mixture, then bread crumbs. Cover and refrigerate 2 hours longer.

In a deep-fat fryer, heat oil to 375°. Fry croquettes, a few at a time, for 2-3 minutes or until golden brown, turning once. Drain on paper towels.

Meanwhile, in a small saucepan, melt butter. Stir in the flour, salt and pepper until smooth; gradually add milk. Bring to a boil; cook and stir for 2 minutes or until thickened. Stir in mustard. Serve with croquettes. **YIELD:** 1 dozen.

minty lime granita

I like to balance the heat from spicy meals by serving scoops of refreshing lime granita. Keep a batch in the freezer to enjoy any time!

Rochelle Schmidt | KENOSHA, WI

1 package (3 ounces) lime gelatin

1 cup boiling water

3/4 cup lemon-lime soda

1/4 cup rum

2 tablespoons minced fresh mint

2 tablespoons lime juice

In a large bowl, dissolve gelatin in boiling water. Stir in the remaining ingredients.

Transfer to an 8-in. square dish; cool to room temperature. Freeze for 1 hour or until edges begin to firm; stir. Freeze 2 hours longer or until firm.

Just before serving, transfer to a food processor; cover and process until mixture resembles finely shaved ice. Spoon into dessert dishes. **YIELD:** 4 servings.

tres leches cake

(PICTURED AT RIGHT)

During our extensive travels to Central America, my husband and I have sampled all sorts of the popular tres leches dessert. We think this is the absolute best.

Joan Meyers | PALOS PARK, IL

6 eggs

1-1/2 cups sugar

1 teaspoon vanilla extract

2 cups all-purpose flour

2 teaspoons baking powder

MILK MIXTURE:

1 can (14 ounces) sweetened condensed milk

1 can (12 ounces) evaporated milk

1 cup 2% milk

3 egg yolks, beaten

1/4 cup rum, optional

FROSTING:

1 cup sugar

3 egg whites

1/4 cup water

1/4 teaspoon cream of tartar

In a large bowl, beat eggs for 3 minutes. Gradually add the sugar and vanilla; beat for 2 minutes or until the mixture becomes thick and lemon-colored. Combine the flour and baking powder; fold into the egg mixture. Spread the batter into a greased 13-in. x 9-in. baking dish.

Bake at 350° for 20-25 minutes or until golden brown. Place on a wire rack. Poke holes into the cake with a skewer, about 1/2 in. apart.

In a small saucepan, bring the three milks to a boil over medium-low heat. Remove from the heat; gradually stir a small amount of the hot mixture into egg yolks. Return all to the pan, stirring constantly. Stir in rum if desired. Bring to a gentle boil; cook and stir for 2 minutes.

Slowly pour milk mixture over cake, allowing mixture to absorb into cake. Let stand for 30 minutes. Cover and refrigerate for 8 hours or overnight.

In a large heavy saucepan, combine the frosting ingredients over low heat. With a hand mixer, beat on low speed for 1 minute. Continue beating on low over low heat until frosting reaches 160°, about 14-18 minutes.

Pour into a large bowl; beat on high until stiff peaks form, about 7 minutes. Spread over the cake. Store in the refrigerator. **YIELD:** 15 servings.

$\mathcal{H}$alloween isn't just for kids anymore. In fact, it's a terrific time for adults to gather with friends for an upscale yet fun-filled bash.

Some folks can become terror-stricken at the thought of planning an elegant, eerie event.

But with fall-flavored recipes and not-so-gruesome games, this chapter takes the guesswork out of party preparation...and you don't even need to look into a crystal ball!

Champagne and apple brandy turn sparkling glasses of Autumn Fizz into a spirited beverage.

Cast a spell on your guests' palates with fantastic foods such as Roasted Beet Salad and Cider-Molasses Pork Tenderloin with Pears.

UNEXPECTED TASTES
(PICTURED AT RIGHT)

Autumn Fizz (p. 238)
Roasted Beet Salad (p. 238)
Cider-Molasses Pork Tenderloin
With Pears (p. 240)

fortune telling
HALLOWEEN

roasted beet salad

(PICTURED ON PAGE 237)

A subtle citrus dressing beautifully coats tender beets in a lovely warm salad.
Goat cheese lends a bit of tang while almonds provide some crunch.

Alissa Stehr | *GAU-ODERNHEIM, GERMANY*

7 medium fresh beets (about 2-1/2 pounds), peeled and cut into wedges

5 shallots, quartered

1 tablespoon cumin seeds

2 tablespoons olive oil

1/8 teaspoon salt

1/8 teaspoon pepper

VINAIGRETTE:

1-1/2 teaspoons lemon juice

3/4 teaspoon minced fresh parsley

1/2 teaspoon grated orange peel

1/2 teaspoon honey

1/8 teaspoon salt

Dash pepper

1/4 cup olive oil

GARNISH:

1/4 cup slivered almonds, toasted

1/4 cup crumbled goat cheese

1 teaspoon minced fresh parsley

Place the beets, shallots and cumin seeds on a double thickness of heavy-duty foil (about 24 in. x 12 in.). Drizzle with oil; sprinkle with salt and pepper. Fold foil around beet mixture and seal tightly. Place on a baking sheet. Bake at 400° for 45-55 minutes or until tender. Open foil carefully to allow steam to escape.

In a small bowl, combine the lemon juice, parsley, orange peel, honey, salt and pepper. Gradually whisk in oil.

Transfer beet mixture to a large bowl. Drizzle with vinaigrette; toss to coat. Sprinkle with almonds, goat cheese and parsley. **YIELD:** 6 servings.

autumn fizz

(PICTURED ON PAGE 236)

Champagne infuses sweet apple brandy with fun fizz in our recipe specialists'
festive cocktail that adds a delightful surprise to celebrations throughout the year.

1/2 ounce apple brandy

1 teaspoon sugar

1 mint sprig

2 ounces unsweetened apple juice, chilled

2 ounces Champagne or other sparkling wine, chilled

Place the brandy, sugar and mint in a champagne flute or wine glass; gently crush mint with a small spoon. Add the apple juice and Champagne. **YIELD:** 1 serving.

pumpkin soup with cinnamon croutons

(PICTURED AT RIGHT)

I was a caterer for years, and this soup was always a favorite with clients. The crisp, cinnamon-sugar croutons complement this smooth, savory soup.

Ellen Conrad | SALEM, OH

1 large onion, chopped

2 tablespoons olive oil

2 garlic cloves, minced

2 cans (14-1/2 ounces each) reduced-sodium chicken broth, divided

1/2 teaspoon salt

1/4 teaspoon ground cinnamon

1/4 teaspoon ground nutmeg

1/8 teaspoon ground ginger

1/8 teaspoon pepper

2 cups 2% milk

1 can (15 ounces) solid-pack pumpkin

1 cup half-and-half cream

CROUTONS:

3 cups cubed French bread

3 tablespoons butter, melted

1 teaspoon brown sugar

1/8 teaspoon ground cinnamon

In a large saucepan, saute onion in oil until tender. Add garlic; cook 1 minute longer. Stir in 1 can of broth and seasonings. Bring to a boil. Reduce the heat; cover and simmer for 15 minutes.

Cool slightly. Transfer mixture to a blender; cover and process until smooth. Return to the pan. Stir in milk, pumpkin, cream and remaining broth; heat through.

For the croutons, place bread cubes in a greased 15-in. x 10-in. x 1-in. baking pan. Bake at 425° for 5-8 minutes or until toasted. Combine the butter, brown sugar and cinnamon; drizzle over croutons and toss to coat. Bake 3-5 minutes longer or until golden brown. Serve with soup. **YIELD:** 9 servings (2-1/4 quarts).

cider-molasses pork tenderloin with pears

(PICTURED AT FAR RIGHT AND ON PAGE 237)

If you want to perk up your usual pork tenderloin, bake it alongside pears and drizzle it with a robust molasses sauce. Family and friends will be thrilled with this beautiful fall dish.

Lisa Renshaw | *KANSAS CITY, MO*

2 pork tenderloins (1 pound each)

3 tablespoons olive oil

4 teaspoons minced fresh rosemary
or 1 teaspoon dried rosemary, crushed

1 teaspoon salt

1 teaspoon pepper

6 medium pears, peeled, halved and cored

1 cup apple cider or juice

1/2 cup molasses

1/4 cup balsamic vinegar

Place pork on a rack in a shallow roasting pan. Combine the oil, rosemary, salt and pepper; rub over pork. Arrange pears around pork. In a small bowl, combine the remaining ingredients; pour over the top.

Bake at 425° for 25-30 minutes or until a meat thermometer reads 160°, basting occasionally with pan juices. Let stand for 5 minutes before slicing. **YIELD:** 6 servings.

olive and herb toasts

Tangy olives pair nicely with mild fresh mozzarella for crunchy, savory snacks that can be assembled in no time.

Laura Moran | *FRIENDSHIP, WI*

16 slices French bread (1/2 inch thick)

1/4 cup olive oil, divided

1 pound fresh mozzarella cheese, cut into 16 slices

1-1/2 cups Sicilian green olives, pitted and chopped

2 tablespoons minced fresh basil

Place bread on an ungreased baking sheet; brush with half of the oil. Broil 3-4 in. from the heat for 1-2 minutes or until lightly browned.

Top with cheese. Combine the olives, basil and remaining oil; spoon over bread. Broil for 2-4 minutes or until cheese is softened. Serve warm. **YIELD:** 16 appetizers.

STORING FRESH MOZZARELLA

With its increasing popularity, fresh mozzarella can be found in many large grocery stores. The cheese is typically sold in a brine; store it in this solution until ready to use. Always buy the freshest cheese possible and eat it within 2 to 3 days. Freezing is not recommended.

pumpkin and plantain mash

(PICTURED AT RIGHT)

*Delicious and simple to prepare,
this pumpkin-and-plaintain mash
is perfectly seasoned with roasted garlic
and caramelized shallots.*

Donna Noel | *GRAY, ME*

1 medium pie pumpkin, peeled and cut into 1-1/2-inch cubes

1 ripe plantain, peeled and cut into 1-1/2-inch cubes

4 garlic cloves, unpeeled

12 shallots, sliced

1 tablespoon olive oil

2 tablespoons white wine or chicken broth

1 teaspoon brown sugar

1/8 teaspoon plus 1/2 teaspoon salt, divided

1/8 teaspoon plus 1/4 teaspoon pepper, divided

1/4 teaspoon chili powder

1/3 cup chicken broth

3 tablespoons butter

Place the pumpkin, plantain and garlic in a greased 15-in. x 10-in. x 1-in. baking pan. Bake at 375° for 30-35 minutes or until tender.

Meanwhile, in a large skillet over medium heat, cook shallots in oil until tender. Add the wine, brown sugar, 1/8 teaspoon salt, 1/8 teaspoon pepper and chili powder; cook and stir for 6-8 minutes or until shallots are golden brown.

Squeeze softened garlic into a large saucepan; add broth and bring to a boil. Remove from the heat; add pumpkin and plantain. Mash with butter and remaining salt and pepper. Top with shallots. **YIELD:** 6 servings.

honey & spice roasted almonds

(PICTURED AT FAR RIGHT, BOTTOM)

Store-bought seasoned nut mixes can be expensive. So I buy unblanched almonds to toast and season at home. The sweet honey and spicy cayenne pepper come together beautifully.

Patty Getzin | WENATCHEE, WA

1-1/2 cups unblanched almonds

1/2 cup sugar, divided

1 teaspoon salt

1/4 teaspoon cayenne pepper

1 tablespoon canola oil

2 tablespoons honey

Arrange almonds in a single layer in an ungreased 15-in. x 10-in. x 1-in. baking pan. Bake, uncovered, at 350° for 10-15 minutes or until golden brown, stirring once.

In a small bowl, combine 1/4 cup sugar, salt and cayenne; set aside. In a large skillet, heat oil over medium heat. Add roasted almonds and honey; cook and stir for 2 minutes. Sprinkle with remaining sugar; cook 1 minute longer or until sugar is dissolved. Remove from the heat; add reserved sugar mixture and toss to coat.

Immediately spread onto waxed paper; cool completely. Break into pieces. Store in an airtight container. **YIELD:** about 2 cups.

wisconsin cheddar-cider spread

Aged sharp cheddar balances the sweetness of apple cider in this spread that's served with apple wedges and crackers. Or place some on bread and broil for excellent open-faced sandwiches.

Wolfgang Hanau | WEST PALM BEACH, FL

1/2 cup apple cider or juice

2 tablespoons reduced-fat plain yogurt

1 tablespoon prepared mustard

2 cups (8 ounces) shredded cheddar cheese

2 teaspoons caraway seeds

Apple slices and/or rye crackers

In a blender, combine the apple cider, yogurt, mustard and cheese; cover and process until blended. Stir in caraway seeds. Cover and refrigerate for at least 1 hour. Serve with apples and/or crackers. **YIELD:** 1-1/4 cups.

sweet potato tartlets

(PICTURED AT RIGHT, TOP)

My family can't resist sweet potatoes when they're mashed, placed in crunchy phyllo shells and topped with marshmallows. The bite-sized tarts are fun to eat, too!

Marla Clark | MORIARTY, NM

1 medium sweet potato, peeled and chopped

1 tablespoon butter

1 tablespoon maple syrup

1/8 teaspoon ground cinnamon

1/8 teaspoon ground nutmeg

1 package (1.9 ounces) frozen miniature phyllo tart shells

15 miniature marshmallows

Place sweet potato in a small saucepan; cover with water. Bring to a boil. Reduce heat; cover and simmer for 10-15 minutes or until tender. Drain.

In a small bowl, mash sweet potato with butter, syrup, cinnamon and nutmeg.

Place 1 tablespoon potato mixture in each tart shell. Place on an ungreased baking sheet. Top with marshmallows. Bake at 350° for 8-12 minutes or until marshmallows are lightly browned. **YIELD:** 15 tartlets.

SOMETHING ABOUT SWEET POTATOES

Sweet potatoes (which are not the same as yams) can be purchased year-round, but their peak month is November. Select those with thin, smooth skin and tapered ends. Avoid any with shriveled skin, soft spots or bruises. Store sweet potatoes in a dark, cool, dry and well-ventilated place for up to 1 week.

When ready to use, scrub with a vegetable brush under cold water; peel and cook as directed.

butterscotch-apple crisp

My delicious take on traditional apple crisp combines the tartness of fruit with the creamy sweetness of butterscotch. Add a crunchy pecan topping and you have an instant hit!

Peggy Jackson | LINWOOD, MI

1 package (10 to 11 ounces) butterscotch chips

1/4 cup all-purpose flour

1/4 cup packed brown sugar

1/2 teaspoon ground cinnamon

2-1/2 pounds tart apples, peeled and sliced

TOPPING:

1/2 cup all-purpose flour

1/4 cup packed brown sugar

1/4 cup cold butter

3/4 cup old-fashioned oats

1 cup chopped pecans

In a small bowl, combine the butterscotch chips, flour, brown sugar and cinnamon. Place apples in a greased 13-in. x 9-in. baking dish; sprinkle with butterscotch chip mixture. Bake at 375° for 20 minutes.

In a small bowl, combine flour and brown sugar; cut in butter until crumbly. Stir in oats. Sprinkle flour mixture and pecans over apple mixture; bake 30-40 minutes longer or until filling is bubbly and topping is golden brown. **YIELD:** 8 servings.

cranberry-glazed chicken

Our Test Kitchen staff infuses bone-in chicken breasts with autumn flavor by topping them with a crimson-colored cranberry sauce. The meat always turns out moist and tender.

1/4 cup dried cranberries

1-1/4 cups whiskey, divided

1/2 cup butter, softened

4 teaspoons minced fresh thyme
or 1 teaspoon dried thyme, divided

1/2 teaspoon salt

1/4 teaspoon pepper

1 cup cranberry juice

2 tablespoons brown sugar

6 bone-in chicken breast halves

In a small saucepan, combine cranberries and 1/4 cup whiskey. Bring to a boil; cook until liquid is evaporated. Transfer to a blender. Cover and process until blended. Place in a small bowl; stir in the butter, 2 teaspoons thyme, salt and pepper. Set aside.

In the same saucepan, combine the cranberry juice, brown sugar and remaining whiskey. Bring to a boil; cook until liquid is reduced to about 1/3 cup. Stir in remaining thyme.

With fingers, carefully loosen skin from each chicken breast; rub butter mixture under the skin. Place in a greased 15-in. x 10-in. x 1-in. baking pan. Bake, uncovered, at 350° for 30-40 minutes or until juices run clear, basting occasionally with cranberry mixture. **YIELD:** 6 servings.

magical crystal ball

(PICTURED AT RIGHT)

We predict your Halloween bash will be a smashing success...especially if this charming crystal ball appears on your table!

Stop by a hardware store and pick up an 8-in. frosted ceiling globe light fixture.

At home, remove the globe from the base. Place the base on your table; center an 18-in. square of crushed velvet over the top.

Turn on a small flashlight or crack a glow stick to light it up; place inside the glass globe. Set the illuminated globe on top of the fabric-draped base. Wrap beads around the crystal ball.

For added fun, gather guests around the table and pretend to "see" their future in the crystal ball. Pick up a book on palm reading and make some predictions. Or play one of the fortune-telling games described below.

FORTUNE-TELLING FUN

Have a little harmless fun on Halloween by pretending to predict the futures of your party guests with these game ideas:

MELTED WAX GAME. Cut wax candles into small pieces; place some pieces on a metal spoon. Hold the spoon over the flame of a candle until melted. Immediately pour the melted wax into a container of cold water. When hardened, remove the wax. The shape of the wax is said to indicate the person's future. (You can find many online sources that tell you what different images represent.)

APPLE SEED SECRET. Cut apples in half and give each half to a guest. Have each guest count the seeds. Two seeds means an early marriage; three seeds, a legacy; four seeds, wealth; five seeds, a long journey by sea; 6 seeds, fame; 7 seeds, a wish fulfilled.

FATES FORTUNE. Encourage guests to look for a penny, ring and feather that you've hidden in the main party room. The guest who finds the penny is promised wealth, whoever finds the ring will soon marry and the person who finds the feather will have good health.

reference index

Use this index as a guide to the many helpful hints, food facts, decorating ideas and step-by-step instructions throughout the book.

general recipe index

This handy index lists every recipe by food category, major ingredient and/or cooking method.

alphabetical index

Refer to this index for a complete alphabetical listing of all recipes in this book.

Here's Your Chance to Be Published!

Send us your special-occasion recipes, and you could have them featured in a future edition of this classic cookbook.

Year after year, the recipe for success at every holiday party or special-occasion celebration is an attractive assortment of flavorful food. So we're always on the lookout for mouthwatering appetizers, entrees, side dishes, breads, desserts and more...all geared toward the gatherings you attend or host throughout the year.

Here's how you can enter your family-favorite holiday fare for possible publication in a future *Holiday & Celebrations Cookbook*:

- Print or type each recipe on one sheet of 8-1/2" x 11" paper. Please include your name, address and daytime phone number on each page. Be specific with directions, measurements and the sizes of cans, packages and pans.
- Please include a few words about yourself, when you serve your dish, reactions it has received from family and friends and the origin of the recipe.
- Send to "Celebrations Cookbook," 5400 S. 60th Street, Greendale WI 53129 or E-mail to recipes@reimanpub.com. Write "Celebrations Cookbook" on the subject line of all E-mail entries and include your full name, postal address and phone number on each entry.

Contributors whose recipes are printed will receive a complimentary copy of the book...so the more recipes you send, the better your chances of "being published!"